Psychotherapy and Culture

Psychotherapy and Culture

Theodora M. Abel
Rhoda Metraux
and
Samuel Roll

University of New Mexico
Albuquerque

18⁴⁰

Library of Congress Cataloging in Publication Data

Abel, Theodora Mead, 1899–
  Psychotherapy and culture.

  Rev. ed. of: Culture and psychotherapy. c1974.
  Bibliography: p.
  Includes index.
  1. Psychiatry, Transcultural.   2. Personality and
culture—Cross-cultural studies.   3. Mental illness—
Social aspects—Cross-cultural studies.   I. Métraux,
Rhoda Bubendey, 1914–   .   II. Roll, Samuel, 1942–
III. Abel, Theodora Mead, 1899–   —Culture and
psychotherapy.   IV. Title. [DNLM: 1. Culture.
2. Psychotherapy. WM 420 A141c]
  RC455.4.E8A23   1986   616.89'14   86-19191
  ISBN 0-8263-0893-7
  ISBN 0-8263-0894-5 (pbk.)

Design by Barbara Werden

Contents

Foreword to the first edition by Margaret Mead   ix
Preface to the second edition   xv

1.   *Orientation*   3

2.   *The Culture and the Individual*   16
Cultural Universals   24
Enculturation: The Process of Learning   28
The High Point and the Low Point of Life   35
Redundancy in Culture   37
Ruth Benedict: Cultural Relativism and the Abnormal in Culture   38
Deviance: The Contemporary View   40
Culture Change and Conflict   45
The Choice of Ethnic Pluralism   46

3.   *Psychopathology in Cultural Contexts*   48
Culturally and Regionally Limited Types of Psychopathology   52
The Windigo Psychosis   53
The Eskimo: Arctic Hysterias   54
Gururumba "Wild Man" Behavior   56
Eastern Iatmul "Lost Hunter" Sequence   57
Psychoses in Rural Ashanti   58
Psychopathology and the Cultural Belief System   60
Specialized Roles of the Mentally Ill   60
Cultural Responses to Psychopathological Behavior   63
Projective Techniques in the Study of Culture and Psychopathology   64
New Directions in Research   66

4.   *Psychoanalytic Theories and Culture*   70
Freud's Contribution   70
Géza Róheim   72
Abram Kardiner and Basic Personality   74
Erich Fromm   76
Erik H. Erikson   77
Opler's Critique of Psychoanalytic Theories   79
Anna Freud   81
The Oedipus Complex   83

5. *The Interview*   *94*

    Cultural Differences   95
    Studies of Culture at a Distance   100
       Eastern European Jews   100
       The Chinese   102
       The French   105
       Syrians: Christians and Muslims   108

6. *Attitudes toward Treatment of Mental Illness*   *117*

    ✓Treatment and Socioeconomic Level   121
    Attitudes Toward Therapy in Different Societies   123
    Choosing a Therapist   128

7. *Communication in Therapy*   *130*

    Treatment Goals and Cultural Factors   132
    Therapy in Japan   134
       Morita Therapy   135
    Communication Between Patient and Therapist   136
    Nonverbal Communication   136
    Time and Space: Aspects of Communication   139
    Cross-Cultural Values in Communication   140
    Resistances in Cultural Contexts   144
    Limitations on the Goals of Therapy   145
    Group and Family Therapy   148
    Other Ethnic Groups   152

8. *Transference and Countertransference*   *154*

    Misunderstanding of Transference   155
    Transferential Variables in Cultural Communications   156
    Therapy Between Black and White Americans   160
    Some Effects of the Caste System on Blacks   163
    Socioeconomic Problems   167
    Transference Problems Among Plains Indians   169
    Transference in Other Cultural Groups   171

9. *Dreams*   *176*

    Psychoanalytic Theory and Dreams   177
    Culturally Determined and Expected Dreams   183
    Dream Communications to the Therapist   187
       The Dream of a Plains Indian Patient   188
       Dreams of a Chinese Patient   191

10. *Training in Cross-Cultural Therapy*   *196*

    Organized Training Programs   199

Notes 205
References 212
Index 230

Foreword to the First (1974) Edition

Ours is a collaborative age. Our knowledge has grown so fast and in so many specialized ways that a single life is seldom time enough to encompass what it is necessary to know in any general field. When the responsibility for therapy of individuals and wise counseling of professionals in therapeutic and learning situations is added to the knowledge needed for theoretical work, there is an even more urgent need to draw upon more than one skill, combined with as many contributory and significant differences between the collaborators as possible.

The two authors of this book present just such an enriching complementarity of knowledge and experience. I have known and worked with both for a long time, but the two are a generation apart in the field of culture and personality.

Theodora Abel and I were graduate students together at Columbia University in the early 1920s. Because her maiden name was Mead—we are probably not closer than a putative seventh cousinship—we used to be seated side by side, so that I had the benefit of her *sotto voce* demurrers when some professor pontificated, secondhand, about the work of the French psychologist, Janet, with whom she had studied in France. In fact, she came to be called by the French pronunciation of her nickname, Théo, and later the spelling was changed to Tao (rhyming with Mayo).

In the years after graduate school, we used to thrash out, with other students, some of the problems which were arising then for an experimental psychologist, as Tao was at that time, or for one who studied infants or taught adolescents, trained social workers or practiced as a psychiatrist. The way theory and practice were to be blended formed an integral part of our discussions as well—how to reduce the anxiety of the obstetricians unused to non-MDs in the delivery room, how to study the recognition of pattern, how to test Piaget's claim about child thought, which Tao did on conversations between adult Americans, and I among primitive children. It was actually Tao's experimental work with the psychogalvanometer at Cornell, as a National Research Council Fellow, that made me realize the inappropriateness of this instrument as a field tool.

In a period when psychologists were explaining that our expression of negation by shaking the head was due to the baby's turning away of its head from the breast and psychiatrists were worrying about the need of an infant to have experience with wet diapers—both views very naive and uncorrected by any knowledge of cultural diversity—Tao was already interested in cultural differences, intrigued, for example, by the portion of verbal habits remaining from the mother tongue or the intricacies of helping to translate a complex Arabic text, or the use a colleague had made of Australian initiation ceremonies during recovery from a psychotic episode. Meanwhile, her work with various special groups—subnormal and normal girls in an industrial school, severe mental defectives at Letchworth Village, and Sarah Lawrence College students—was adding to her sensitive knowledge of the way differentially gifted or socially specialized individuals responded within the American culture in which she herself had grown up. Marriage to Theodore Abel, who grew up in Russian Poland, and who, as a sociologist, kept alive critical ties with Germany and Poland, provided another context within which her cultural sensitivity could flourish. So it was as a culmination of a long process of intellectual open-mindedness that she did her first Rorschach analyses on groups from other cultures, the Chinese subjects who had been tested by Francis Hsu and also the Mexican subjects of Oscar Lewis in Tepoztlán. This inaugurated the period of her cooperation with anthropologists and psychologists, including the studies of the French, on which Tao and Rhoda Metraux worked together, the studies of Syrians, on which she worked with me, and the pathfinding study, with Frances Macgregor, of responses to facial disfigurement and plastic surgery.

Over the years, many of us have drawn intellectual nourishment from Tao's varied interests, nourishment so much the stronger because we could speak a common language, as she included culture within her psychological comments and psychology within her cultural ones. When the Postgraduate Center for Psychotherapy was started with an eclectic openness which was fresh and inventive, Tao became one of its central figures, organizing the psychological teaching and combining clinical work with an extraordinary diversity of patients—Chinese, Hindus, Italian-Americans, black and white Americans—and teaching aspiring therapists from many disciplines and of many cultural backgrounds.

Rhoda Metraux and I first worked together during World War II, on the Committee on Food Habits of the National Research Council in Washington. Here she developed her unique method of qualitative analysis of elicited verbal materials, which she was to use later during her anthropological studies of American character. With her Swiss anthropologist husband, the late Alfred Metraux, a South American specialist, she did field work in Haiti, Mexico, and Argentina. Returning to New York after the war, she worked with Tao Abel in the French project of Columbia University Research in Contemporary Cultures and, subsequently, on German culture.

Out of the relationship with Tao Abel in the French project grew the work-congeniality which resulted in shared field work on the island of Montserrat in the West Indies. She, entering anthropology twenty years later than I did, with original rigorous training in English literature, entered it at a time when the inclusion of psychology and psychoanalysis in anthropological work was taken for granted. She became an inheritor of the tradition which Tao had been one of the pioneers in establishing.

This book, almost ten years in the making, is, thus, a particularly felicitous collaboration. The materials were tested and retested in the real life situations of therapy and teaching by Tao and of teaching and writing by Rhoda, and of the joint interpretation of their own shared research as well as the research of others. This was done both in small research seminars, where the interviews, tests, and clinical reports of different members of the research group had to be organized and combined into a significant whole, and in the field situation of Montserrat, where Tao was able to enter a culture, very different from her own, because the version of English spoken there was simple enough to grasp quickly and Rhoda's intensive knowledge of the small village community provided background and context.

An interest in music has also provided a recurrent background to the work of both authors. When I first knew her, Tao was a violinist who first studied professionally and continued to play the violin as an ardent amateur in small concert groups, and this book was finished against the background of Rhoda's ongoing analysis of the imagery of the Iatmul culture of New Guinea, based partly on recordings of their music made in 1967–1973. The people of Montserrat, moreover, were delighted that highly respected field workers could dance, an ability which seems to have established a different kind of rapport with those who might, otherwise, have been awed into unresponsive silence. Speaking the unfamiliar cadences of Montserratian English requires the same kind of delicate ear and ability to get in step that dancing does.

So it seems to me that one of the essential strengths of this collaboration is that the two authors have shared so intimately and so differently in the same experiences; their theoretical conclusions and therapeutic illustrations have been worked out by reference to the same subjects, known in the clinical context by Tao Abel and in the social context by Rhoda Metraux. There is none of the kind of patchwork that occurs so often when one point of view is labeled cultural and another psychological. Like coproducers of a play, Tao and Rhoda can refer to the same actors and the same scenario. We will need more and more such collaborations, aimed at a unity of understanding so that those who read come away less internally divided, more secure, more able to use all that they have experienced and known in what they now propose to do. This is doubly important, as the field of culture and personality provides an important background to more and more kinds of work as worldwide travel and culture contact increase.

The need to provide those concerned with individuals enough cultural understanding to enable them to deal with the diversity of peoples with whom they would work, as colleagues, as patients, as students, has been of great concern to all of us since the 1920s. The psychoanalyst Brill's suggested solution was to offer what he called "cultural cases" to a trained anthropologist. Others advocated providing anthropologists with psychoanalytic training; still others, sending psychoanalysts into the field. But all of these are drastic solutions that require very gifted and energetic individuals who have time in their lives for specialized graduate training, psychoanalysis, and field work. Such lifetimes of special interest in such problems are found occasionally as in the authors of this book, but this is severely impractical for those who wish to devote their lives completely to mental health practice, whose primary drive is to help those in need of help now.

How were we ever to give to the mental health practitioners enough sense of the part their own culture would play in their therapeutic skills and enough background so they would allow for the extraordinary range of cultural differences they would encounter among their patients and clients and pupils? We couldn't ask them to complete the kind of cultural self-analysis which intensive anthropological field work gives to the anthropologist; we couldn't ask them to do months and years of research on the culture of Sicilians or Eastern European Jews, even if they could be sure they would be working with patients from Europe and would not be transferred next month to an area where their patients were Spanish-Americans, or black Americans from the Deep South, or migrants from Appalachia. There just wasn't time for all this. And yet it was desperately important that a Sicilian in Chicago, who felt he was being conspired against, should not be treated as if he had a paranoid delusion if, in fact, he was involved in some local feud. And it was equally important for a young New York-born, left wing Jewish analyst to know, when his aristocratic White Russian patient expressed fears about communicating with her relatives in the Soviet Union, that although she might have delusions on other subjects, this was real.

It is also important, however, not to overemphasize cultural insights in teamwork. For example, when a young psychoanalyst, who had just become enthusiastic about how important culture was, wanted to explain the sleep-walking of a Puerto Rican patient as due to "culture contact," someone had to reconcentrate her attention on that patient's idiosyncracies, by pointing out that all Puerto Ricans in New York City suffered to some degree from culture contact, but that the many thousands of them were not walking in their sleep.

This book is, thus, the distillate of actual experience in providing students who are to be mental health workers with enough material about the way their own lives and the lives of their patients express different cultures or different versions of American culture so that they will be wiser and more skilled in their endeavors.

Our educational institutions are plagued by the very human desire of each specialist to make all those with whom he comes into contact into his own image, as university professor or psychiatrist or research worker. But these two authors share a characteristic reticence and reserve; they both have too much respect for other people to try to do this. This same respect for the uniqueness of every individual informs and illuminates the way they have, in collaboration, respected each other's contribution and point of view.

MARGARET MEAD
American Museum of Natural History
New York
September 22, 1973

Preface to the Second Edition

Ten years after the publication of *Culture and Psychotherapy*, the authors—Theodora Abel and Rhoda Metraux—invited Samuel Roll to join in the preparation of a new edition tuned to the emerging interests and needs of today's clinical psychological and psychiatric practitioners, their students and their fellow researchers, patients and clients.

Samuel Roll shares with others of so many generations the difficult experiences of all who have become Americans in their own lifetime. He himself was born in 1942 in Medellin, Colombia. His mother had been born into a traditional Catholic family in the conservative Antioquia region of Colombia, his father into a Jewish family in Beirut, Lebanon. As a child he came with his parents to New Orleans and began there the long process of enculturation. His, therefore, is a background that has given him special insight into the problems of culture conflict in the development of self-identity and mature personality in the contemporary version of American culture.

Roll is, however, unique in the breadth of his research and experience in working with Americans of two continents: with the Quechua of Puno, Peru, laboring and middle class Colombians in Medellin, Mexicans in Mexico, D.F. and Monterrey and, in our own country, with Native Americans—Mescallero Apache, Jicarilla, Utes, Navajo, Laguna, and others—and members of several Hispanic cultures, as well as with his university students of many backgrounds. Since 1970 he has taught at the University of New Mexico, where he is currently professor in the departments of psychology and psychiatry. He is simultaneously a faculty member of the Instituto de Salud Mental, a psychoanalytically-oriented training center in Monterrey, Mexico, and a consultant to the Justice Department of the Navajo Nation.

In the intervening years, the original authors—Abel and Metraux—have continued and broadened our work in our respective fields of research and practice as well as our work together. Now, looking ahead, we welcome Samuel Roll as a companion collaborator and as a friend, for the immediacy of his understanding of new approaches to the theoretical and practical problems we share, for the freshness of his vision and the sureness of his voice as he addresses members of his own and a still younger generation.

Although work on the several chapters of this edition were divided among the three coauthors, all of us have, in one way or another, contributed to all the chapters, and we share a joint responsibility for the ideas expressed in this new volume.

We share also in our gratitude and thanks to Helene Pleasants who gave up a long summer holiday to the difficult editorial task of creating unity of style in our diversity, and to Eleanor Orth and Penelope Katson for their patience and excellence in the actual typing of the manuscript.

THEODORA M. ABEL
RHODA METRAUX
SAMUEL ROLL
August 1984

Acknowledgments

Grateful acknowledgment is made of the use of unpublished files of Columbia University Research in Contemporary Cultures, a project funded by the Human Resources Division, Office of Naval Research, 1947–1951; to the American Association for the Advancement of Science for support of research on conceptions of science and scientists in American culture, 1958–1960; to the National Institute of Mental Health, Research Grant MH-3303-01, 1961–1965, "The Factor of Mental Health in Allopsychic Orientation"; to the National Science Foundation, Research Grant GS-642, 1966–1969, "The Cultural Structure of Perceptual Communication"; and to the Jane Belo Fund, American Museum of Natural History, New York, for support of research in Papua New Guinea, 1971–1972, "A Comparative Study of Cultural Style in Communication."

One

Orientation

We are living in a time of transition.

Looking back on our lives, few of us can say—as others could who grew up in an untroubled period in a stable and homogeneous society—that our childhood expectations prefigured our adult experience. Consciousness of discontinuity is one of the marks of our time. Significantly, all around the world, those who turn to the past, as well as those who are engaged in social protest, whether as innovators, activists, or dropouts from their society, include not only groups and individuals who know that they have been cheated of their birthright, but also many who are privileged and socially secure.

At the end of World War II, Americans felt that faith in their kind of society was vindicated and hoped to use their great strength for good purposes in the world—even though they did not necessarily agree in defining "good purposes." Today we are struggling with a new awareness that Americans, as members of a world community, are facing the need for change far more profound than any we have lived through in the recent past. It is coming home to us that the well-being—even the very existence—of future generations depends not only on the uses we now make of existing material and technological resources, and on our care for the natural environment, but also on a disciplined concern for all life.

We are living, today, in an interconnected and intercommunicating world. In the past, most events took place within localities in which actors and audience, adversaries as well as allies, shared the same or related cultural premises. Events that transcended the local community involved only a small number of persons as actors and the vast majority as passive onlookers whose destiny might be drastically altered, but who had little or no part in determining the course of events. Now, instead, local events may be played out on a worldwide stage and have repercussions among peoples far from the initial scene of action. Events that are symptomatic of discontinuity and dysfunction—such as strikes by public employees in essential services, riots in ghettos, student disorders, terrorist attacks, guerrilla fighting, and civil war, as well as the upsurge of individual crime, the widespread use of hard drugs, personal violence and suicide, invasions of personal privacy, and threats of nuclear destruction—all trigger parallel events in very different societies, and increasingly involve individuals everywhere as participants, as victims, and, less directly, as audience and critics.

We are coming to recognize that modern technology has made possible societies in which people can live with a far greater appreciation than in the past of the worth and dignity of the individual; even in the most remote parts of the world, men and women aspire to a dignified place in their own changing societies and in the wider world.

Inevitably, change for which we already recognize the necessity involves change within ourselves. Americans, as a people, are experiencing a crisis of identity. The attempts of individuals and groups to expand their personal, internal consciousness have their parallels in attempts—and resistance to attempts—to expand the consciousness of the social and cultural frame of human existence.

The crisis we are living through finds expression most conspicuously in the experience of alienation that has been called the "generation gap" and in the heightened self-consciousness and activist orientation of black Americans, Native Americans, descendants of immigrant groups, and those who were long denied citizenship, women (who, unlike the others, are not a minority), homosexuals, the poor and the uneducated, the elderly and, not surprisingly, members of the so-called Establishment. At other periods in our national history, Americans have attempted to work out social problems and support the individual's sense of worth by muting awareness of racial, social and cultural differences. Today we react strongly against this dead-end road to mutual understanding and respect. Protest groups regard the "melting pot" theory of cultural assimilation as a fraud and the glossing over of differences as a form of social oppression. We are becoming aware, once more, that we are a pluralistic society and that there are many versions of our national culture—to only some of which we have granted full recognition.

Clearly, one of the prerequisites for coming to terms with the problems we face is a better, especially a more dynamic, understanding of who we are as individuals and as members of a society. Fortunately, we have the resources—the scientific resources—to do so. In contrast to the past, we need not depend on stereotypical representations of the nature of human nature or the well-springs of human behavior. Our images of the individual and of society need no longer be static and absolutist. We know a good deal more about the development of individual personality and the cultural framework of individual development, as well as something about the evolution of social institutions. We can, if we will, apply this knowledge to our pressing problems.

Moreover, Americans believe in the possiblity of constructive change and an open future. However bitterly and violently protesting groups may phrase their accusations, their demands for change are based in a culturally shared expectation that the outcome of change can be for the good. It is part of our world view that human beings can act on their own behalf. This is the basis of our faith in the therapeutic process and of our conviction that knowledge is intended for application. While we are made aware of problems of cultural differences and of the plight of the disadvantaged in our midst, we are also aware that we can incorporate an understanding of culture in the disciplines that have to do with human behavior.

This book brings together some current thinking about the relationship of the cultural patterning of character structure and personality to the well-being of the individual. It has been long in the making, having grown out of collaborative work over more than thirty years.

Coming from different disciplines—clinical psychology and cultural anthropology—the two original authors, Theodora M. Abel and Rhoda Metraux, found areas of common interest in the research program inaugurated in 1947 by Ruth Benedict, Columbia University Research in Contemporary Cultures (Metraux 1980). In this project, small overlapping groups of researchers from a wide variety of disciplines explored seven different cultures through work with informants, analysis of themes in novels and films, use of projective techniques, and so on. The full sharing of all research materials and interpretations by all members of each research team, as well as discussions that involved the whole research group, made possible a continuing comparison of very different world views and ways of living and of contrasting types of cultural character structure (Mead and Metraux 1953). Two of us worked on an intensive analysis of French culture (Abel, Belo, and Wolfenstein 1954; Metraux and Mead 1954). One psychologist author was also a participant in a group that explored Chinese culture (Abel and Hsu 1949).

Later, the anthropologist author (Metraux) drew on this work in a program of medically oriented research on Chinese culture at New York Hospital–Cornell Medical Center (Hinkle *et al.* 1957; Metraux 1955b).

In 1953–54, while the anthropologist author was doing field research on the rural culture of Montserrat, a small British West Indian island, the psychologist author (Abel) also lived and worked for a month at midpoint in the research in the village that was the locus of the study. There she herself carried out a series of testing procedures among a representative group of adults and adolescents with whose daily life she became familiar and on whom the anthropological work provided a complementary body of organized data (Abel 1958, 1960; Abel and Metraux 1959; Metraux and Abel 1957).

This work, in turn, suggested that their cross-disciplinary collaboration could be carried over into teaching. Over a period of ten years, various methods of developing an interdisciplinary framework were worked out in a joint seminar at the Postgraduate Center for Mental Health (formerly the Postgraduate Center for Psychotherapy). The combined teaching techniques included the presentation and discussion of major themes in American culture and the enculturation process as experienced by American children, analysis of cultural expectations as expressed by patients and clients of various cultural backgrounds, and anthropological interviews on personal life history with student volunteers in the seminar. These interviews, conducted in class, brought out vividly cultural contrasts represented within the group itself and conflicts of understanding that occurred as the seminar participants found that they were taking for granted interpretations of culturally patterned behavior that were not, in fact, shared by others within the group or by their patients or clients.

The third author, Samuel Roll, comes from a later generation and a different culture. He was born in Colombia, but was trained in clinical psychology in the United States and has conducted research in this country and in Mexico, Peru, and Colombia. His work includes cross-cultural studies of dreams and psychotherapy (Roll, Hinton, and Glazer 1974; Roll and Brenneis 1975; Roll, Rabold, and McArdle 1976; Roll, Millen, and Martinez 1980) and cross-cultural studies of cognition and intelligence (Roll 1970; Roll and Irwin 1974; Gomez-Palacio, Padilla, and Roll 1982; Melgoza, Roll, and Baker 1983).

Like the two original authors, the third author has become involved in problems faced by mental health practitioners and their patients in a pluralistic society. Shared concerns and converging experiences have led to the current volume.

Our overall goal is to demonstrate the relevance of cultural patterning to the many kinds of situations with which mental health professionals from different disciplines—psychoanalysis, psychology, social work, psychiatry, psychiatric nursing, guidance, and so on—are concerned.

Our first aim is to provide these professionals with an awareness of the cultural patterning of human behavior as well as the processes of encultura- tion in the development of personality in their patients and clients and in themselves. Chapter 2, "The Culture and the Individual," is intended to show how individuals come to embody the culture in which they are reared and so provide a working basis for placing two-way communication within a sound and realistic therapeutic framework. It would be inappropriate to discuss, except by way of example, the content of the great many cultures and ethnic adaptations with which the mental health professional may come into contact, whether within the United States or in a working situation abroad, but it is hoped that this discussion may provide the reader with a model for gaining insight into the culturally patterned behavior of individ- uals who come from unfamiliar groups or societies. Therapists working with patients from specific cultural and ethnic groups should, of course, avail themselves of existing anthropological and psychological research on the specific groups.

In succeeding chapters we have indicated some problems that must be met with in every culture, at whatever level of complexity. We have also discussed the question of deviance within a cultural framework, differences in types of deviant personality, and the place of deviants in various societies. In many situations, it may be critically important to know whether an individual from a particular ethnic group who, from the American view- point, has a deviant personality structure is also a deviant within his own culture (and so in his self-estimation), and to know what his expectations are about the handling of his deviance—expectations that may be quite different from our own.

Our second aim is to indicate ways in which cultural patterning of be- havior enters into the occurrence and manifestations of behavioral dysfunc- tion and psychopathology in different cultural contexts. In Chapter 3, "Psy- chopathology in Cultural Contexts," we have reviewed rather specifically types of research on cultural manifestations of psychopathology, and we have indicated some difficulties that may be encountered in evaluating men- tal illness in very different societies—literate and preliterate, Western and those we ethnocentrically term "non-Western."

The problems of appraising, understanding, guiding, or treating (and, of course, training) an individual can become diffuse in their expansiveness and almost unlimited in their complexity. For this reason, the mental health professional must set some limits to his ideas and procedures so that he can order his data in an intelligible way, whether the data consist of diagnostic test results, rating scales, responses to open-ended interviews, psychiatric interviews, free associations, or other verbal or nonverbal communications.

But the professional, given his specific skills and training, may set too many restrictions on his appraisals. His judgment of personality may be bound by his particular orientation, such as his theory of operant conditioning or psychosexual development, or by his culturally determined conceptions of normality and good mental health. He may leave out of consideration essential factors that affect the functioning of the individual, just as a physician can be so intent on his specialty that he may overlook the total physiological, emotional, and social functioning of his patient. The tasks of one mental health profession may be helped by insights from another discipline. Thus the several disciplines complement and supplement one another—they throw light on the problems of the person who seeks guidance or aid for emotional difficulties, and they illuminate the problems of a group with which mental health professionals are working as consultants.

However, it still is very common for those who are working in the mental health professions to make assumptions about the culture of their clients or patients. The fact that an American patient uses unfamiliar idioms or that a foreign-born client speaks "broken English" does not necessarily raise questions about the version of American culture within which the patient was reared or the familiarity of the client with American expectations about testing or treatment. Frequently, what seems to be unusual behavior on the part of a client or patient is treated as idiosyncratic, rather than as an expression of beliefs or values that the person shares with members of another culture or a different version of American culture.

It is not safe to presume mutual understanding unless the professional and his client or patient, having been reared within the same culture, share related values, expectations, and modes of communication—including the nonverbal communication of posture, gesture, and timing, as well as imagery and the more subtle meanings of words. But in our complex American society there are several versions even of the basic culture. In addition, persons from other societies—or from enclaves within the American one—will have learned American culture as adults or only as it impinged on some part of their lives, for example, at school but not in the home.

Of course, our experience of our own culture also affects the way in which as therapists we estimate and react to our clients or patients. Although a therapist may be acting objectively or neutrally in therapeutic work, he or she inevitably responds, consciously or unconsciously, in terms of culturally determined criteria and may convey value judgments by a nod of the head, a smile, or a stiffening of the neck; these communications, in turn, may be misinterpreted by a client or patient accustomed to a different set of body-motion signals (Birdwhistell 1970).

The tools used by psychologists, social workers, psychiatrists and members of other disciplines are culture-bound, so much so that without careful exploration it may be difficult, if not impossible, to evaluate correctly the results of a test performance (Alland 1971; Samuda 1975; Padilla and Ruiz 1975). The test situation, the content of the test material, the method of responding (using paper and pencil or manipulating objects), and the specific phrases used (even when these are translated into the subject's own language) may have different valences and varied meanings (semantic differentials) for subjects reared in a culture other than the one in which the test was developed and standardized.

For example, in administering the Rorschach test, it is well to understand something about the cultural background of the subject who is responding to the inkblots or, at least, to recognize that the imagery on which he draws has cultural components. A mentally ill student from one of the smaller African nations was sent to a state hospital near New York City, where he was given a Rorschach test. After looking at Card III, he refused to respond to the blots, for in this card he perceived a portrayal of the gods. He explained that he was not allowed to look at such a picture. His response would be considered pathological in an American; it had to be evaluated within a different cultural frame of reference.

The individual's learning, as a member of a culture, necessarily influences the attitudes with which he or she approaches an interview situation, as well as overt and latent modes of communication, and transferences and countertransferences during interviewing, counseling, and therapy. We shall show how an interview, including an initial psychiatric interview, needs to be geared to meet the specific frames of reference of clients or patients from different cultural groups. For example, the timing and phrasing of questions must take into consideration the person's cultural background. In an initial psychiatric interview, a first-generation Irishman may refuse to reveal details of the conflicts in his personal life; only to a priest would he expect to expose himself in this way. A Chinese patient may withhold details about sickliness during his infancy, needing first to establish that this is not intended as an attack on his parents' attitude toward him. So we shall be concerned with such problems as the phrasing of questions, the understanding of responses and the evaluation of the relationship, including both an awareness of how the subject or patient perceives the interview and the interviewer, and a sensitivity to the values imposed on the interview by the mental health professional himself.

Again, attitudes toward treatment vary so much from culture to culture, and from one social group to another within a culture, that the mental health professional can be nonplussed by the situation in which he finds himself, especially if he is unaware of his own cultural expectations. In particular, transferences and countertransferences in therapeutic settings may reflect the regularities of American cultural patterning, but they can also bring out the values of the two different cultural groups to which patient and therapist, respectively, belong.

Since dreams play a large role in understanding latent content in the psychological makeup of an individual, they will be dealt with psychodynamically and culturally. We shall show how an understanding of the patient's culture can be important in approaching the intrapsychic conflict reflected in dreams. Also we shall demonstrate how dreams have been interpreted with psychotherapeutic intent in different cultures.

Situations may occur in which the culture, as such, is minimally relevant, as when, for example, an analyst is exploring some of the deeper aspects of intrapsychic conflicts. But even then the patient may reveal problems through the use of content whose meaning is culturally highly specific. A young Jewish patient, who had been brought up in an Orthodox home, but who was living apart from her family, dreamed that she had returned to her parents' house for the Friday night meal. In the dream she herself lighted the Sabbath candles. The culturally appropriate question was why the girl dreamed that she herself lighted the candles; within the Jewish tradition this was an inappropriate act, since her mother was alive and present in the dream.

An American analyst who had been brought up in a middle-class Protestant home, but who had had a varied experience of other social and cultural settings, had a vague, uneasy feeling during several analytic hours with a Jewish patient who repeatedly used phrases such as "God willing," or "God bless you." The analyst wondered why she had the impression that the patient was not serious in making these references to God. Finally, she recalled that, in her childhood, prejudice against Jews was vaguely connected with their repudiation of Christ as the Messiah. As a child, the analyst had equated Christ with God and so had gained the impression that Jews were atheists. As an adult she knew this idea was irrational. When she became aware of her childhood associations, her feeling of unease left her permanently.

But cultural misinterpretation may also have profound effects on the therapeutic relationship. A young woman of Old American descent, who was pursuing an independent career, was the patient of a European analyst. Discussing her relations with her brothers and sisters and their children, she described how they kept in close communication with one another through the letters they wrote the mother, still living at home, who passed on news to the others. As she saw it, the mother kept alive the affectionate intimacy of a large, scattered family. But the analyst perceived the mother as a grasping and controlling woman (as she might have been in the analyst's own culture), and she conveyed to her patient that she saw her as a kind of witch. Unfamiliar as she was with American culture, the analyst could not modify her own culturally determined image, and in the end the trust based on good communication broke down.

It is the central theme of this book that mental health professionals must continually take into account their own culture, the culture of the person being interviewed, tested, or listened to with the "third ear," and the relevance of culture to the medium used—tests, questions and answers, constructions, dreams, or associations.

It is a corollary to this theme that each of us is embedded in our own culture and that our personal experience of this culture is embedded deeply within each of us. In other words, an individual brought up in only one culture has difficulty becoming aware of the extent to which his learning—conscious and unconscious—differs from the conscious and unconscious cultural patterning of a person reared in another society. Individuals from different societies may learn to accommodate to each other in interactions, but they may miss many of the contrasts.

The psychological orientation of this book is psychodynamic, based largely on Freudian psychoanalytic theory. For this reason it seems essential to discuss very briefly the history of psychoanalytic theory in relation to the theory of culture.

Freud broke away from the preoccupation of earlier psychologists with cognitive processes and concentrated instead on motivations. He postulated unconscious processes that affect the individual's behavior, perceptions, thoughts, and feelings. In the course of his investigation of these processes, Freud speculated on the ontogenetic psychosexual development of the child and on the possible phylogenetic mental functioning of human beings. These speculations led to a consideration of group behavior; to studies of the personality dynamics of historical persons, such as Leonardo da Vinci; to the analysis of myths, such as those surrounding figures like Oedipus, Electra, and Moses; and to interpretations based on some of the thinking of his time about "primitive hordes" and a "primeval" father figure. He was greatly impressed by the work of Frazer and of Lang, on which he drew for his discussions in *Totem and Taboo* ([1913] 1959). He saw culture as a neurosis in which defenses were built up in specific ways to counter instinctual demands, libidinal and aggressive.

Freud viewed the world from the position of a middle-class Jew living in Vienna during a period in which the problems of his largely Austrian Catholic middle-class patients were responses to the highly formalized, socially circumscribed, repressive culture of the period, which was characteristic in many respects not only of Austria but of the Western world.

Darwin's theory of the descent of man was already well known, but knowledge about actual human evolution was limited to speculation about a few fragmentary finds. As we now know, these were the remains of men close to modern man (*Homo sapiens*) who, in fact, had relatively well-developed cultures (Johanson and Edey 1981). There was also exceedingly little good firsthand information about exotic and primitive societies, though explorers, missionaries, traders, travelers, and others had made contact of sorts, in some cases centuries earlier. Systematic knowledge of cultures, based on scientific methods of investigation during extended periods of observation in the field, living in the community of the people studied, is almost entirely a product of anthropology since the turn of the century. Only in the 1930s did anthropologists turn seriously to consideration of the complex cultures within which they themselves were reared and trained as social scientists.

Róheim was the first analyst to test Freudian theory in the field, especially castration fears and unresolved oedipal conflicts. Some successors of Freud modified certain of his formulations and dealt with psychodynamic problems in cultural contexts: Kardiner, Fromm, and Erikson. The first research worker who fully incorporated the training—and, more importantly, the practice—of the two disciplines, was George Devereux.

In spite of the massive research on culture and personality, professionals influenced primarily by a Freudian (or modified Freudian) viewpoint still tend to separate "culture" and "personality." It is their assumption that the core personality of the individual is influenced largely by the idiosyncratic behavior of parents, rather than by the style of child rearing that parents have consciously or unconsciously adopted and modified. According to specialists in the various mental health disciplines, what the child introjects is not unconscious attitudes common to the cultural group in which the child is reared, but only the more individual attitudes of the parents—particularly the mother, as she attempts to satisfy her libidinal and aggressive needs.

Here the analyses of the development process by Erikson, on the one hand, and by Devereux, on the other, are critically important. Erikson (1963) demonstrates how cultural learning, as it is mediated by the mother (and other significant figures), is incorporated into the infant's earliest experience. Devereux (1969) demonstrates how this early experience is modified and elaborated by experience during later childhood, especially in the interpretation—that is, the meaning—of behavior, including motivation. He points out that certain parallel ways of handling the child in early infancy (such as swaddling) have quite a different outcome in character formation in terms of different cultural interpretations of the "same" practices. In fact, the dichotomization of behavior that is and is not culturally determined is an artifact. In practice, all behavior is taught and learned by individuals, and whether one looks at behavior as an expression of cultural regularities or as the expression of an individual's unique learning experience is a matter of approach.

More recently, Devereux has suggested that all societies can be investigated within the frameworks of the complementary disciplines of anthropology and psychoanalysis. At the same time, he states that the sociological (anthropological) datum and the psychological datum are interdependent in that, "starting from the same *raw* fact, each of these data is *created* by the manner in which that fact is considered." But, Devereux continues, it is necessary to postulate the autonomy of the two discourses "precisely by showing that these discourses are *complementary*. It is hardly necessary to add that it is precisely the interdependence and complementarity of these two discourses which makes all 'reductionism'—the one which seeks to reduce ethnology to psychoanalysis or vice versa—absolutely illusory" (Devereux 1978: 2–3).

In the United States at the present time there are those who believe that a white therapist cannot treat or counsel a black patient or client, or vice versa, because the therapist or counselor does not "understand" the culture of his patient or client. Actually, therapist and patient share the same cultural heritage, as do Americans from areas of the country having regionally different versions of the same cultural heritage.

The problem for black Americans today is better phrased as one that has to do with autonomy, a major value for the individual in American life. The situation is much the same, but also somewhat different, for members of other ethnic groups—Mexican-Americans, for example—who have been assigned subordinate positions in the social class structure. They, too, have formed activist protest groups today in search of autonomy, that is, the freedom to move and live in accordance with personal choice.

This means that in counseling and therapy today, the mental health professional is faced with the complex problems of working with members of our society who are struggling toward a *personal* identity that is defined, at least at a conscious level, by membership in a group seeking recognition of a new *cultural* identity. In addition, there are the complications of coming to grips with the problems of those who intend to retain their older and separate cultural identity.

One of the difficulties of the therapist's or the counselor's position vis-à-vis members of ethnic groups is that this position involves a partial reversal of what Americans still expect. In the past we expected the newcomer and the outsider—the immigrant—to learn our language and modes of behavior. It was the immigrant and his children who were bilingual (at least until the children "forgot" the language of their foreign-born parents), and who had to struggle with the difficulties of living simultaneously in two worlds and of communicating across vaguely recognized cultural boundaries. It is something of an innovation, in viewpoint as well as in practice, to extend the responsibility for learning a second language and understanding the premises of a second culture to the teacher, the government official, the doctor or nurse, the employer or supervisor, the minister, social worker, counselor, or therapist. And when the person who has to cope with this reversal of expectations is someone who has gone through the process of Americanization himself, this may set up a kind of rivalry: "Why doesn't *he* have to do what I have done?"

Most discussion of generalized—and in some cases regional—American culture, as presented by anthropologists and others, deals with the culture as it was incorporated in the personality and behavior of the older living generation (see, for example, Dollard 1937; Gorer 1964; Mead 1965; Riesman 1973; Singal 1982; Warner and others 1941–59; West 1945). For younger men and women this represents the world view of parents, teachers, and other significant older adults. It is still the culture into which adults, often with doubt and vacillation, have attempted to induct their children. It is now obvious that they have also communicated their own doubts and difficulties. In many cases they have communicated their sense of failure to maintain a mode of living in keeping with their earlier expectations or to adopt one more in keeping with their perceptions of change.

As Margaret Mead (1978) has pointed out, children in the past learned a mode of life, including a picture of a whole life span, from their parents, grandparents, and other adults important in the community. In our society, in which adults have expected the life of their children to be different from their own, children learned from their elders to look to their own peers for the development of a suitable life style. This is still the case in our culture, but in certain ways their peers today are members of their own generation in many parts of the world—a generation that rejects the past and is unclear about the future.

It is necessary for us to incorporate some understanding of the enculturation process in our thinking and in the practice of disciplines that bring professionals into critically important contact with individuals and groups from cultures other than our own. It is the goal of this book to demonstrate by exemplification the relevance of a knowledge of cultural character, cultural values, and cultural styles of communication in those situations in which mental health professionals, whatever their discipline, take responsibility for judgment, evaluation, guidance, and therapy.

Cross-cultural communication is the more important in a world where geographical and national boundaries have become artifacts of thought instead of barriers to experience. The only model we have at present for thinking systematically about change is the conception of culture and ethnicity as systems within which character is formed and a way of living is learned, and through which the individual is enabled to express his deepest needs, conflicts and satisfactions.

It is the authors' conviction that mental health professionals who can fully incorporate within their specialized skills the model of culture and the ability to make systematic cross-cultural comparisons will increase the effectiveness of their communication within and across cultural boundaries and, perhaps, across the generation gap. It follows that they may become innovators in the development of techniques leading to a more systematic understanding of the processes of change as they are expressed in the problems of individuals and social groups.

Two

The Culture and the Individual

Culture is both the product and the process of humanization. The world as it is known to us is a human world. In this sense there are as many coexistent worlds as there are living traditions through which experience is shaped, mediated, and interpreted. Each individual, unique in his or her specific genetic endowment, becomes a full human person through the process of being reared as a member of an ongoing society. Through learning, in the broadest sense of this term, the individual becomes a carrier of a culture who shares with others in the society values, modes of perception, access to a body of skills, knowledge and symbolic representations, a style of physical movement, ways of formulating experience, and a sense both of community and of himself or herself as a person.

Learning, as we understand and use the term holistically, is based in innate—that is, biological—capacities that are shared by members of our own species, *Homo sapiens*. Individuals differ—even the closest kin—genotypically and phenotypically, but over all it is the fact of shared human capacities that makes possible the valid comparison of cultures, however widely they differ in complexity and world view, and of individuals, men and women, who are the living carriers of different cultures.

Race, a term that has a great many contradictory meanings as it is used in our own and in many other cultures, here we define as a social, not a biological, form of categorization. We agree with Alland (1971:133) that in its ordinary usage today race "is clearly a folk category. The criteria for placing individuals in one or another racial group are determined not by biological but by current ethnically defined rules." It is the *cultural* concept that race is biologically determined which still has great power to shape our thought and our actions.[1]

Every historically distinct culture represents a special version of the complex processes through which human personality comes into being and is sustained, human relationships are established and supported, forms of communication are maintained and elaborated, systems of belief and knowledge are produced and transmitted, viable communities are organized, and the natural world is transformed into and maintained as a man-made world. The cultures of contemporary societies—American, Chinese and Eskimo, for example—differ in their historical traditions, in the complexity and style of their social organization, in their emphases on the organization of human capacities, in their ways of handling communication within and across cultural boundaries and in their conceptualization of man's place in the universe. Yet in each of them, as in all societies, individuals become full human beings and in turn transmit their life experience to others who come after them.

We can know about the culture of some societies only fragmentarily. From a few objects that their members, long since dead, have made—from house sites and rubbish heaps, food storage pits and pottery sherds and tools, graves and offerings to the dead—we can extrapolate some very meager clues as to the way of life of an unknown people who lived thousands of years ago. We can learn a great deal more about the culture of any vanished society that made use of some form of written communication. We may even get a tantalizing glimpse of an individual from an essay inscribed in cuneiform on a clay tablet by a Sumerian schoolboy some four thousand years ago.

Anthropologists' studies of living preliterate peoples—peoples in various parts of the world who, until recently, have been cut off from the mainstreams of communication—have given us, by analogy, some slight insight into the past and some grasp of the vast variety of ways in which human beings have been capable of organizing experience.

Equally importantly, field research on very small societies has made possible the study of a whole way of life, of the way in which different aspects of living interlock and are mutually reinforcing, and of the processes of learning through which those born in a society come to embody and later transmit to a new generation appropriate behavior. Comparative studies, both of societies in the same environment and sharing in some of the same traditions, and of societies in different parts of the world, have given us insight into the specificity of learning styles on the one hand, and, on the other, into the universality of cultural integration.

Until recently, anthropologists had only limited resources other than words and very partial assemblages of material objects to present a picture of the life of a people. Today, new methods of observing and recording, particularly the use of films, videotape, and sound recordings of ongoing life, have given us ways of making available to others aspects of a cultural style that can be recorded and communicated in words only with great difficulty, if at all. Regularities in the fine details of the patterning of posture and gesture and intonation, and in such things as the rhythms of movement, speech, and music, can be recorded and communicated to others at a distance from the actual scene only by means of the camera, the tape recorder, and the new methods of analysis that these have made possible. In fact, the new technology has made it possible to study simultaneously sequences of events, some of them widely separated in time, which hitherto could be recorded only in some personal form of shorthand and carried in memory. This does not mean that the data obtained in the past by skilled observers were less accurate. What is new is the kind of record, which is available for analysis and reanalysis, as our knowledge grows, long after the event.[2]

The use of projective techniques in field research can also provide data on cultural regularities as well as on individuals, which can be shared for purposes of later study and analysis. Particularly useful are tests, such as the Lowenfeld Mosaic test and the Kaleidoblocs, both developed by Margaret Lowenfeld,[3] in which subjects are asked to produce something tangible, and both the process and the product can be visually recorded and reproduced. Though such tests are artifacts from the culture of the observer, when used sensitively they open channels of communication about systematic ways in which a cultural style is embodied in and expressed by individual members of a society.

However, the development of research methods such as these has served only to emphasize what is central to anthropological studies: the recognition that full understanding of a culture as it is embodied in members of a society depends on direct observation of and communication with the members of a living, ongoing society. Even a single individual, reflecting on his own life and the life of his society as he has experienced it, can give the skilled investigator access to a version of his culture that is inaccessible by other means.[4] But the fact that in all cultures only some aspects of learning enter into awareness and only some parts of behavior can be articulately described—and what is outside awareness or beyond the range of articulateness varies from one culture to another—means that understanding and inter-pretation depend also on observation of people in action.

A culture exists, essentially, as it is embodied in living people. It has continuity as the members of older living generations interpret and pass on their experience to those younger than themselves. It changes as living members of the society alter their beliefs and ideas and practices, develop or adopt new techniques, invent new ways of exploiting or conserving the social organization, reinterpret their traditional social organization, rein-terpret their traditional values and through their symbolic system create a new vision of the universe and of man. It ceases to exist when a people who once had a social identity die out or merge with another, different social community. The merging of peoples of distinct cultures and the emergence of new cultures, as people form new kinds of societies—or radically change the form of their own society—and develop a new style of living in which they rear their children to become different kinds of human beings from their ancestors, are both continuously ongoing processes.

Today, in our intercommunicating world, we are the witnesses of, and participants in, the development of a world culture of which, in time, it is possible that our diverse and conflicting local cultures will become special versions. Worldwide communication deeply affects not only the great post-industrial national cultures, but even the cultures of small, remote tribal peoples. Today, in Tambunam, a village of the Iatmul people in the East Sepik Province of Papua New Guinea, a middle-aged man, who knows only his local river country, can say, "Soon black men and white men, our chil-dren and your children, will walk one road." Two generations ago, Iatmul men were headhunters; elderly adults still vividly recall the last headhunting raids in which their fathers and uncles took part. But Iatmul children now growing up are entering a transformed world. Music and news and the most varied kinds of information reach them daily on their transistor radios, and government secondary schools are bringing together the children of many different Papua New Guinea peoples; what they are learning relates them to their contemporaries growing up in Europe, Asia, Africa, and the Americas. Iatmul schoolboys are still their parents' children, with a deep sense of their Iatmul identity. At the same time, as members of a whole generation group, they are becoming new kinds of men and women, the first representatives of a newly emerging national culture.[5] In Papua New Guinea, a new nation, peoples of many cultures and speaking more than 700 languages are facing, just as we are, very complex problems of reordering experience and values.

In a certain sense, of course, culture is an abstraction. The "patterns of culture" about which Ruth Benedict wrote (1934) are extrapolations from ways of life, standardizations that are arrived at through the anthropologist's analysis of regularities in the behavior of members of a society, distilled from the details of the behavior of many individuals. Looking at the people around us, we do not see "American culture," but individual men and women working and playing, quarreling and making up, running their homes and carrying on their business activities, bringing up their children, caring for the sick and the indigent, making laws and flouting them, teaching and learning in schools, voting and holding political office. What we see is individuals carrying on their everyday lives, no two of them doing exactly the same thing in the same way, entering into controversies, meeting crises or breaking down under the impact of unbearable conflict. Without much conscious thought, we continually categorize those we come in contact with, making differentiations, some very gross and simple and others too subtle to put into words, but all learned through our individual experience as Americans.

Nor do we see "French culture" when we watch French men and women going about their lives. Yet we begin to respond to—and over time perceive—regularly recurring differences between the French and ourselves when we interact with individuals. We discover that the "same" acts—calling a man by his given name or visiting a family at home, for example—have different meanings for the French and for us. We gradually discover that their conceptions of masculinity and femininity, childhood and adulthood, friendship and intimacy and so on, do not coincide with ours. Knowing only one or two French men or women well, it would be easy to attribute characteristic modes of emotional response, thought and behavior to their specific and idiosyncratic experience. Only over time, living and working in a French setting, do we begin to discern, first, that we are hindered in our perceptions by standardized American ideas about the French, and second, that there is a community of thought and feeling, a patterning of behavior that is French (Metraux and Mead 1954).

The greater the differences between two cultures, the more difficult it is for the outsider to discern differences between individuals. "All Japanese look alike to me" is the very commonplace response of American tourists on a three-week visit to Japan. The sense of strangeness blurs one's ability to grasp detail. But the closer two cultures are, the more likely it is that members of one culture will misinterpret the behavior of members of the other. Nominally speaking the same language, English, and sharing many historical traditions, Americans and Englishmen or Scots or Australians assume a state of mutual understanding that breaks down as words and actions are interpreted according to differing and conflicting expectations.

It is possible to present the core themes of a culture as abstractions, that is, as a set of propositions incorporating the basic beliefs of a people, derived from actual, observable behavior. Thus it can be said: *Americans believe that men and women can transform themselves in the course of their own lives.* This is a statement that can be derived from many kinds of characteristic American behavior: from our acceptance (and rejection, at different periods) of immigrant groups and our management of the processes of Americanization; from our conceptions of social equality and our difficulties in realizing our own ideals of an egalitarian society; from our definitions of success and failure; from our handling of sickness and incapacity; from our optimistic belief in progress and our pessimism in the face of determined opposition to change; from the long history of adult education in the United States; from our facilitation of geographic and social mobility; from the ambiguities of our attitudes toward the criminal and the aims of penal institutions; from our handling of marriage and divorce; from our interest (from the most faddish to the most serious) in therapy; from our tendency to deny death and the value of mourning; from our claims of belief in the possibility of happiness. Our belief in the possibility of self-transformation is relevant to our handling of the landscape and the cityscape—to our willingness to bulldoze what exists in order to build anew. In the past, this belief infused the work of American missionaries abroad, and today it sustains the more sophisticated efforts of Peace Corps workers and many others in their efforts to help disadvantaged peoples transform their own modes of living quickly. It is expressed in our fear of revolutions and our desire, sometimes our gnawing anxiety, to be modern and keep up with the times. It is one of the marks of being an American.

Such basic beliefs motivate a wide range of behavior. They also are the source of crucial conflicts for individuals and large social groups within a culture. Hofstadter and Wallace (1970) have documented the frequency with which violence in America—vigilantism, lynchings, strikes ending in bloody conflict, terrorism, and riots—has been touched off by religious, regional, ethnic, and race conflict. Americans deeply believe that people can transform themselves (the basis of the "melting pot" image), but they are also capable of suddenly turning against any group defined as outsiders, intruders, or invaders. At various times they have lashed out with lethal ferocity against the Irish, the Germans, the Italians, the Japanese, Mexican-Americans, Catholics, Mormons, black Americans, carpetbaggers from the North, hillbillies from the South and, more recently, Haitians and Vietnamese—almost any group that did not conform to the contemporary and local versions of American living. Our very belief in our capacity to change through learning makes us very vulnerable to prejudice against, and fear and distrust of, those we see as "different" and so possibly dangerous.

It is contact, direct or indirect, with the living reality of a culture that gives it meaning for most of us. Abstract statements provide a way of ordering data, but we need to be able to visualize the actual behavior to which they refer. Even a brief film depicting, for example, interaction in a French or a Japanese family can give us a vivid sense of cultural style that no verbal formulation can give. McNeill's *Four Families* (1959),[6] which depicts a day in the life of four comparable families—Indian, Japanese, French and English Canadian (representing North America)—as they care for their children, eat, work, and move around their homes, illuminates, by the use of contrast, the reality of cultural style.

To a great extent the presentation of a culture by anthropologists is based in a middle ground of standardized behavior. Descriptions of concrete details of behavior and of variations in individual personality serve mainly to bring to life the regularities by which the culture is defined. In such a presentation only an occasional illustration can suggest the range of variations of which the anthropological field worker, living with the people he is studying, is so intensely and continually aware.

As one result of this style of presentation, readers of ethnographic accounts sometimes question whether the people of another culture, especially a "primitive" culture, have individualized personalities. This doubt reflects the nineteenth-century Western conception of "stages" of social evolution and an accompanying belief that there are intrinsic mental differences between "primitive" and "civilized" man.[7] Conversely, they may question whether, considering the personality differences among individuals in our own and other complex societies, we have a culture. Or they may come to think of a culture as if it were, in some way, like a suit of clothes that people wear in public and take off when they relax at home. Or, reifying the culture, they make statements such as, "The culture makes women feel inferior to men," or they ask, "What is the conflict between the culture and the individual?"

These are common responses of Americans, who are conscious of the diversity of our plural society and, today, are fully aware of the fact that they themselves and those around them—their parents and children, neighbors and friends, near kin and strangers—are struggling with the issues of social and cultural change.

Occasionally, we equate our culture with our ideals of what life should be, in contrast to what it actually is in our society in the different experiences of the rich and the poor, the intelligent and the stupid, black and white, the farmer, the white-collar worker, the scientist and the artist, the family living in a small stable community, in a single-class suburb, and in an inner-city ghetto. This equation of culture and ideal is itself an expression of one American way of handling discrepancy, by treating a part as the whole.

Or we fragment the culture in terms of social groups and institutions. For example, we speak of "the values of middle-class American culture," or "the culture of black Americans" (as though the social designation "black" could equate the experience of a child of a sharecropper in the deep South, a family subsisting on welfare in Los Angeles or New York, and a family on the campus of a midwestern university), or "youth culture"—as though all these versions of the culture existed independently of one another. We also speak of "the culture of the hospital" (or of some other institution, such as the school or the army) and even "nursery school culture"—as though institutions exist, as they are sometimes studied, in a vacuum.

What gives society cohesion is the culture as it is embodied in its members and as it is expressed through their activities in the institutions through which the tasks of the society are carried out. Even in the most simple and homogeneous society, all individuals do not have equal access to the content of the culture; differentiation of roles carries with it a corresponding differentiation of knowledge, activities, skills, and viewpoint. In a large, complex society there are many versions of the culture that differ from, but are on the whole congruent with, one another. To the extent that those reared within any particular version of the culture also participate in institutionalized activities involving members of other groups or the society as a whole—are subject to the same laws, attend schools, belong to churches, serve in the armed forces, form audiences for the mass media, take part in local and national politics, vote, pay taxes, obtain medical care, receive welfare, work in the larger community—they are drawn within the orbit of the more generalized national culture and share in the behavior forms and the character structure of members of the society as a whole. In a caste society the individual's sense of identity, as a person and as a life member of a group, includes not only who he is and what he can do but also who others are (members of other castes) and what they can do that he must not.[8] In contrast, in an open society in which there is emphasis on mobility and change, as in the United States, and in the casteless Chinese society, the individual carries as part of his sense of identity some conception of what he may become, as well as what he is at the present time.

In most complex societies it is not uncommon to find cultural enclaves—groups living in closed communities that stand in some special relationship to the larger society. European gypsies still form such a closed group, but one that is attached to no single locality. Maintaining a tenuous network of relations in many countries, gypsy bands everywhere have been barely tolerated outsiders. At different periods of European history, there have been many closed or partly closed religious communities, of which perhaps the most stable was the Jewish community, that have existed in symbiotic relationships to the countries in which they were located.[9]

Cultural Universals

All cultures must meet certain problems of ordering experience that are related to innate human capacities and the nature of the world itself. In this sense one can think in terms of cultural universals that take into account all variations of specific cultural content.

For example, in all cultures there is a formalized system of verbal communication, that is, a language. All languages must fall within the range of possibilities of human physiology, and all natural languages (as opposed to the special languages invented for particular purposes, for example, mathematics) must be such that they can be learned and adequately used by any normal individual. This tells us nothing, however, about the organization of any specific language or (since the boundaries of speech communities and cultural communities do not coincide) about cultural differences in the use of language. It merely alerts us to the fact that speech communities do exist and that normal human beings learn to speak and to respond to speech.

Additionally, it does suggest that deaf-mutism is a major handicap in any culture. For this reason, attitudes toward and ways of handling deaf-mutism in different cultures can give us a certain insight into culturally specific beliefs about and ways of handling physical incapacity. Thus some awareness of human universals can help to clarify our understanding of the specificity of their expression in our own culture and others.

In considering the universals of culture we cannot go beyond the crude material indicators of vanished cultures and whatever inferences they permit us to make. Nor can we exclude the possibility that there are human capacities as yet untapped by any culture in a systematic way. Thus it is only in modern, scientifically oriented, technological cultures that we have culturally systematized man's capacity to innovate and invent, although, of course, all human culture involves discovery and invention.

One belief that all peoples have in common is that their familiar behavior is the "natural" way for human beings to think, feel, and act. All peoples have made the discovery that there are also others, aliens and strangers, who behave differently—people who walk differently, speak a different language, laugh when "no one" would laugh, eat food no human being would touch, and have beliefs that no right-thinking person could accept. Some societies have solved the problem of like and unlike, familiar and strange, by defining themselves as "the people"—that is, as human beings—and by treating alien groups as somehow more or (more commonly) less than human. Other peoples have been inclusive in their conceptions and have been able to identify and incorporate aspects of the strange and the unknown within their own human universe. The differentiation may be a relatively subtle one, as when in traditional Hispanic cultures "Christian" and "human" are equated, or as when in traditional Judaism one people is singled out as the chosen of God.

The recognition that all are human—that is, belong to one species and are differentiated by their systems of learned behavior—is a very slowly emerging reinterpretation of the awareness of difference. It is significant that this is coming about in a period during which, on the one hand, there are no more wholly unexplored regions (and so no more unknown peoples) in the world and, on the other hand, ethological studies of animal communities place humans in a new way within the framework of all living beings. But the problem of the cultural dimensions of the human world is, of course, only part of the more general one of dealing in some systematic way with the familiar and the strange, the known, the unknown, and the unknowable in the individual's relation to himself, to other persons and to other living creatures, and in humans' relation to the man-made and the natural world.

All peoples have had to come to grips with patterning in the natural world: with periodicity, regularity, and variation; with day and night and the systematic changes in sunrise, moonrise, and the movements of the constellations in the night sky; with the winds and the tides; with the seasons and the seasonal processes of germination, growth, and decay, and the vicissitudes that alter or interrupt these processes; and with recurrent and progressive changes in the landscape.

All peoples have had to organize time and space. The world may be the center of the universe, one planet in a solar system, or a small island in an unbounded sea. Time may be conceptualized as a flowing river or as an endlessly turning wheel. A people may have a sense of unbroken continuity back to the beginning of things, when the world was created and human-kind came into being, or time, like space, may be unbounded. The past, as a Golden Age, may provide men and women with models of a good life in the present; or a Golden Age located in the future may give them a vision of what they are moving toward; or past and present and future may be, as it were, an endless replaying of the same record.

All peoples have had to deal in some way with what we in Western cultures term the unforeseeable, the accidental. But accident, as such, may not be conceptualized. People may see the event as brought about by magic or witchcraft; as the effect of one's own (or another's) actions in another lifetime; as predetermined by one's own luck; as coming about by super-natural intervention; as a moral judgment; or as the arbitrary working of a blind, impersonal fate.

As far as we know, the family exists in some form in all societies. It is within the family, with all its echoing relationships, its reflections of a larger world, and its responsiveness to the internal world of each of its members, that initial learning takes place. Although from time to time attempts have been made to separate the child partially from the family, so far there has always been a drift back toward family living.

The family as a living unit may take a great variety of forms. Within any given type of family structure—the extended family, for example, within which three or even four generations live in one household, or the nuclear family, from whose household all kindred other than parents and children may be excluded—interpersonal relations can be structured in many ways. In some societies the family is the nucleus of the principal recognized rela-tionships; community and kinship are coextential. Hypothetical ties of kin-ship, extending into the unremembered past, may link together even a very large population, as in West African kingdoms in which ruler and ruled were bound by kinship ties. Or, as in traditional Chinese society, the network of kindred may provide the individual with a safe route through the world of strangers. Organized kinship provides one of the models on which people may draw in establishing new kinds of relationships, and the existence of a kin group can provide the basis for new forms of organization.[10]

In no society, however, do the family and the organized kin group provide the only institutionalized models for interpersonal relations. Moreover, there are types of relationship that are not made explicit—that is, that are not given formal recognition—but that are highly significant in the life of the individual. For example, in societies where relationships among men are explicitly stylized so that events are described in terms of the men who take part in them, but where no associations among women are given overt recognition, there may nevertheless be informal relationships among women or involving women that are learned and passed on from generation to generation.

All cultures must come to grips not only with infant helplessness but also with growth, maturation, senescence, and death, and must in some manner deal with the problem of how the individual comes into being and what his fate is after death. In cultures that treat time as circular, the end of life is also the beginning of a new phase that leads to a new birth. Death may be seen as the end, as a new beginning or as a transition to some alternate form of being that occurs only once or that occurs repeatedly as the person moves back and forth between two worlds. The person lost to this world may be living in another world, leading a life like or unlike that on earth. The dead may be concerned with events on earth and influence their course, or their well-being may depend on others still living or they may be wholly beyond the reach of life on earth.

Every culture marks off stages of living, each with its appropriate experiences of learning. Young people learn how to be lovers and married couples. Couples with children learn how to be parents. The aging learn how and when to become elderly and how to die. In a very stable homogeneous society every stage is prefigured in the individual's experience with other persons—grandparents, parents, older and younger brothers and sisters, peers, teachers, public leaders, notable men and women, the successful and the failures. The elderly re-experience childhood and parenthood in new ways in caring for their grandchildren and in their relations to their own adult sons and daughters as the parents of children. Children learn about the past, which they will never experience, and the future, which will be theirs, as they are cared for by their grandparents and parents. (See Mead 1978.)

Only a small part of this cross-generational learning is ever made explicit. Tone of voice alone may convey to the listening child that the past holds all that is admirable and good in life or, on the contrary, that hope for the future is what makes present hardship bearable—or unbearable. What it means to be a man or a woman, what it means to be old and the point at which the individual defines himself (and is defined by others) as old, may be conveyed mainly by posture, including changes in posture of men and women in each other's presence and the bearing of those not yet old in the presence of the aged. Later, in other situations—in school and at work, in intimate situations and in public life, among friends and among strangers—others will express parallel attitudes toward past and future, femininity and masculinity, maturity and old age, by tone of voice and in their stance.

In cultures in which individual creativity is valued, the work of the gifted artist shocks and delights by giving new expression to some part of what is carried nonexplicitly in the voice, in bodily movement patterns, and in other modes of communication, including dreams, of those who are reared as members of the culture. However, it is in song and dance, universal human activities that are created for and shared by large numbers of people, that one finds perhaps the most highly patterned and redundant recreations in symbolic form of the cultural style of a people.

Cantometrics and choreometrics are very new, complex techniques developed by Alan Lomax and his collaborators for the stylistic analysis of song performance and dance and movement style. Discussing the analysis of song, Lomax (1978) writes: "Each song style . . . portrays some level of human adaptation, some social style. Each performance is a symbolic re-enactment of crucial behavior patterns upon which the continuity of a culture hangs, and is thus endowed with the emotional authority of the necessary and the familiar. Moreover, many levels of this symbolic behavior are brought into congruency with some main theme, so that a style comes to epitomize some singular and notable aspect of a culture, by which its members identify themselves and with which they endow many of their activities and their feelings. This is why an expressive style may become the focal point for cultural crystallization and renewal." (See also Lomax and Pauley 1976).

Enculturation: The Process of Learning

Each individual becomes a person, a human being, through enculturation—the process of learning how to live in the society into which he was born. This process involves not only the individual but, reciprocally, all living generations. Each individual's life is shaped by the way in which the culture is mediated to him by others, and each person, in turn, participates in the shaping of his culture through his interactions with others, his parents and other adults, but particularly his peers and those younger than himself.

Even a very brief discussion of cultural universals suggests, on the one hand, that all cultures are based in the responses of the human organism to the environment and, on the other hand, that each culture builds selectively on human capacities and on the environment as it is perceived and thus is made into a humanized world. But it is the individual who is the carrier of culture.

In Western Europe, as in other parts of the world, there is a long tradition of stories about finding children who appear to have survived in a nonhuman setting. Kipling's stories of Mowgli in *The Jungle Books* are derived from Indian versions of ancient folk tales about children who, it was believed, were reared by wolves, bears, or other wild animals. But it is now well known that the nightmare that a potentially human infant, having been stolen from or abandoned by its parents, might be reared in a mode characteristic of some other species, and the daydreams that a child, so reared, might triumphantly assert its humanity are not based in reality.

In the eighteenth century, Linnaeus classified these children as a separate species, *Homo ferus*. Reading the scattered records today, it seems clear that they were autistic children who were abandoned or permitted to wander away (see Bettelheim 1959a and 1959b; Itard 1932; Mandelbaum 1943, Mead 1959b; Ogburn 1959). François Truffaut's film, *The Wild Child*, based on Itard's account (1932) of an effort to rehumanize such a child found in France in 1798 during the hopeful period of the Revolution, is a poignant evocation of French attitudes toward the handicapped and toward formal education.

The human environment, created over thousands of generations and re-created in a contemporary version in every generation, is essential to the survival and development of the human organism. The prolonged helplessness of the infant and the tremendously rapid growth during infancy of innate capacities for learning (in its broadest sense, the development of the capacities for perception, organization, interaction, and communication) together determine the need for care and the kinds of interaction that are crucial for enculturation, which begins long before conscious learning and teaching enter into the process.

Erikson (1963), basing his analysis on the bodily orifices, has outlined how the developmental processes enter into learning from the first days of life and has shown how learning is shaped both by the special emphasis given to one, rather than another, set of bodily functions (for example, oral as compared to anal functions) and by the special emphasis upon one, rather than another, stage of development (for example, active as compared to passive sucking or intake). Erikson's analysis provides one model for studies of the relationship of organism and environment in the shaping of the developmental processes. But our knowledge is as yet very incomplete. For example, we now know that infants are capable of pattern discrimination at a very early stage, but little is known as yet about the incorporation of visual patterns in the early weeks of life.

Nevertheless, evidence of very early enculturation is clear. It appears, for example, in a study reported by Caudill and Weinstein (1969), part of a longitudinal cross-cultural study of Japanese and American children, in which a comparison was made of mother-infant interaction in a carefully matched sample in the two cultures. A major finding of this research was that "largely because of different patterns of interaction with their mothers in the two countries, infants have learned to behave in different and culturally appropriate ways by three to four months of age. Moreover, these differences in infant behavior are in line with preferred patterns of social interaction at later stages as the child grows to be an adult in Japan and America" (p. 13). It should be realized, of course, that studies of this kind must be placed within the context of the total culture as a way of relating what is significant in the infant's experience with significant patterns of behavior in adults.

Field studies, particularly those that are photographically recorded, have permitted us to analyze stylistically distinct cultural modes of adult–infant interaction, taking fully into account the idiosyncratic variations of individuals, both mothers and infants.[11] Treated comparatively, the most important findings are, first, that what is learned is not confined to what is conventionally called "socialization," but is global (that is, involves all aspects of the child's development); second, that modes of behavior learned in infancy are in some sense congruent with later life styles; third, that individual differences are essentially variations on a given style; and, finally, that the basic learning about the handling of the body, the involvement of the senses in experience, modes of interaction, and climax structure are all essentially preverbal.

In fact, the stylization of life begins before birth in the preparatory activities of the mother, in the prescriptions and taboos that define her state and, in many cultures, that of the father as well. In all cultures, as far as is known, rules concerning the mother's activities—what she must and must not do, what she must and must not eat, whether she must, or may, or may not have sexual intercourse at different stages of pregnancy, what sights and sounds are beneficial or harmful to the unborn child, and so on—are believed to have impact on the child's safety, future well-being and, in many cultures, its character structure and personality. In traditional Chinese culture, in which character formation was believed to begin with conception and the newborn infant was reckoned to be one year old, the infant was treated as a partner in an interaction system long before its birth. In some cultures, personality traits are attributed to the child before birth. Thus a Iatmul mother chided her husband, who was impatient for the birth to take place: "Do you think your child is a pig or a dog? No. It is a human being and will be born when it is ready."

Birth, then, is the beginning of a second stage of life, whether or not this is given formal recognition. The way attending adults respond to the birth cry, the way the newborn infant is cleaned and wrapped, lulled against a warm body, laid on a coarse mat or placed in a sterile, mechanically heated crib, and the infant's initial experience of being nursed by a fully lactating woman, or of being kept hungry and demanding until its own mother's milk comes in, or of being fed a formula through a plastic nipple at scheduled intervals, are all events that enter into enculturation. However skillfully or awkwardly, carefully or negligently, warmly or coldly the individual mother carries out her tasks, she is beginning the process of communicating to the child what a human being is and what that child—girl or boy, wanted or unwanted, first-born or tenth-born—may expect of life.

Although the actual requirements for sustaining the life of the neonate are exigent, they are few and relatively simple. Yet cultures differ extraordinarily even in their handling of the newborn. The infant may be defined as very frail and sensorily susceptible, and so may be protected from all but the most essential forms of stimulation for a week, two weeks, a month, or even longer. Or, since the child may be seen as menaced by dangers from the outside world with which it cannot cope—cold, germs, loud noises, and other much more vaguely defined dangers—adults may continually hover over the child in efforts to protect it. Or the child may be regarded as a visitor from another world to which it may be snatched back or to which it may elect to return. So there may be a trial period of days before it is ceremonially lifted up, given a name, and formally acknowledged as a new member of the family and the living human community. Or the newborn infant may be conceived of as strong, so strong that it must be tightly swaddled to protect it from harming itself.

Individually, of course, infants vary in their robustness, their responsiveness, and their adapatability to the kind of care given them. But actual fragility will be treated differently in a culture in which it is taken for granted that all infants are fragile and in one in which it is assumed that newborns are normally strong, active, and demanding. And special sensitivity to auditory stimulation will be treated differently in a culture in which it is assumed that all infants are endangered by too early stimulation, in one in which adults engage in auditory mimicry of the infant's own vocalizations, and in one in which all infants are expected to be essentially passive and nonresponsive.

The neonate may be subjected to various forms of ritual treatment, such as purging or, for a boy, circumcision, as a way of marking its incipient humanity. Or the earliest emphasis may be on setting up a reciprocal relationship between the infant and the world around it as the mother or nurse insists that the infant initiate interchange (for example, feeds the child only on the infant's demand) or as the adult continually responds to observed changes in the infant's state by modifying the way it is rocked, carried, fondled, fed, or wrapped. Or from the first weeks the infant may be subjected to a fixed, externally established routine of care in the belief that this is "natural" (in accordance with nature's "orderly" processes) and is a necessary prefiguration of later obedience training. (See Mead and Wolfenstein 1955, Part 3.)

Whatever the specific methods of infant care, two very significant considerations are the conception of what a child is and should become and the style of relationship that is established initially between the infant and other persons—the setting into motion of the processes of interaction and communication in which the humanity of both partners is involved. In comparing Japanese and American attitudes toward the child, Caudill and Weinstein (1969) comment that the Japanese see the infant "as a separate biological organism who from the beginning, in order to develop, needs to be drawn into increasingly interdependent relations with others," whereas Americans tend to see the infant "as a dependent biological organism who, in order to develop, needs to be made increasingly independent of others" (p. 15).

In current American thinking about socialization, great stress is laid on the very early years, and the principal focus is on the child itself. Other persons related to the child tend to be treated as aspects of the setting in which socialization takes place. For example, the "rejecting" mother as a mediating figure has become a familiar personage in American literature on childhood. The idea that a young mother might be traumatized by her experience with a rejecting infant has been much more difficult for Americans to formulate. We give lip service to the idea of the individuality of the child, but at the same time we strongly believe that the particularities of the setting (including the mother and her handling of the child) are determining factors. The child reared in a "good" environment will grow up to be an autonomous, mature individual; the child reared in a "bad" environment will in some sense be a damaged person.

Our attitudes are most clearly expressed in our handling of the physically handicapped or psychologically disturbed child. Thus the physically handicapped child must be given prosthetic devices and any special care necessary so that it can be "like other children"; the blind child should learn to move around freely and live a "normal" life like that of a sighted child; the deaf child should learn to speak "like other people." That is, we aim to create not an environment geared to the special needs of the handicapped child, but rather learning situations intended to help the child live in the ordinary environment.

In a sense we treat the child's experience as if it were a form of nourishment. The image is striking as it is used in connection with contemporary educational programs for disadvantaged children that are intended to "enrich" the environment or the learning experience, much as vitamins are intended to "enrich" their diet. Such treatment of the environment has the effect of muting the play of personality in the partnership of parent and child.

In certain other contemporary cultures the dominant role of the parents, particularly of the mother in the early years, is less ambiguously phrased. In France and Germany, for example, the infant is regarded as essentially passive and dependent on the mother's initiative and control.[12] The French, especially, are amused, but also distressed, by the active, exploratory behavior encouraged in infants by American parents; Germans see this as evidence that American children are "spoiled."

The stage of development at which the child is conceived of as entering actively into interpersonal relationships, beginning with its parents, and into a specifically educational partnership in learning, varies culturally with the conception of what is crucial in growth and development. The German child, for example, is expected to become active through opposition. Mothers are advised to carry the child through what is regarded as an inevitable battle of wills (at about 2½ to 3 years) by the previous establishment of firm discipline, so that the child will already take for granted obedience to impersonally stated rules. Success in getting through this crisis, during which the child has become conscious of his own will, ensures that he will thereafter direct his efforts toward the self-enforcement of obedience. It will also help him through the second crisis of will, as Germans see it, in adolescence, when he must begin to formulate his own life goals. The central aim of German child rearing is character building: it is assumed that the young adult who is prepared to meet life's tests (*lebenstüchtig*) will exercise self-control just as earlier his parents and teachers controlled him.

From infancy on, French children are urged to be *sage* and *raisonnable*, but these are qualities that are acquired over a long time. A child is not expected to differentiate truth and falsehood before the age of five or six or to be capable of abstract reasoning before early adolescence. It is the responsibility of parents and teachers to "awaken" the child's mind and sensibilities and, in doing so, to teach the child correctly before it has a chance to make mistakes. Spontaneity, for the French, is safe and creative when it follows, but not when it precedes, training in skills. Left to experiment on its own, the child is both endangered and dangerous to others. Discipline, for the French, is a continuous process of transformation: the obligation to eat what is set before it teaches the child the enjoyment of good food; the obligation to listen silently to good conversation teaches the child to enjoy verbal skills; the obligation to "fight with words, not with fists" teaches the child to enjoy verbal combat. As a partner in the learning process, the French child is an apprentice human being who, under the guidance of others, learns to become himself. Only then can he enter into fully reciprocal relations with his peers and exercise initiative in self-expression and as the teacher of other apprentices.[13]

In the comparative isolation of the American home, it is easy to believe that all experience is mediated first by the mother (or, today, by both parents—if both are in the home) and later by parents interacting with the child and with siblings older and younger than himself. But, in fact, the whole setting of the home, what it incorporates of a wider world and what it excludes, early enters the child's experience and sets up complex expectations about the larger world. For example, the architecture of the house itself, the use of space, the assignment of activities to certain parts of the house, the parts of the house to which strangers, kin or friends, only members of the household or only certain members of the household are admitted, the limits of privacy—all these give the child cues about the ordering of life not only in the home but also within the self and in the community.

As far as is known, neither learning nor learning to learn is limited to any one stage of life. Unquestionably, there are certain constants—periods in the development of the human organism when particular kinds of specialized physical and mental skills are best learned, as well as various skills that must be learned early if even the most talented individual is to become fully proficient. Nevertheless, enculturation is essentially a lifelong process, in spite of vast cultural differences in expectations about what is proper to childhood learning and what the span of learning is among adults.

Not every culture defines the young human being as qualitatively different from the adult, as we do. Instead, the difference may be perceived as an essentially quantitative one; the child may be regarded as an adult in miniature, as Phillipe Aries, in his study *Centuries of Childhood* (1962), has shown that children were regarded in medieval Europe. Or children may be grouped together with women as different from adult men. Or the point about children may be that they are not yet ritually incorporated within the community.

In many, but not all, cultures the child's status changes abruptly, once or several times—at a definite age, at some clearly visible stage of development when the child demonstrates certain accomplishments, or when it has undergone a ritual marking a change in status. The designation of stages of development and the time scale within which development is seen to occur vary considerably from one culture to another. The Eskimo boy, who began to use miniature adult weapons and to take part in adult activities before the age of ten, and the Chinese man, who in the traditional culture arrived at the stage of full, active responsibility only in the fourth decade of life (long after his marriage, but long before he would arrive at the stage of unquestioned authority), exemplify the working out of two highly contrasting, culturally determined time scales of individual life. But one of the most revolutionary changes of our time has been the extension of the human life span, a point which must always be taken into account in reconstructing age relationships in any earlier period. There have always been a few really old people; the change is in the proportion of men and women who are long-lived and in the age at which a person becomes "old."

The High Point and the Low Point of Life

Cultures differ also in the definition and the placement of the high and low points in human existence. The high point in living may come early, as in the West Indian culture of Montserrat, where both men and women look back with nostalgia all their adult lives to "the happy careless days" of older childhood and early adolescence, before they had taken on the irksome burdens of responsible autonomy. Or the high point may come late in life, as in Haitian culture, where the old speak with authority and must be deferred to. The low point in life may also come at any stage: in the apprentice years of childhood in French culture; in the early years of marriage for the woman in traditional Japanese culture, when she was at the beck and call of all other adults in the family; in old age in Polish peasant culture, when the man and his wife, having given over control of the land to a son, were merely tolerated in the household.

In some cultures most individuals will arrive at the high point of existence. In others it can be achieved only by the exercise of effort. In still others arrival at the high point may be a matter of chance or fate. Success opens the way to authority and deference earlier for the Haitian, but simply by staying alive long enough, most men and women (but not all, for there are recognized exceptions) will reach the goal. In traditional Chinese culture, too, the full flowering of personality and the high point of individual existence were believed to come late in life. But no exercise of skill could ensure that an elderly couple would be fortunate; that is, that husband and wife would both survive into old age, that they would be healthy, and that they would then be surrounded by children and children's children.

The ideal may be such that everyone, as in Montserrat, must inevitably move on to a less desirable stage of life; indeed, as in Montserrat, the recognition that one has already passed life's high point may come only in later years. Or the ideal may be so narrowly defined that only a few can ever hope to reach the pinnacle and all others must define themselves as, in some sense, failures.

Each man may hope, as in French culture, that he will be able to reach a limited, self-selected goal, beyond which his ambitions do not take him. Or, as in American culture, the main emphasis may be on movement itself, so that no one, child or adult, can long remain on any plateau of achievement. For Americans, not to move on is to fall back; the man who is content to stay where he is remains "stuck in a rut." In the past, retirement for the Frenchman did not mean that he was taking a back seat to life; if he was fortunate, he had arrived at the position of his choice at which he hoped to stay. For Americans, it meant that a man was on the downgrade. Today we are attempting to rephrase retirement as the beginning of a new stage in living, with its own special attributes and aims.

The cultural conception of the total life span always has a bearing on the way in which the individual interprets his existence at any period of his life. Set in the framework of a belief in reincarnation (which, of course, takes many forms), events in this lifetime are not absolute; misery and ill fortune may be tempered by the hope for a better fate in the next. Attitudes toward the events of one's life are qualitatively different in a culture in which one's acts in this life determine one's eternal salvation or damnation. So also attitudes toward the worth of the individual, as well as toward accident, suffering, illness, and early death, are very different in cultures in which the individual believes he lives many successive lives, and in those in which he has only one life, bounded by birth and death in this world. The secularization of life in modern societies has the double effect of altering the boundaries of existence and of setting a very high value on the individual at all stages of his life, which, it is believed, begins and ends in this world.

Redundancy in Culture

No two individuals, even identical twins, share exactly the same life experiences in their society. No two families are exactly alike; the timing of learning varies; the individual capacities of parents and children differ; parents and other key persons die; natural and man-made catastrophes—floods or droughts, famines or epidemics, wars or dissension—disrupt the life of the community; the individual suffers some disablement that temporarily or permanently cuts him off from some aspect of experience he would normally share with his peers. All such things mean that the child, growing up, experiences the life of his society in a way that is, in some respects, unique. It does not, however, mean that he has grown up *outside* his culture, but only that he (like every other individual, to a greater or a lesser extent) learns his culture from a special vantage point. The orphan, the child in a single-parent home, and the child in a series of foster homes, learn about families through what they, as individuals, lack; the child growing up in a long period of famine learns about plenty through the experience, shared with others, of deprivation.

Even more important, however, is the fact that every culture is exceedingly redundant. The "message" is conveyed to the individual in many different forms and contexts of experience. While he is growing up, the orphan may never experience in its most intense form the relaxed intimacy—or the formal distance or the covert rivalry or the rebellion—of the expected relation of father and son. But he will experience, however imperfectly, what it is to be a son in other relationships that are modeled on father-son relations (with a guardian, teachers, employers, leaders and, later, with his own pupils, employees, followers and so on); he will also learn about it indirectly from the plots of stories and the whole imagery of the culture that draws on the father-son relationship and on the predicament of the orphan, the fatherless, and the homeless child.

There is also the situation in which, for whatever reason, the learning experience miscarries: the boy learns to flee from, rather than to accept as a challenge, the games in which boys learn courage, endurance, loyalty to a peer group, and other attributes of masculinity and male relationships in their culture; the girl overestimates the anxiety surrounding childbirth and sees it not as a temporary state that is resolved in the warmth of welcome to a new life, but as a permanent threat to a woman's existence. The aberrant belief and behavior, the "incorrect" picture of what is involved, the idiosyncratic adjustment made by the individual still are systematically related to the expectations, the patterning of behavior to which the individual is responding.[14]

All cultures provide alternative routes to the same ends and provide alternative roles for at least some of the deviants who are born in the society or who are likely to develop in deviant ways in response to the expectations of the particular culture. Given the conditions of life or the cultural definition of what is crucial for life, some do not survive early infancy. In most cultures the infant with a severe physical anomaly, visible at birth, is likely to die very early. In a culture in which only the mother can suckle her own child, the newborn infant whose mother has died in childbirth will not survive. Until recently, this was likely to be the case in most cultures; the exception was the culture in which the idea of the wet nurse existed. There have also been a few cultures in which techniques were known for inducing lactation in a nonlactating woman.

In all cultures there are some marginal roles into which certain recognized deviants may be fitted, roles that may be honored, tolerated or despised, protected or surrounded by devices for protecting others from persons in those special roles.

The relationship of deviance and abnormality to normality within a culture, and viewed across cultural boundaries, is a concern common to the social scientist and the practitioner who, today, may be called upon to work with people of many different cultural origins and in unfamiliar settings in many parts of the world. The problem becomes acute in situations of abrupt change, where the premises and viewpoints of two generations may be in violent conflict.

Ruth Benedict: Cultural Relativism and the Abnormal in Culture

In the 1920s and early 1930s—a period when, as in the present, traditional values were under heavy attack—anthropologists attempted to generalize the principle of cultural relativism, that is, the theory that values and beliefs, modes of behavior, and conceptions of the nature of the world must be understood within the framework of the culture in which they occur. In this connection, the problem of the deviant and the abnormal individual was treated, in a sense, as a test case.

In developing her theory of cultural diversity in *Patterns of Culture,* first published in 1934, Ruth Benedict hypothesized that each culture draws selectively on the "great arc" of human potentialities and that each cultural configuration is an elaboration of certain "selected" potentialities at a period. She hypothesized further that while most individuals, owing to the malleability of their original endowment (as she phrased it) are able to function adequately in the society within which they are reared, cultures are differentially congenial to those born within them. Essentially, it is those for whom, in terms of their inborn temperament, the emphases of the culture are uncongenial, who are the deviant individuals in that culture. As she herself put it: "Just as those are favored whose congenial responses are closest to that behavior which characterizes their society, so those are disoriented whose congenial responses fall in that arc of behavior which is not capitalized by their culture. They are the exceptions who have not easily taken the traditional forms of their culture" (1934:258).

Further, in her discussion of contrasting cultural styles in her seminal paper, "Anthropology and the Abnormal" (1966), she stated that "most of those organizations of personality that seem to us most incontrovertibly abnormal have been used by different civilizations in the very foundations of their institutional life. Conversely the most valued traits of our normal individuals have been looked on in differently organized cultures as aberrant" (p. 276). In *Patterns of Culture* she demonstrated the point in sketches of the Kwakiutl Indians of Vancouver Island, the Melanesian Dobuans and the Zuni of the western Pueblos, whom she compared with other American Indians, particularly those of the Plains—cultures which contrasted extremely in their ethos, the organization of their institutions, the focus of their interests and the personality structure of individuals.

In fact, Ruth Benedict was not interested in constructing an over-all cross-cultural typology of cultures or personality structures (Mead 1959a: 201–212). The terms she used—Dionesian and Apollonian—were to be understood metaphorically, as a device to focus awareness on a well known major stylistic contrast between certain large groups of American Indian societies. It was her acute awareness of individual personality differences in the culture to which she had access, as well as her own sense of herself, that allowed her to recognize quite precisely that those persons for whom the patterned expectations of their culture are temperamentally uncongenial and whose responses to these expectations are unusual—whether or not they are psychopathic—are, in this sense, aberrant. And as Margaret Mead, whose views differed on this problem, wrote:

> From the first Ruth Benedict resisted any idea of schematization in terms of a given number of temperaments—Jung's fourfold scheme, for instance. She

saw the relationship between a culture, which was "personality writ large" and "time binding," and any individual, who might or might not fit in, as a way of so phrasing all deviation that the unfortunate could be pitied and the world seen as the loser because of gifts which could not be used. She wanted to leave the future open (1959a:206).

It was the possibility of openness—of an infinite variety of cultures—that captured her imagination (personal communication).

Contemporary readers have some difficulty in accepting Ruth Benedict's use of terms in *Patterns of Culture,* without recognizing the lack, at that period, of a precise, clearly understood vocabulary. But this reflects the originality, then, of her search and the difficulty of matching insight and formal statement. Her handling of the problem was an exploratory one, based on an immense knowledge of the anthropological literature interpreted by an extraordinarily sensitive and perceptive investigator. The questions she raised prompted other anthropologists to develop new approaches in their own field research.[15]

Today, the principle of cultural relativism is taken for granted. The focus of interest has shifted to problems of process. Ruth Benedict's hypothesis about the relation between temperament and cultural "fit" still stands. But contemporary investigation places greater emphasis on the nature of experience, in different cultures, that may lead to maladaptation in a particular setting or, cross-culturally, in many settings.

Deviance: The Contemporary View

Today there is general agreement that the major psychoses are found in all cultures in which relevant investigation has been carried out, but there are, in addition, what George Devereux (1961) calls "ethnic psychoses." There is also agreement that manifestations of psychosis are modified by cultural patterning and by the way in which the particular type of psychosis is characterized by members of his own culture.

The problem of the deviant individual is an extraordinarily complex one, particularly in the matter of whether or not he is necessarily, by the standards of his own culture or in terms of psychological theory, abnormal and emotionally disturbed.[16]

Clearly, more than one type of deviance may occur in any culture. The individual may be a temperamental deviant, or he may be singled out in his society as a particular kind of deviant because of some physical trait or condition that is recognized as a significant variation from the normal in his culture. Blindness, deaf-mutism, albinism, left-handedness, convergent or divergent strabismus, having erupted teeth at birth or being born in a caul, having an extra digit or elflocks—all these and many other major and minor anomalies, as well as being a twin (same or opposite sex) or the child born after twins, have been seized on in various cultures as evidence of aberrance; the child so born (if he is not immediately killed or allowed to die) is expected to follow some special path in his development that differentiates him from others as a person and often in the roles that are open to him.

An individual may also be categorized as a deviant because of some special social circumstance. In a mild way, in American culture the only child has been thought of as deviant. And in Western societies in general the illegitimate child has been regarded as deviant, but there are radical differences in these societies in the definition of illegitimacy and in beliefs about the character structure, personality, and expected fate of the illegitimate child.

There are also circumstances in which an individual or a whole family may come to be regarded as aberrant by the community. In American culture this may happen, for example, to the family of a man who has embezzled money or the children of a person who has committed a murder; in fact, particularly in smaller communities, the immediate relatives of any respected person who has become notorious tend to be treated (and, as they share in the attitudes of the community, come to think of themselves) as deviant. The question of whether the family of the individual whose behavior has resulted in notoriety is or is not, in fact, deviant is not relevant here. But the fact that deviance of some kind is likely to be ascribed to members of such a family in itself alters the community's perception of them, as well as their perception of themselves, and has consequences for their later behavior.

A crucial question in considering deviance, whatever its origin, concerns the kind and intensity of intrapsychic conflict experienced by the deviant individual and the psychological mechanisms employed in attempts to manage conflict. Looked at as a cultural phenomenon, what is important is that the deviant's responses fall—or are believed to fall—outside the range of the expected and the comprehensible, at least in some aspects of life. The person's responses may be misinterpreted (as when the excessively passive little girl is treated simply as a "good" child, or when a gifted young boy in American culture is suspected of having homosexual tendencies because of his unusual tactile sensitivity), and efforts to elicit "normal" (culturally regular) responses may be, or may be felt to be, excessively punitive. It would appear that confusion and disorientation result from a breakdown in communication insofar as the individual's preferred responses and attempts to handle conflict do not receive support in the culturally patterned methods of child rearing, standardized types of conflict expression and resolution, or the institutionalized forms of adult behavior.

The problem must be viewed in a somewhat different light where aberrant behavior appears to be congruent with some type of deviance that is institutionalized in the particular culture; that is, the individual "fits" into an unusual but acceptable place in the society.[17] The role open to the man or woman may be an honored one, as in the case of the celibate member of a religious community. It may be one that involves considerable power, as in the case of shamans in some societies. It may be essentially protective, as in the case of an old woman who is a solitary in peasant Haitian society, who is both feared and deferred to and, by this means, is provided with human contact. It may be very marginal and despised, but socially necessary, as in the case of the beggar in the Eastern European *shtetl* or in Spain who, by his existence, permits others to perform enjoined acts of charity. A role may emphasize incapacity and dependence, as in the case of women in Victorian England who were confined to an invalid's life on a sofa (Elizabeth Barrett Browning is a well-known example). It may also put the individual beyond the pale of respectable society, as in the case of the compulsive thief who spends a major part of his life behind bars.

Stated in an oversimplified way, the problem is not that the deviant and the abnormal individual suffer from intrapsychic conflict whereas the normal individual in the same society does not. It is rather that the methods of handling conflict, as these are shaped by and expressed in characteristic patterns of behavior and in the institutional arrangements of the culture, are not in the same way available to the deviant or the abnormal person—whose learning is in some sense distorted—as they are to those whose learning experiences have been relatively felicitous and successful.

The most obvious case is that of the child born with a serious defect, such as total blindness or deafness, or suffering from a major birth injury, such as cerebral palsy. The child's self-model (Devereux 1967) differs from that of the physically normal child in ways that reflect cultural attitudes toward the particular defect. The existence of the defect affects not only the child's dependency needs, perceptions, learning processes, and sense of himself, but also the attitudes of parents and other adults toward the child and their handling of the child's enculturation. Parent–child and teacher–child relations are altered in terms of adult expectations for such a child, as are peer relations, courtship relations, career expectations, and so on.[18]

In Britain it is not uncommon for the parent of such a child to ask, "What have *I* done?" as if the disability were a judgment on the parent for some earlier act. In France the mother of a blind infant may forego any formal attempt to teach the child (that is, "the mother just sits all day holding the baby"), so that socialization may be postponed until very late; later, the blind child's formal education carries to an extreme the tactile and kines-thetic training that is part of the normal French child's early education. The very different attitudes of most Americans (both parents and professionals who work with different groups of handicapped persons) toward the blind and the deaf child—their determinedly optimistic assessment of what the blind individual can and should accomplish and their pessimism and, very often, punitive attitude where the deaf child is concerned—demonstrate clearly contextual differences in the handling of various types of physical incapacity. In our society there is a very high demand for autonomy in the blind individual—so much so that he may be cut off from some normal forms of dependence (in contrast to Spain, for example, where it is taken for granted that the blind can survive only in a very protected setting). But the blind, in our culture, are not alienated as are many deaf individuals, who tend to retreat into the partly closed community of nonhearing persons like themselves. This is, however, changing.[19]

The problem of the person who is a temperamental misfit in his society, particularly someone who cannot (or will not) adopt one of the alternative roles recognized in the culture, is much more complicated. One difficulty is the technical one that while such individuals have been observed, few have been carefully studied.[20] But it is possible to illustrate the problem. For example, in Haitian peasant and proletarian culture not everyone experi-ences trance (possession by a god), but there are a few people who seek and never attain a trance state. Although these deviants participate—even play formal roles—in the ceremonies of Voodoo (the folk religion), they are cut off from the major mode of expressive communication in the culture; that is, they are cut off from using certain culturally regular ways of—among other things—symbolizing and working out intrapsychic conflicts. It is significant, in this connection, that there are also those who temporarily or permanently abandon Catholicism and become Protestant converts (in sects that are strongly anti-Voodoo) in an attempt to evade and escape the too exigent demands, even the persecution, of Voodoo deities. Some succeed in avoiding trance possessions, others do not or, alternatively, begin to "speak in tongues," a practice that is permitted them.[21] However, for educated Haitians even the remote possibility of a trance episode is a source of anxiety.

Today in Montserrat rural culture, which draws on much of the same African cultural heritage as Haiti, trance is not a type of experience that is widely available. In fact, in the very few ceremonial situations in which trance is still expected, such as the ceremonies of the marriage night, individuals may be resistant to going into trance. While it is very standardized in form, trance has become a kind of experience and a mode of communication that is characteristic only of certain deviant individuals, whose preference for this expressive mode of communication is regarded with great ambivalence by most people. In overt behavior Montserrat culture heavily emphasizes personal choice and denigrates the use of coercion and constraint in compelling compliance. It is just this sense of a compelling force that leads most people to reject—and some to be attracted to—trance experience.[22]

In considering the problems of cultural patterning and deviance, one must also realize that no cultural configuration is wholly integrated. A culture totally in balance would cease to be human. Persons reared in such a culture would no longer be capable of cultural innovation—that is, of the kinds of "breakthrough" behavior that lead to culture change—or of the adaptive behavior involved, for example, in learning a new culture as an adult.

In actuality, however, the conditions for ideal stability are not attainable. Very few societies have existed for any length of time in full isolation. (A partial exception was Easter Island where, owing to the extreme geographical isolation of the island, contact was lost with other Polynesian societies.) Ongoing contacts with the peoples of other societies—through trade, warfare, the capture of women and children or regularly institutionalized marriage exchange, the purchase or exchange of not only utilitarian goods but also ornaments, techniques, ritual complexes, objects made by specialists—means that there is a more or less continuous flow through which change can take place in the handling of details of style, in ideas, and in cultural emphases over time. Also, the presence in each generation of people who, through some special set of circumstances, may bring new talents into play (Mead 1964, Part 2) keeps open possibilities of change. Moreover, in every culture there are characteristic discontinuities, discrepancies, ambiguities, and contradictions, as well as what might be called blank spots—contingencies that are unprovided for. Part of learning a way of life consists of learning that there are alternative ways of handling the discontinuities, and acceptable modes of handling intrapsychic conflict—including, in many cultures, suicide as the expected outcome of certain forms of conflict.

Culture Change and Conflict

The culturally defined situations that evoke conflict and the overt behavior through which conflict is expressed and resolution of conflict is sought are a matter of special concern when one is attempting to understand the difficulties experienced by immigrants and the children of immigrants, who are in the process of adapting themselves to an alien way of life. They are also centrally important in any attempt to understand the processes of very rapid, far-reaching culture change and the effects of such change on the personality organization and institutional arrangements of a people who are in the process of adapting themselves to a new and as yet unknowable way of life (Mead 1978). Both are situations in which it is essential to have some conception of what are the normal (and the recognized abnormal) ways of responding to crisis and also to the new, the strange and the unforeseeable.

Immigrants, living in a society different from the one in which they grew up, must learn new styles of courtship, marriage, parenthood, maturation, aging, and dying, for which they have had no childhood preparation. As individuals, some will have an easier time than others in making an adequate adaptation to a particular new style of living. But there will also be distinct differences among immigrant groups that arise from differences in the attitudes which are characteristic of the cultures from which the immigrant groups come—attitudes toward stability and change, continuity and discontinuity, learning at different ages and learning by men and by women and, especially, the relationships of adults and children and the expected outcome of childhood learning. Coming from one culture, immigrants may believe that stability is ensured by flexibility; coming from another, they may experience change as fragmentation. In one culture there may be a very deep belief that the whole course of life is set at birth or by a certain age; in another there may be an expectation that men and boys learn new ways outside the home and the home community, but that women carry through their whole lives what they have learned from older women who are close to them. For some it will seem possible to maintain at home a style of living that has become inappropriate outside the home in the new country. For others change is an all-or-nothing matter, involving all aspects of living, as far as they are understood, or none.

The children of immigrants, especially those whose parents try to rear them in ways related to their own upbringing, have a very complex learning experience. They must somehow manage the double task of imagining the organization of a culture of which they have at best only a partial experience at home and of translating the requirements of their upbringing into the different requirements of the culture into which they are moving as school-children, as adolescents in search of a peer group among whom they will find friends and companions, and as adults who must leave home and enter the working world and possibly the world of marriage and parenthood. They must learn to "hear" two languages and to interpret two sets of expressive patterns, each of which they experience only in some parts of their lives. And as a way of fitting their own lives together, they must to some extent reverse the normal process and become the teachers of their parents, who have never experienced the new culture from the vantage point of childhood. In doing so, they must somehow convey to their parents what they can understand about a future of which they themselves have no prefigurative experience.

The Choice of Ethnic Pluralism

In contemporary American society—as in other societies in which cultural pluralism is recognized, whether positively or negatively—a new kind of understanding is emerging which has to do with the status of groups, large or small, that exist simultaneously within and outside the national culture as it is conceived. Throughout our history Americans have had very strong—and very conflicting—attitudes toward the true natives, American Indians; toward African forced immigrants and their black American descendants; and toward the various immigrant groups and the refugees from different areas of the world that have flooded into the country at different periods. Designated as a "minority"—a characterization that carries mixed, but generally negative, messages—each group has had forced on its members, or its members have worked out for themselves, some form of adaptation that has made survival possible. But for as long as minorities have been seen and have seen themselves socially and culturally in an anomalous relationship to the larger cultural community, the possibilities for alienation have been very great. So also have been the possibilities of sudden individual and group rejection, a form of double alienation (such as the actions of the Ku Klux Klan at various periods and in various settings and the panic reaction and incarceration of Japanese in World War II).

Today, instead, we speak of ethnicity, and the changes rung on this word and the contexts in which they appear make clear the current popularity of the idea. In addition, for some years there has been a growing literature on the subject (see, for example, DeVos and Romanucci-Ross 1982). Triggered in part by the strength and passion of the Civil Rights movement and the movements that were part of the 1960s counterculture, there has been a reevaluation of the place of minority groups in the society. Ethnicity carries positive overtones at present, and there is a recognition that a sense of clear ethnic self-identity carries with it feelings of pride and self-worth.

Schwartz (1982), discussing his intensive research on the contemporary relationships of the "at least twenty locally recognized linguistic groups in the Admiralty Islands, each associated with cultural differences other than language" (p. 109), suggests that as "identity is always problematic and consequently dynamic, not only in modern, rapidly changing societies but in primitive societies as well . . . ethnic status (like sexual status but perhaps with even greater priority) is one of the bases upon which identities are constructed" (p. 128). For such reasons, he concludes, the more closely different peoples are associated in interaction, the more likely they are to value and preserve the special marks each people has of its own ethnicity which also singles out each individual member as having a recognizable social self-identity.

Three

Psychopathology in Cultural Contexts

The brilliant and widely publicized 1920s debate on the question of the universality of the Oedipus complex as defined in Western cultures was engaged in by the psychoanalyst Ernest Jones and the social anthropologist Bronislaw Malinowski, on the basis of their radically different reading of Malinowski's pioneer field work among the matrilineally organized Trobriand Islanders. It ended more or less in a draw, yet it was a debate that continually provoked further debate up to the present (see, for example, Parsons 1969b and Weiner 1976 and 1985). In the interim the problem itself has been recognized to be far more complex than it appeared to be at first, when the argument depended on data—and, as it turned out, not the full, relevant data—primarily on one matrilineal society, and very little was known in any detail about other Melanesian cultures.

The original debate also suggested to research-minded clinicians and field-oriented cultural anthropologists concerned with problems of personality how much more might be accomplished by drawing on the combined skills of men and women trained in these disciplines, particularly in work among peoples whose cultural heritage is rooted in traditions very different from those of more familiar Western societies. The further recognition that these complementary skills could be illuminating in combined application to problems of personality in Western cultures still lay quite far in the future.

Although the development of method and theory in the practice of interdisciplinary and collaborative research has been sporadic, the several disciplines, particularly since the 1950s, have drawn with increasing sophistication and success on one another's research data. In this period a great deal has been written about psychopathological behavior in different societies and within the same society at different times. This is, so far, the area within which the methods and viewpoints of cultural anthropology and dynamic psychology, taken together, have perhaps been most productive. Where appropriate research has been carried out, occurrences of the major psychoses as defined in Western medicine have been identified in preliterate and so-called traditional societies as well as in societies undergoing radical change and, to some degree, among ethnic groups living in enclaves in a culturally different, larger society—for example, the "guest workers" everywhere present in Western Europe. In older psychological studies, especially those based in Western societies, the culture was, as a rule, treated as given; in contemporary research, account is taken of the cultural setting in which a specific psychopathology occurs. Both psychologist and cultural anthropologist place the identified individual within a living context.

That there are both quantitative and qualitative changes over time in the occurrence of mental illnesses and their manifestations is well known. In Europe stigmata (such as bleeding from the palms on Fridays) do not occur as they did in earlier centuries. But belief in the occurrence of stigmata lingers on in some marginal groups in Europe and elsewhere, usually displaced onto such figures as the dying Christ, the Virgin, or various saints represented by miraculous statues in churches. The idea, even now, remains available for further elaboration or reinterpretation.

Even within very brief periods, shifts in emphasis in the occurrence of mental illnesses have been observed. In World War I, for example, American soldiers suffered from conversion hysterias. In World War II other ways of coping with severe conflict—such as physiological reactions, anxiety states and depressions—were much more common in the American armed forces. Still more recently, in Vietnam, the use by members of the armed forces of various readily available drugs as a generalized escape device reached almost epidemic proportions.[1]

In the same period radical changes have taken place in worldwide communications. First radio and then television—especially as combined with satellite transmission—and the worldwide availability today of small, cheap, battery-operated radios that are equally at home on city streets and in very remote villages in Papua New Guinea and elsewhere have deeply affected ways of life in almost every setting. For inevitably people's awareness of others who are like—but especially unlike—themselves is bringing about alterations in their sense of personal and ethnic identity as well as in their own views of the identity ascribed to them by others, nearby or far away.

In the light of such changes as these, data on the more distant past, particularly data in which the cultural setting was disregarded, cannot now be reviewed in search of answers to questions that were not asked and records of observations not made or noted down. At best, what is known may be no more than suggestive. We can, therefore, only speculate about forms of behavioral disturbance that occurred long ago, even in societies on which relatively good historical and other sources exist. For example, in Western Europe in the period of intense culture change in the sixteenth and seventeenth centuries, which we think of as a time of extraordinary aesthetic and scientific enrichment, preoccupation with witchcraft as a phenomenon of the real world (as it was believed to be) had great influence on contemporary thought and shaped not only normal modes of behavior, but also interpretations of the abnormal in ways that have become exceedingly rare—and even now defy analysis.

Older data on the occurrence of dysfunctional behavior, especially in preliterate societies, must be viewed with caution. Often the only persons who recorded information or reported what they had heard secondhand about members of a preliterate society were casual travelers, traders, missionaries, and the like. Untrained in any scientific discipline, they were seldom well informed about behavioral norms outside their own circle of experience and were unable to distinguish correctly between behavior that appeared bizarre, from their point of view, and behavior that was abnormal within the context of the native culture, or to evaluate and fully record interpretations presented to them by native speakers.

The same strictures apply to reports on normal behavior by unqualified observers, whatever their discipline. In the late nineteenth century social theorists hypothesized that Australian aborigines represented man at an early stage of human development, and accounts of Australian tribal life were distorted in the direction of assumptions then current about the way of life of "early man." Thus it was reported that the family, as a concept and as a functioning social unit, was lacking among these peoples—who, in fact, had built up some of the most intricate sets of rules of marriage and kin relationships that are known. It required both a more scientific understanding of human evolution and a more objective view of human capacities to open the way to a more exact appreciation of Australian aboriginal cultures.[2]

Furthermore, relatively few anthropologists trained a generation or more ago had the double training that would have allowed them to undertake cultural studies that involved work in depth with individuals. Moreover, much of the basic data on American Indian cultures, for example, was obtained through very intensive work with informants—many of them quite elderly, some of them talented, many of them not—living a restricted life on reservations at a time when the cultures were broken and Indian populations decimated. Where emphasis was on saving what could be saved—on attempting to reconstruct the culture of a fully functioning society—opportunities for direct observation were limited and accounts of behavior, including dysfunctional behavior, were obtained at second- or third-hand, distant in time and often far from the place where the alleged events took place. Where this kind of research was carried out by sophisticated, experienced anthropologists, as for example by Franz Boas on Northwest Coast Indian societies or by Robert Lowie on the Crow and other Plains Indians, the method was a highly productive one. It provided us with quite detailed, critical analyses of the *formal* culture. But such analyses seldom include in-depth accounts of the life of individuals. Rarely, as in Lowie's last, most general book on the Crow Indians (1935), which followed on a series of formal monographs, one comes on a passage describing the man who became a "Crazy-Dog-wishing-to-die" (pp. 330–34), that is, a man who voluntarily acted out the ritualized suicidal behavior in warfare. Then one recognizes that, after all, the field research was based in friendship and intimate personal understanding. Students also were well aware of this.

Although the history and circumstances of contact with societies in other areas of the world are very different from those that affected American Indian ways of life, the same cautions apply to earlier work carried out in South America, Africa, Polynesia, and elsewhere. Unquestionably, the lack of usable data means that some expressions of human potentialities in societies that have vanished, even within our own lifetime, are beyond our reach. Yet, in spite of these limitations, we do have a body of information that, used with care and discrimination, provides a base for thinking about the occurrence of psychopathology in cultural contexts.

The point of view, the necessary skills, and the capacity for trained insight were acquired in different ways by anthropologists who became interested in problems of personality. Some were initially caught by the way in which their teachers talked informally about their field experiences, in contrast to the way they wrote their formal published monographs. In the early days very few were psychoanalyzed. Kroeber was for a short time a practicing lay analyst (T. Kroeber 1970); George Devereux, a student of Kroeber, combined the two disciplines throughout his career (for example, Devereux 1961, 1967, 1969, 1978, 1980). A. Irving Hallowell moved only slowly from social work into anthropology and, on the wave of 1920s excitement about Freud and psychoanalysis, developed and taught a new style of fieldwork (Hallowell 1976a). Erik Erikson (1963) writes of his "long talks" with an-thropologists—talks that also had a profound influence on *them*—and of his introduction to "the field" by Scudder Mekeel and Alfred Kroeber, who guided him in his exploratory research on the Sioux and the Yurok. These are, of course, only a handful of the people who were attracted by the possibilities of dynamic psychology and played parts in opening the way to cross-disciplinary and cross-cultural studies of personality.

This does not mean, however, that earlier work must be discarded. In some cases, carefully directed research in the earlier literature together with intensive fieldwork can, in fact, be extremely rewarding, as, for example, in recent work by a young medical anthropologist on the syndrome commonly known as *koro* (Edwards 1983; see below). In addition, methods of contem-porary fieldwork that incorporate new techniques of combined visual and aural recording provide invaluable data on which members of several disci-plines can work simultaneously, in this way expanding the areas within which members of each discipline are effective.

Culturally and Regionally Limited Types of Psychopathology

In different regions of the world, in societies, most—but not all—of which have long had contact with at least some aspects of Western cultures with-out, however, losing altogether their own distinctive culture, forms of psy-chopathological functioning have been identified that have been variously described as culturally or regionally limited. They are recognized as abnor-mal states within the belief systems of the peoples among whom they occur, and the behavior of those afflicted elicits standardized cultural responses also in keeping with the belief system—just as in our own society. In terms of Western medicine they appear to be equivalent to psychotic episodes, anxiety states, or hysterical manifestations observed in our own societies.

A number of these abnormal states have become well known in the literature, and they appear to be passed on from one survey or discussion to another without significant alteration of content or interpretation, simply as cultural aberrations. Occasionally, however, a new explanatory analysis is offered, which may or may not be based on new first-hand research, but which usually provides, as substantiating evidence, more information than may otherwise have been given about the cultural context in which the dysfunctional behavior occurs. Again, a significant cross-cultural comparison, like Parker's (1962) comparison of the occurrence of Arctic hysterias among the Eskimo and of the windigo psychosis among the Algonkian Ojibwa, sharpens our perception of the cultural setting in which a particular psychological disturbance occurs, but does not necessarily increase our understanding of why one individual is at greater risk than another. Here a brief discussion of several such pathological manifestations, some better reported than others, may demonstrate some aspects of the "fit" between cultural configuration and manifestation of abnormality.

THE WINDIGO PSYCHOSIS

The windigo psychosis, which is believed to involve cannibalistic acts, as far as we know is (or was) limited in its occurrence to the Algonkian-speaking Indians of central and northeastern Canada (Ojibwa, Cree, and Montagnais-Maskapi).[3] Cases of windigo have been reported from the period of the earliest contacts with these Indians in the seventeenth century, but no modern research worker has observed an instance of a full-blown windigo psychosis. Some descriptions are extraordinarily vivid, but are in fact based on secondhand reports, some by persons who had witnessed the killing of an individual believed to be a windigo, others by persons who had known a recovered windigo or had heard episodes described by still others. Teicher (1960) assembled data on seventy reported cases, on which more recent speculation has depended. However, from a reading of these cases it cannot be determined whether the affected person, the windigo, ever in fact committed cannibalistic acts or whether the accusation rested on the belief that he had done so, which was accepted as verdical by the individual himself, his relatives, the community, and those who later heard about what had taken place—whether the victim was killed or, as sometimes happened, recovered.

According to Hallowell (1934:7–8):

> The initial mental phase of the "Wihtigo psychosis" appears to be a morbid state of anxiety on the part of the subject, directly traceable to the native interpretation of certain physical symptoms. These are distaste for ordinary types of food, nausea and perhaps vomiting. When these symptoms continue . . . anxiety develops, and, if they fail to disappear, rapidly reaches a climax. This is because repugnance to food is construed as positive evidence that the person is becoming a "wihtigo," i.e., a cannibal. The person afflicted with anxiety, therefore, soon becomes the object of the projected

fears of a number of other human individuals. . . . The individual affected is usually watched day and night by some relative and, in former times, a medicine man would probably be consulted.

In cases reported by Hallowell (1934, 1936, 1938) the disturbed person suffered only the earlier symptoms and was often cured. But even at this preliminary stage, the victim might ask to be killed, or those around him, carried away by their own fears, would kill him before he became violent. Elsewhere Hallowell (1976b:434–35) contrasts the Ojibwa view that killing a windigo was an act of self-defense and the horror experienced by Canadians in learning about such "murders," as they defined the situation.

The windigo psychosis was related, for the victim and all those around him, to beliefs that were, in their world view, crucial for survival. The Ojibwa lived (and still live) in a harsh, cold environment in which the game they depended upon for food, shelter and clothing—and, more recently, as an economic resource—was scarce at the best of times. Both boys and girls were very early taught self-sufficiency and the suppression of emotions; boys, especially, were also trained to fast. In their lives, starvation was a real possibility, and although people expressed horror at the thought of eating human flesh, starvation cannibalism did occur. It was in the winter season that windigo acts of cannibalism also were said to take place.

Judging by reports that in some cases successful efforts were made to cure the afflicted man (or woman), whereas in other cases there was no deliverance from death, Hallowell suggested that more than one syndrome might have been included within the windigo designation.

Condensation of detail within a single construct, such as windigo, is a possibility that cannot be overlooked. It can happen in at least two sets of circumstances where the main sources of information are secondhand reports: the native informant, a member of the culture, fits a variety of details into a whole, as this is integrated in the total belief system; or the person recording the information lacks the knowledge of the culture (and, most often, of the language) that would enable him to differentiate nuances in separate accounts of illness. It is more difficult to understand the continuing fascination with the idea of windigo, in spite of the fact that, given the nature of the data available, only speculation, nowadays only remotely related to ongoing Ojibwa life, is possible.

THE ESKIMO: ARCTIC HYSTERIAS

The Eskimo, whose New World habitat extends from Greenland to Alaska, are in one area neighbors of the Algonkian Ojibwa; indeed the word Eskimo is an Algonkian term for "raw meat eaters." The Eskimo speak dialects of one language and, in spite of their enormously wide dispersal, Eskimo cultures are essentially versions of the same culture, adapted to the particular terrain where each group lives. Above all, the Eskimo have in common their very successful adaptation to what is one of the world's most difficult natural environments.

The literature on the Eskimo is extensive, even in English, and references to psychopathological behavior, observed and described, goes back to the latter part of the nineteenth century. According to Parker (1962:77) "the most frequent symptoms noted by different observers have been convulsive hysterical attacks and, less frequently, conversion symptoms." It is generally agreed that aggressive behavior is absent—in extreme contrast to the behavior that the Ojibwa attribute to the supernatural monster and to the living person who is believed to be a windigo. Clearly, although the natural environment is relevant to the experience and imagery of Ojibwa and Eskimo forms of mental dysfunction, the aspects of the environment to which members of the two cultures respond are very different.

Both Parker (1962) and Freeman, Foulks, and Freeman (1978) agree that arctic hysteria is the characteristic psychopathology in Eskimo culture. The latter are concerned with a special version that affects some men in a North Alaska group, while the former attempted a more general survey over time and space.

Freeman, Foulks, and Freeman define arctic hysteria as "an acute dissociative reaction, precipitated by separation or loss of the object, in an individual who has not been able to complete the psychological processes of 'separation-individuation' in childhood, and is not able to deal with threatened or actual object loss." Parker suggests that the difficulties faced by women are such that the focus of their disturbance is somewhat different from that of men. Both, however, emphasize the nurturant care given the infant and small child and the relatively low frustration, and Parker notes the lack of restraint that continues into adult sexual life. Both emphasize the interdependence of members of a group, the high development of skills (Parker) that ensure a man's security, but the anxieties that assail an individual who, in a difficult situation, can call on no one for help (Parker). It is the view of Freeman, Foulks, and Freeman that it is the man who never achieves autonomy in relation to his parents and/or wife (and whose attitude may be one of deep ambivalence) who falls prey to the characteristic form of hysteria, which is calmed by the return of the lost or absent person(s). The role of the father in this situation is not made clear.

It is not the intention here to elaborate on arctic hysteria, but to indicate that in contrast to the existing data on windigo psychosis, data on Eskimo arctic hysterias are grounded in actual observation and informed discussion—research that permits new questions to be asked and testable hypotheses to be framed with the expectation that further study will be rewarding.

GURURUMBA "WILD MAN" BEHAVIOR

There are forms of psychopathology and therapy that may be particularly difficult for the psychologist to appreciate insofar as the difficulty that precipitates disturbed behavior in a certain person is located within the community and, by the same token, the community as a whole becomes, as it were, the therapist. One example of this kind of relationship is provided in fieldwork carried out by Philip Newman among the Gururumba, a horticultural people living in the Eastern Highlands of Papua New Guinea. In a relatively brief article, Newman (1964) describes a syndrome which he calls "wild man" behavior, a figurative translation of the native term for the disorder.

Although "wild man" behavior shows a certain resemblance to the amok syndrome, no life threatening violence is involved. The evidence, fully documented by observation and discussion, shows that the "wild man" is not feared and that the principal effect of the episode is to modify community attitudes in the direction of lifting the weight of too heavy responsibility from the man's shoulders. In all cases the "wild man" is a young adult married man.

After marriage a young man in this society is heavily burdened by debt to those who arranged the marriage for him and to the family of his wife, but the new husband does not yet have the economic resources to meet the demands for payment easily or to make economic contributions to coordinated group activities. "Wild man" behavior seems to occur when a man feels that he cannot cope with the heaviness of the burden.

Initially, for several days, the man forces his way into houses and carries off objects of minor value. Anticipating his coming, people try to hide their chickens, pigs, and valuables. At this stage he is hyperactive and clumsy in his movements, and he may have disturbances of speech and hearing. Great crowds follow him, curious and amused, but ready to draw back when he threatens to attack them. There are also a few men who watch him solicitously, ready to protect him and others from harm. People express "expectant excitement," not fear or anger. He himself speaks of the things he has stolen as if they were rare objects of great value. Finally, the "wild man" runs off into the forest where he remains alone for some days. When he returns to the village, without his loot, he takes up his normal life. No one discusses the episode with him and he appears not to remember what has happened. He gets on with life.

Newman (p. 18) comments that in this episode the "wild man"

is presenting his view of the way the everyday actions of others look to him. His aggressive collection of the belongings of others, his excessive valuation of objects having small worth, his refusal to hear objections to his acts, his refusal to speak about his acts, and his disregard for the way his acts may affect others . . . are dramatic expressions of the way certain patterns of everyday life appear to him. Although Gururumba beliefs portray human nature as highly aggressive, people do not habitually act as if it mattered to them. By forcefully calling attention to this aggressiveness the performance of the wild man makes it clear that he is an individual who cannot fully accept it. What others know about this man—his current situation, his past performance, his character—is seen in a new light and given a new interpretation.

What is perhaps the most significant aspect of "wild man" behavior is that viewed from within the cultural setting, it is clear that while the aberration temporarily sets an individual apart from his peers, it also focuses the attention of the community on his plight and provides an accepted, well-understood way back into the community.

EASTERN IATMUL "LOST HUNTER" SEQUENCE

Among the Eastern Iatmul people of the Sepik River in Papua New Guinea there is a disturbance that has no name but that might well be known as the "lost hunter" sequence. A man who is depressed and withdrawn from everyday social life, usually because of veiled criticism of some act of his, will go hunting alone in the bush. Iatmul men usually treat hunting as a sporting activity and make up large parties to go to the more remote fens or a distant mountain. Going alone, following a game animal off the beaten track, is dangerous; the hunter may lose his way in the featureless marsh terrain.

This is what happens in the "lost hunter" sequence. Later the man will describe how he tracked a large game animal, which suddenly and inexplicably disappeared, and then, one after another, four more, each of which led him on—and disappeared. (Five is the "magic" number for the Iatmul.) Now he realizes that he has been tricked and led astray by supernaturals in animal form. Benighted and lost, he recognizes that "they [the supernaturals] closed the road to me."

In the village, people are alerted to his protracted absence. The men of his clan, sitting in their men's house, discuss the problem but take no action. The next day young men, out on the river in their canoes, rove restlessly, hoping to sight the lost hunter on the shore. Finally, a small party of responsible men, his close relatives and clansmen, paddle gloomily toward the place where the hunter is believed to have entered the bush, planning to beat through the bush looking for signs of his passing. In one case observed, the lone hunter made his way back near the river, where he was found. The whole party returned home in exuberant spirits, much as if they were celebrating the rescue of a man who, out alone, might have been attacked and killed by an enemy party of headhunters—as often happened in the past.

Iatmul men are proud and touchy; they value autonomy and do not easily admit dependency needs. They rely on highly formalized situations for joint action in any group enterprise. "Lost hunter" behavior is histrionic. On the surface it emphasizes a man's belief that he can stand alone. At a deeper level it is a cry for help and solace, a demand that his relatives and clansmen demonstrate their awareness of him and his predicament and that the most responsible men react to his need by coming to his aid. (They do not always do so. Then the man knows that he is alone, an exile within his own community—and he may, in fact, go away temporarily or permanently.)[4]

PSYCHOSES IN RURAL ASHANTI

Particularly valuable are studies in which the fieldworker has the double training necessary to make a comparative psychological analysis across cultures. M. J. Field (1958, 1960), in the course of research on rural Ashanti in West Africa, carried out a study of the supplicants who came to the shrines of native deities, to which pilgrims from all the Akan tribes of Ghana traveled. The existence of shrines among the Ashanti is ancient, but of the twenty-eight shrines studied by Field, twenty-two had been established within the ten years preceding her research. Most pilgrims were healthy individuals who came in search of protection and blessing in their enterprises, but Field also was able to observe and interview individuals, men and women, who were suffering from either of two types of psychoses. One of these she characterized as a "frenzied guilt-and-fear" psychosis and the other as a depressive psychosis that affected mainly women, some younger and others older. The priest at the shrine, in a state of trance, obtained advice from the deity of the shrine on the basis of which he diagnosed the patient's trouble and prescribed treatment.

The guilt-and-fear frenzies, the most common cases observed by Field, occasionally were precipitated by physical illness, particularly fevers. Typically, the patient believed that the deity was punishing him for some offense, became frightened and then frenzied. A little later he was quieter, but he became "inaccessible, hallucinated, smiling, giggling, posturing, crawling, dancing, singing, tearing off his clothes, eating faeces" and so on (1958:1045). Brought to the shrine, the patient expected to be given help; the priest offered pardon, and within a week complete recovery took place. However, Field found, on following up cases, that some such patients later developed an unobtrusive schizophrenia.

Women suffering from depression, the most common mental illness among rural women, invariably accused themselves of witchcraft—of having become witches and of bringing harm to others without conscious intent. The middle-aged patients were hard-working, able women who had successfully reared their children and worked in their gardens and as traders. Among younger women depression associated with self-accusation of witchcraft was often precipitated by a difficult childbirth following a chronic, debilitating illness, or by the death of a sickly infant, for which the mother felt she was responsible through some act of witchcraft, but without willing the child's death.

Commenting on similar cases observed earlier among middle-aged women in Gold Coast villages, Field (1955) pointed out the resemblance to agitated depressive cases which are very common in British mental hospitals, also among middle-aged and elderly women. They, too, often accuse themselves of doing harm to others. There is, however, a crucial difference. In the British cases the emphasis is upon the subjective character of the self-accusations. But in the Ghana villages the deranged woman and the members of the community in which she lives treat the idea that an individual may inadvertently become a witch and do injury to others as something that is based in reality, for which a specific cure exists, involving supernatural help, which will protect both the victim and the community where she lives.

This African research was carried out by an anthropologist who later also became a qualified psychiatrist with experience in modern hospital settings. Equally important is the fact that Field based her interpretations on first-hand observations in several settings. Working in a well-studied culture, she combined observations of stricken individuals and the treatment given them by native practitioners (the priests at the shrines) with observation and interviewing of the same persons in their home setting, including a follow-up of her cases at a later time, and placed their behavior within the larger framework of their culture.

Psychopathology and the Cultural Belief System

By and large the literature on special forms of abnormality as these occur in preliterate and traditional societies has emphasized the more spectacular types of psychopathology, such as the windigo psychosis or amok. The social disturbance that amok behavior evokes—when the afflicted person suddenly enters the stage of violent, random attack—is obvious, and attention is concentrated on the details of the immediate, external event. But in other forms of disturbance, far less spectacular, the reported behavior may be so deeply imbedded in the belief system that unless the observer is actually present during the occurrence of an episode, it is virtually impossible to distinguish between actuality as it is represented by the participants and as it must be interpreted by an uninvolved observer who is familiar with the belief system.

The distinction may be clarified by an example from Haitian culture. In the ceremonies of Haitian Voodoo (A. Metraux 1959) participants in trance take on the personality of the various gods whose presence has been invoked. For the Voodoo believer the god is literally present; it is Legba who comes and speaks for all to hear. Later, participants report that "Legba did and said such and such things." The punishment for faking ritual trance is the threat of sudden illness and death. The observer who does not share these beliefs must nevertheless recognize that actuality has to be located within the belief system in order to be understood and correctly interpreted. But this is not the only difficulty. Clearly, even for the most articulate believers a great deal of what is believed is outside of awareness. Thus it becomes necessary for the interpreter to relate belief and action, spontaneous or ritualized, in such a manner that the relationship becomes comprehensible to others at a distance. (See Boyer, below.)

Specialized Roles of the Mentally Ill

In many societies there are specialized roles that permit the individual who has suffered from mental illness to play an active and sometimes powerful, but more often marginal, part in the community. Students of American Indian cultures have pointed out that in both North and South American Indian societies, as well as among Siberian peoples, the shaman entered into the specialized role of curer, visionary, seer, and so on, following a long and severe illness, the symptoms of which suggested such an outcome to members of the society.

The term *shaman,* applied originally to visionary curers found in Siberian societies, has been generalized in the literature to apply to a broad category of—usually—religious specialists in a great many preliterate societies. Typically he (or she) is a curer and a visionary; usually he is a medium who has direct access to the supernatural and who acquires or learns techniques of control over spirits. The shaman may—or very well may not—also be versed in witchcraft or sorcery. However, there are significant differences in the kinds of individuals, male or female, who become shamans, in the manner in which their powers are acquired and used, and in their formal status in their society (see Lessa and Vogt 1965, for a discussion of the subject). Curers, with visionary and other powers—including the power to kill as well as to cure—are found in a great many literate and preliterate societies; almost every modern language has a name for such a specialist, whose role predates that of the physician in caring for the sick, however culturally defined.

Róheim (1939) discussed some of the psychopathological modes of functioning of a Siberian shaman who behaved in a more dependent manner than other men in his tribe and who showed hysterical manifestations by sweating blood from his forehead and temples. Róheim himself (1941 and 1943), in the course of an investigation among Central Australian aborigines, made a study of their "medicine men." He found, for instance, that they hallucinated "phallic demons." His conclusion was that they were what he called "dissimulating paranoiacs" who had not broken contact with their environment. In his view shamans are unstable members of a group who have been able to convert their maladaptive behavior into activities in harmony with their interests; shamanism is therefore an art based on mechanisms adopted by persons whom we would designate as neurotic or psychotic. It must be added, however, that the individual who selects—or who is selected by his community as someone who is predisposed for—the role of curer, by whatever name, engages in activities that are well defined in his culture.

It is known that there are within well-described cultures—and very likely within all cultures—institutionalized roles for at least some individuals who do not fit the culturally accepted model. Among many Plains Indians tribes, for example, whose male ideal was the active, aggressive, competitive, and touchy warrior, the role of *berdache*—a male who performed female social roles, though not necessarily a transvestite and/or overt homosexual—was available to the man who would not adapt himself to the game of warfare and male competition. Often he was an able, intelligent man who developed special skills inadmissible in the warrior. Devereux (1969) points out that complementary roles of this kind are likely to be found where, as among the Plains Indians, "the socially sanctioned impulses and attitudes . . . are *over-institutionalized*—i.e., if they make excessive demands upon the individual" (p. 128). Such roles, like the role of the shaman, are a resource for individuals, men or women, who, temperamentally or as a result of their unusual life experience, depart in expected ways from the normal in their society.

Of course, in a great many societies only certain persons, culturally defined, can fill specific roles or carry out particular activities. For example, among the Mundugumor of New Guinea (Mead 1935), only a male child born with an umbilical cord twisted around his throat could become an artist; anyone else who attempted to develop an artistic talent would have been ridiculed.

The individual who does not fit the culturally accepted model, or who is disturbed, does not create a role, such as that of shaman or berdache. He can only fit himself into an existing socially recognized role or accept the decision made for him by others that he is the kind of child, young adult, sick person, elderly person, leader, or visionary who is right for the role. The role is culturally determined. It exists within the culture as a resource— sometimes a critically important one, sometimes one that is marginal within the particular society. Thus men or women who are identified as fitting such roles remain, however marginally, functioning members of the community. The extreme deviant is everywhere a different problem.

But the roles—and the prevalence of particular forms of psychopathological disorder—are not necessarily continuous over time. In a restudy of Eastern Iatmul culture, the anthropologist co-author found that the curer-sorcerers who had played a conspicuous part in the life of Iatmul villages studied a generation earlier (Bateson 1958; Bateson and Mead, unpublished research, 1938) had no successors in Tambunam Village in the next generation. The quarrels and rages that had ripped through this and other villages earlier were muted, and Tambunam men said about the curer-sorcerers "They all died." Men of their kind belonged to the past, but belief in their powers was in no way diminished; it still remained as an explanatory resource.[5]

In many societies there are also multipurpose institutions within which deviants may find a place. In Burma the Buddhist monastery provided, among other things, an institutionalized setting in which somewhat deviant individuals could find a secure niche. In the villages studied by Spiro (1965), Rorschachs were administered to the village people and the monks. Analysis of these records by James Steel revealed definite psychopathology among the monks. Among other characteristics, they showed marked regression in manifestations of aggressive and oral needs, hypochondriasis, "erotic self-cathexis," great fear of female or mother figures, great defensiveness, and apparently latent homosexuality. Nevertheless, their test results differed in degree, rather than in kind, from those of ordinary village males.

It should be recognized that the Buddhist monastery is one of the central institutions of traditional Burmese society. Particularly at the village level, the monastery provided a refuge for men who were actually or potentially mentally disturbed. But the monastery also carried the responsibility for Buddhist religious activities and, especially in the past, for literacy, learning, and scholarship. All young male Buddhists spent a period of time in a monastery, traditionally for educational purposes; in the present, as in the past, mature men from all walks of life can go into temporary retreat in a monastery during any period of difficulty in their lives. When the monastery served as a therapeutic community, it was fulfilling only one of its multiple functions, as, in other societies, the religious shrine also served the needs of the sick. It can be said that all the major religions have at different periods of their history provided settings in which actually or potentially disturbed individuals of various types have found safe refuge—as prophets, seers, hermits, wandering mendicants, warriors, artists, cloistered nuns and monks, scholars, missionaries, nurses of the sick, and so on.

Cultural Responses to Psychopathological Behavior

One aspect of certain forms of psychotic behavior is seldom commented upon in the literature: this is the extreme and fully patterned response of those who are confronted by the disturbed individual. In the windigo psychosis, for example, the expected outcome is the death of the victim at the hands of some person or persons in the community. Even in the absence of more adequate data, it is evident that the total "plot" includes the response of deep disturbance evoked in those in contact with the central figure (the man or woman who becomes a windigo). That is, the phenomenon involves a crucial group, not merely an isolated, mentally disturbed individual, and it should be studied from this viewpoint.

In other types of disturbance, such as the "wild man" behavior described by Newman, the disturbed behavior sets in motion what must be regarded as a therapeutic sequence; here, again, the behavior of all those involved in the action sequence is crucial to an understanding of the illness suffered by the individual.

In some societies individual specialists (shamans, for example) or a specified group in the community (members of the individual's kin group, for example) may become ritually involved in the care and treatment of the person who breaks down. In other societies, as in those studied by Field in her research in Ghana, the traditional handling of mental and physical illness is, at least in part, the responsibility of specialists working in institutionalized settings such as the religious shrine (in Ghana) or the Voodoo temple (in Haiti). Here one may correctly speak of the existence of a traditional therapeutic community that includes the well, the sick, and those who carry the responsibility for caring for the well and the sick, as well as the responsibility for supporting the belief system to which all adhere. All these culturally defined contexts of treatment are relevant to the problem of illness and should be part of the comparative study of psychopathologies. Devereux (1969:xxix–xxxi) distinguishes forms of treatment that are based on genuine insight from others that are primarily ritualized. The distinction is important, but it is also relevant to ask, with reference to any culture, how help is given (or withheld) and organized, as well as whether there are differentiations in illness that are reflected in modes of treatment and in the personnel involved.

Projective Techniques in the Study of Culture and Psychopathology

Projective techniques have been used since the early 1930s (see, for example, Mead 1968b) in the study of cultures and for the purpose of testing hypotheses about the occurrence and forms of psychopathology in preliterate societies, societies undergoing radical change, and societies with long cultural traditions other than those characteristic of the West. But the history of their use has been a patchy one, and perhaps researchers have not quite recovered from the disappointments that followed the first burst of enthusiasm a generation ago.

Designed for use with individual members of a familiar culture, projective techniques produced results that were on the whole insignificant when the tests were administered to members of groups about whom little (except age and sex) was known or, alternatively, when the analyst was required to judge test performance "blind," that is, without knowledge of the culture or the individuals tested. Somewhat more useful cultural clues were obtained in studies of culture at a distance when those who tested individuals and analyzed their responses were at the same time working on the culture in a wider context (Abel and Hsu 1949; Abel, Belo, and Wolfenstein 1954). However, there have also been difficulties in research where information was available, but the projective tests provided the only in-depth data, so that little was known about symbolic representation in the culture and the adaptations made by individuals. (In contrast, see Boyer, below.)

The Bleulers (1935) gave the Rorschach test to a group of twenty-nine male and female peasants living on the plains of Chaouia in western Morocco. The test responses were characterized by emphasis on small details and specks as well as by (in Western terms) bizarre and distorted answers. According to the Bleulers, the protocols resembled in some ways those of schizophrenics in Switzerland. Nevertheless, the respondents were normal individuals—rather fussy naggers who were at the same time romantic dreamers.

When Oberholzer (1944) interpreted the Rorschach protocols of a group of Atimelang villagers on the island of Alor in the East Indies, who had been tested by Cora Dubois as part of her field research on the culture, he found that the responses, particularly those of the seventeen male subjects, resembled those of brain-damaged patients in Europe, showing timidity, fear, distrust, and emotional oscillations. They were not, however, brain-damaged; all of them functioned satisfactorily in their small, isolated island society.

These examples are echoed many times over in the records of earlier field research. Similar difficulties of interpretation occurred initially when the Lowenfeld Mosaic test (Lowenfeld 1954), which had been developed with British and continental European subjects, was first presented to American children. The reproductions of Mosaic designs shown to Lowenfeld (who had just arrived on her first visit to the United States) consisted of a large random sample of work by elementary schoolchildren and a small, carefully selected sample of work by gifted children, on each of whom considerable developmental information was available. Looking through the reproductions, Lowenfeld exclaimed in dismay that these were, one and all, certainly the work of highly disturbed children. The American children's use of massed color and their emphasis upon open space as an element of design, for example, differentiated their work from that of normal European children with whom Lowenfeld was familiar; the closest resemblances were to the productions of children in Britain and on the continent who were known to be aberrant. It is not surprising, in the circumstances, that the interpreter herself initially suffered from a kind of intense culture shock. It should be added that Lowenfeld's later cross-cultural interpretations, based on Mosaic designs, are among the best we have on recently preliterate, rapidly changing societies.

The problem of interpretation is compounded, but is not essentially a different one, when persons move from one country to another and must adapt themselves to an unfamiliar mode of life. Basically, it is through our understanding of normal personality structures in any society, including our own, that we are able to perceive and make judgments about deviance that is dysfunctional and psychopathological. Working within our own society, we can more-or-less "hold the culture steady." But working with members of another society, particularly one that is rooted in a tradition different from our own, an in-depth knowledge of the culture is necessary to evaluate individuals and the problems they present.

New Directions in Research

It is rarely possible to date definitely a new approach to research, especially transcultural research that depends on the state of theory and the availability of data in two or more disciplines. A single individual may experiment, as Margaret Mead (1968b, 1972) did with ink blots of her own devising in Manus in 1928 (there being no Rorschach cards then available to a field–worker), and with Rorschach cards in Arapesh in 1932; it takes time, however, for a new approach to take hold. Nor is it possible to summarize at any point in time all changes in research approach that may be significant. Here brief mention will be made only of two directions in which research is moving that are relevant—though not exclusively—to problems of psychopathology that may be culturally or regionally distinct.

The view has generally prevailed that although an understanding of the cosmology and the beliefs about human physiology held by a people are integral to an understanding of the culture, a wholly unscientific "folk" conception of human physiology and mental processes can be ignored in a scientific assessment of somatic and mental aspects of illnesses within that group. Consequently, research on a culturally or regionally bound syndrome may neglect systematic study of the context within which the disturbance occurs.

Edwards (1983), a medical anthropologist, has conducted research based on Indian medical and psychiatric literature, as well as literature on Chinese and Ayurvedic medicine, on the syndrome he calls "semen anxiety," which is very widespread among men in China, India, and South Asia in general.

Among a great variety of disturbances that are related to semen anxiety, there is a panic state which is best known in Western literature by the Malayan-Indonesian term *koro*. The male sufferer believes that his penis is shrinking back into his body and that death may follow. Until recently, although cases occurred sporadically elsewhere, *koro* was generally regarded as a culture-bound disturbance associated with the very complex yin–yang balance, as taught in traditional medicine and as supported by Chinese traditional cosmology. Apparently it was not understood—at least not in the West—as one manifestation of a world view and an understanding of the functioning of the human body which, with variations, is very wide-spread.

The occurrence of three major epidemics of *koro* (called by various local terms) over a period of seventeen years necessitates a change of view. These epidemics took place in 1967 in Singapore (affecting some 500 young men, most of them Chinese, over a period of two weeks); in 1976 in rural Thailand (affecting some 2,000 persons, including some Buddhist priests and some women, but no ethnic Chinese, over a period of two months); and in 1982 in West Bengal and Assam and spreading south to the outskirts of Calcutta (affecting great numbers of persons of different cultural, religious, educational, and social status, including not only men and young boys but also women—who believed their breasts were shrinking—over a period from early summer to autumn). The Indian epidemic "jumped from one village to another; vanishing quickly from one area only to reappear in a neighboring region" in areas "known for their recently severe inter-racial [intercultural?] strife" (Jilek 1984:60).

An understanding of the ethnophysiological belief systems alone, of course, can do little to clarify the relationships between such an epidemic outbreak and other events, or the different ways social panic affects some individuals and not others. But the situation cannot be well understood without this basic knowledge. And on a larger scale, the organization of viable combined forms of Western and traditional medicine in a regional or national health service depends on the availability of carefully researched data, such as that provided by Edwards; for only by this means can trained medical personnel become aware of the particular belief system and its symbolic representations reflected in community and individual responses to illness. The goals of research of this kind are necessarily both theoretical and practical, related both to the particular cultural situation in its changing forms and to human needs in all societies.[6]

There is a movement also in the direction of long-term commitment to research within one cultural setting or a cluster of related—or contrasting—cultures. In an earlier era long-term commitment characterized the work of a number of anthropological fieldworkers, particularly academic Americanists, who almost always had to carry out their research over many years, but for short periods only and almost invariably with very limited field funds. The emphasis, under these circumstances, was primarily on the formal culture.

More recently, as the overseas distances to fieldwork sites increased the time and cost of travel, periods of fieldwork lengthened and the number of field trips to the same site tended to decrease. However, there has been a growing conviction that research in depth—research on individuals as members of a culture, on observed actual interpersonal behavior over time rather than on the stated rules of behavior, on symbolism as a personal expression of an accepted symbolic system, on the involvement of the community with the deviant, the sick person, and the law-breaker, on the play of power within the social system—all this, and above all the development of mutual trust and respect, depends on long-term research commitment. Moreover, whether at home or abroad, researchers have become far more aware of change as a process requiring study, not at a point in time, but over time.

One long-term study of great interest, especially because it combines research by a cultural anthropologist, Ruth Boyer, and a psychoanalyst, L. Bryce Boyer (who functioned both as a student of the culture and as a psychoanalytic therapist), is the Boyers' twenty-year study of the Mescalero Apache (Boyer 1979). Ruth Boyer lived for over a year with a family as a way of following the day-to-day intimate life of family members, especially parents and young children (1964). Psychiatric and psychoanalytic work necessarily concentrated on the ways in which individuals interpreted the ideas, the beliefs, and especially the myths shared in common with the inheritors of the culture. Benedict's (1969) classic collection and study of Zuni mythology and tales is essential to an understanding of Zuni culture, but it is the interweaving of event, folklore theme, and symbol in personal experience, as Boyer has worked out the process over an actual individual's lifetime, that illuminates Apache cultural style and personality.

Long-term research is not of one kind only. Schwartz (1962, 1982), working as an anthropologist in the Admiralty Islands for more than thirty years, followed the development of a political movement that turned the tide of a disastrous cargo cult soon after World War II and analyzed the way in which the several small continuously interacting local societies make use of language differences and minor cultural differences to maintain their separate cultural identities in a period when, at the same time, all are becoming members of a new nation-state. (This, too, provides a setting for studies of health and illness.)

Still another form of long-term research, also ethnopsychiatric in approach, is that carried out in Morocco by Vincent Crapanzano (1973, 1980) in his intensive study of the Hamadsha, a traditional religious brotherhood, which provides the setting for his study of one man, Tuhami, who is "married" to an enslaving female demon, from whom he struggles to set himself free. Here again, one emphasis is on the personal interpretation and manipulation of both traditional and contemporary symbols, for Tuhami is a man caught between two worlds, a man in transition. There is, however, another focus in this research: the analysis of the relationship of the two men, ethnologist and informant, one to the other, so that the position of each becomes clear, in the context of a culture in transition, attempting to communicate across cultural boundaries. This is a new direction.

Anthropologists have long understood that the researcher and the researched—as also, of course, the analyst and the analysand—are equally part of what goes on between them. It is also self-evident that the personal style of each—a style that reflects cultural preferences in personal terms—determines the fused content of the communication. But this is extraordinarily difficult to communicate to uninvolved audiences, among them many who look for an "objective" account. The willingness and the ability to present content in the light of the relationship has seldom been evident in earlier reports of research. Instead, the researcher, struggling to understand what is new, has usually "held his *own* culture steady." The use of film, following the precedent set by Bateson in the research in Bali (Bateson and Mead 1942), provides viewers with more data on which to base a judgment; the deliberate inclusion of the researcher himself provides still another source of insight.

We have come a very long way in the past fifty years in working out the complementary relationships of different approaches to personality and psychopathology. In 1922 Malinowski (1961:25) stated that the anthropologist's aim must be "to grasp the native's point of view, *his* relation to life, to realise *his* vision of his world. We have to study man, and we must study what concerns him most intimately, that is, the hold which life has on him." He hoped that "perhaps through realising human nature in a shape very distant and foreign to us, we shall have some light shed on our own." However differently phrased today, these are still viable aims.

Four

Psychoanalytic Theories and Culture

Freud's Contribution

In his earlier years Sigmund Freud became interested in then-current theories about the origins of group behavior, incest taboos, and totemism, as well as in accounts of rites and ceremonies described as taking place at puberty, at the time of death, and on other occasions in so-called primitive (preliterate) societies. He was greatly influenced by early pre-Darwinian theories of evolution around the turn of the nineteenth century, particularly the ideas of Lamarck, the great French naturalist, and possibly the work of the *Naturphilosophie* (natural philosophy) group of thinkers. Among philosophers and theorists closer to his own generation, he was influenced perhaps by Nietzsche and certainly by Darwin, whose *Origin of Species* was published in 1859, when Freud was a young child.

Anthropologists in whose theories Freud became interested were nineteenth-century forerunners of modern anthropology—Andrew Lang, James Frazer, and E. B. Tylor. These men accepted the prevailing social evolutionist theory, namely that the societies of all peoples everywhere and throughout time have evolved through a series of set stages from a primal horde up to (in late nineteenth-century Europe) highly industrialized civilization. In general, their concern was with the idea of "culture," rather than that of different "cultures" carried by organized groups of human beings who share a common world view and mode of life. Lang was an indefatigable collector and analyst of myth and folk narrative. Frazer, also a collector on a vast scale, had as his principal concern the evolution of religion, and attempted to demonstrate in his monumental works that this had taken place through natural processes, without recourse to divine intervention (Langham 1981). What interested most of Frazer's readers, however, and presumably Freud as well, was the sheer mass of extraordinary second- and third-hand material gathered in his publications from the far corners of the earth. Tylor was the most systematic thinker of the three, and it was "the history of mankind in which he was interested, the history as man has forged it, not as it has resulted from natural causes" (Radin 1958). Although Tylor drew on the same kinds of sources as his contemporaries, he was better able to conceive of highly organized human life. Indeed, he provided his own and the next generation with the first truly scientifically viable definition of the necessary components of ethnographic research in the opening statement in *Primitive Culture* ([1871] 1958): "Culture or civilization, taken in its wide ethnographic sense, is that complex whole which includes knowledge, belief, art, morals, law, custom, and any other capabilities and habits acquired by man as a member of society." Spelled out in that massive work and other publications, this was a view that set students to doing systematic fieldwork.

Freud himself, however, was apparently unfamiliar with the new anthropology, based in a holistic approach and on direct observation within small preliterate communities. There were also, of course, the great expeditions aimed at surveying a whole region, such as the Cambridge Expedition to the Torres Strait and the Jesup North Pacific Expedition (directed by Franz Boas), that set the style and location of much work in Great Britain and America, respectively. But theoretical advance was based in the small preliterate communities where the fieldworker lived and worked in the midst of his subjects—a method pioneered by Boas in his early research and in his published study, *The Central Eskimo* ([1888] 1964). As early as 1904, Boas (1974b) had firmly rejected the evolutionist theory of social development; even earlier, in 1887, arguing from empirical data, he had stated categorically that "unlike causes produce like effects"—and vice versa (Boas 1974a). Thus, indirectly, Boas was a critic of Freud long before Freud's theories became at all well known.

Nevertheless, Freud had a remarkably keen intuitive sense that data on preliterate cultures could provide new kinds of insight into human behavior. But much of the work available to him was based on second-hand, fragmentary, and unsystematically collected materials, highly colored by the theories and prejudices of those who collected and those who attempted to analyze them. Like others of his generation, Freud believed that modern "savages" could provide clues about the life of early man. So, for example, the rituals, taboos and magical practices of "savage" peoples were equated by Freud with the kinds of obsessional behavior and the wishful, magical, or omnipotent thoughts he found among his patients, especially as revealed in their dreams. Thus Freud suggested that oral-aggressive fantasies of patients might represent counterparts of what he believed, from his interpretation of totemism, could have taken place in reality among "hordes" in man's unknown prehistory; then, he theorized, the sons destroyed the father in a cannibalistic feast and took over the manhood role and presumably, by this means, solved the Oedipus complex (*Totem and Taboo,* [1913] 1959).

Again, taking cues from his patients, Freud postulated that, in the course of evolutionary development, ritualistic defenses were developed against the original patricide in the form of taboos of various kinds, such as a taboo against taking the women who belonged to the father (mothers and sisters), against fratricide, and against assuming the father's role. Out of these defenses, he speculated, there emerged the idea of the totem—an animal that had to be respected, worshiped and, at times, eaten—the totem being a ceremonial survival of the original cannibalistic feast.

As we know, Freud accepted the idea that the primal scene a patient reported witnessing might have been an actual event, but it might also have been a fantasy. He felt that just as patients might have disguised wishes with accompanying guilt about killing their fathers, primitive men might also have had fantasies about patricide. Hence Freud speculated that the impulse to kill a father and eat him would have been sufficient to produce strong guilt. On the other hand, he noted how often his patients reported having felt, in their childhood, angry impulses against parents and how they had turned these impulses into acts of hostility without actually committing murder or causing physical injury. One might consider aggressive deeds committed among primitive men both in present-day preliterate societies and among ancient hordes in the past in the same way. Freud was critical of his own formulations about ancient man, however, for he was aware of how tentative they were.[1]

Géza Róheim

Róheim was the earliest of the psychoanalysts to study preliterate societies seriously and directly (1941, 1943). In order to gather materials firsthand, Róheim went into the field in Central Australia, Somaliland, New Guinea, and Arizona (where he worked with Yuma Indians). Thus he was able to discuss analytic theory as it applied to specific groups with which he had had direct contact. He criticized Freud, first of all, on the grounds that Freud, in *Totem and Taboo,* was equating the preliterate and the neurotic, whereas he was actually comparing "savage" cultures with the behavior of neurotic individuals living in Vienna at the turn of the century.

When Róheim first went into the field, he accepted Freud's theories about the way in which the child handles its libidinal strivings and frustrations. He saw culture—or, as he called it, the process of becoming human—as a neurosis (1934). He hypothesized that societies have institutionalized goals toward which behavior is directed, and that these behavioral forms are defenses against libidinal strivings.

Working in the field, where he was able to make firsthand observations of the living behavior, rituals, and daily activities of a specific group and, to some extent, of neighboring tribes, Róheim observed various infantile traumas in different cultures. He also observed that these traumas—for example, separation and castration anxieties, destructive fantasies against or longings for a lost object (the mother)—were handled differently in different groups. He believed that the main infantile trauma in the Central Australian tribes he studied (Pitjentaca, Yumu, Pindupi, and others) was that of the mother lying on top of her infant son, a practice in those tribes. He postulated that in this inversion of the sexual position, the son became fearful of being a female, but repressed his anxiety (a castration fear). Puberty rites, phallic ceremonies from which women were excluded, provided a counter-cathexis to this trauma. One object used in the rites represented a penis ornamented with concentric circles (the womb). Róheim described many further elaborations of this restitutive activity that were given social sanction by these Australian aborigines.

In *Symbolic Wounds, Puberty Rites and the Envious Male* (1962), Bettelheim describes the ritualistic behavior of some severely disturbed children in American culture. One ritual that appears to have been worked out spontaneously consists of a ceremony in which boys and girls share the girls' menstrual blood, thus alleviating various jealousies, envies, and fears. This ritual and others seemed to Bettelheim to be similar to the initiation rites described by Róheim in Central Australia.

Here Bettelheim compares (as did Freud) the behavior of disturbed individuals with the normal cultural tradition of a preliterate society. But, in fact, two different situations are being compared: one deals with the private ritualization of disallowed behavior; the other is built into the way of life of a whole people. Nevertheless, it is useful to realize that when severely disturbed individuals (as in the case just described) attempt to cope with their difficulties of adjustment by a variety of symbolic acts, they draw on some of the same sources of symbolism as have primitive peoples in the development of rituals that express their world view. As Róheim himself said, Australian aborigines, living under hazardous conditions of survival, libidinize the surrounding world so as to make it tolerable.

The Kwakiutl, studied at great length by Boas and briefly described by Benedict (1934), provide another illustration of the unfolding of an infantile trauma. This, Róheim suggested, seems to be severe castration anxiety over-compensated for by boasting, bargaining, and competition. In their traditional feasts the Kwakiutl handed out a great deal of food, which Róheim interpreted as a reaction formation against an oral-sadistic trend, for there was great fear of menstrual blood which, in an earlier period, members of the group had been made to drink.

Róheim concluded that different tribal groups have different cultural "plots," in which specific countercathectic devices are responses to specific infantile traumas. It was his view that an intimate analytic knowledge of all cultures might make it possible to find a common denominator for infantile libidinal strivings in relation to psychosexual development, to parents and to the social group. But, Róheim goes on to say, what one generally finds in different societies are different dominant roles in the infantile situation, and different patterns for handling infantile anxiety and libidinal needs as well as for the establishment of sexual identity through the resolution of the Oedipus complex.

Abram Kardiner and Basic Personality

Kardiner (1945), another psychoanalyst, also became interested in relating libido theory to the comparative study of cultures. Kardiner investigated what he called "basic personality" in several different cultures. He criticized Freud for not being experimental and for having assumed that much human behavior had become phylogenetically frozen and was not greatly influenced by contemporary life. Róheim paved the way for the research that Kardiner pursued and developed.

Kardiner recognized that the institutionalized practices of a society—practices relating to the nurturing of a child, affective relationships, discipline, and attitudes of concern or rejection during a child's early years—all influence personality structure. In fact, in his view, it is not only the developmental years that are crucial; institutional practices affecting the whole life cycle influence personality structure.

What Kardiner called basic personality is actually an inventory of characteristics. In various cultures, basic personalities differ owing to their formation in response to the culturally patterned behavior of the group. When the psychoanalyst came along with the concept of psychodynamics, it was then, according to Kardiner, possible to understand the relationship between institutionalized practices and specific traits and therefore to demonstrate that the basic personality of an individual is not entirely idiosyncratic but is rather a function of culturally patterned institutions within which personality is molded. Kardiner postulated that the personalities thus formed create secondary phenomena characteristic of a specific group, such as folklore, religion, educational systems and healing practices, work constellations, value systems, and types of neuroses and psychoses. To arrive at a definition of a basic personality type Kardiner and his collaborators collected personal life histories and gave projective tests (Rorschachs, Thematic Apperception Tests, and others) to a sample of the population studied.

Kardiner makes a point of differentiating basic personality and individual character. For example, two Indian tribes living on reservations (Apache and Hopi, for instance) can be compared in terms of the basic personality characteristic of each of these two cultural groups, whereas specific character analysis describes how one individual differs from another within the same culture. Thus, in the Rorschach protocols of the Alorese in the South Pacific, Oberholzer (1944) looked for traits that seemed common to the group (which Kardiner called their basic personality) and also for idiosyncracies of various individuals tested (which Kardiner called character traits).

Anthropologists who have carried out field research on problems of personality and culture, however, take the position that Kardiner's analysis is vastly oversimplified. They agree that personality is shaped by culture, as those who are born into the society are reared by others who already embody the culture, but they feel that those traits which Kardiner ascribes to basic personality cannot so easily by winnowed from the character traits of a given individual that are related to temperament and endowment. Also, anthropologists take the stand of fieldworkers such as Hallowell and Devereux that adult as well as child models of behavior are relevant to personality development. Those who have worked in complex societies also point to the further complications that are introduced by the coexistence of variously related versions of the culture. There can be cultural patterns of behavior characteristic of a given society, but not differential basic personality traits per se.

As stated in Chapter 1, Devereux (1978) has demonstrated the complementarity that exists between a psychoanalytical interpretation of a culture
and an analysis of its cultural patterning, that is, its characteristic structural
regularities. The two positions complement each other, and each represents
the particular viewpoint of a discipline. In research on a given society
Devereux (p. 121) writes: "If one is a Freudian, one must explore and clarify
the nexus between the Superego, the Ego Ideal and the patterning of Ego
functions, on the one hand, and the structure of the socio-cultural matrix on
the other hand." Devereux goes on to explain that it is incorrect to transpose
the psychodynamics of a given individual to the sociocultural structures and
processes of his society. He makes an amusing analogy (p. 122), showing
that the Constitution of the United States does not have a superego or ego
ideal any more than the psyche of the individual has a Constitution or a
Supreme Court.

Erich Fromm

Fromm (1949, 1953) applied psychoanalytic concepts to culture in a manner
that emphasizes interpersonal relationships and focuses less on instinct development and childhood training. Fromm takes the position that man is
not an isolated entity entirely endowed with drives, but rather a relational
being whose personality is molded by his kind of relatedness to significant
people in his life, to the larger world and to himself.

Fromm considers child training significant only as a transmission medium; he believes that child training methods can be understood correctly
only as we understand the personality types that are evaluated as desirable
and essential in a given society. In other words, Fromm sees child training as
one of the key mechanisms for the translation of social necessities into
character traits. He postulates a prevailing social character structure—for
example, paranoid, anal, or oral—for a given culture or version of a culture.
His point is that it is important to determine social character structure and
to discover the ways in which it has been transmitted from generation to
generation.

Freud's explanation of a particular character structure—for instance, anal,
stemming from sublimation of, or as reaction formation to, the anal libido—is accepted by Fromm as clinically correct; but in describing an
individual in a society, he adds, it is necessary first to find out whether the
group is predominantly one in which stinginess and parsimony (or, differently phrased, thrift) are highly valued. In that case, that particular kind

of relatedness (not giving, withholding, saving) will be transmitted to the child. In other words, the child conforms to the social character of the culture by developing an anal character. Presumably there are many variations, especially in a complex society in which there are many versions of the culture and many variations in family structure and individual experience.

Erik H. Erikson

Erikson (1963) devised a chart that clarifies and expands the possible sequence of stages of pregenital psychosexual development as set out in Freudian theory. His system represents body zones and the modes and modalities of the different orifices (including the skin). These orifices or erogenous zones become coordinated with the ways parents (initially the mother) and others respond to infants and small children and provide for their needs.

Erikson postulates two oral stages. At Stage I, which he terms the oral-respiratory-sensory stage, the first incorporative mode (receptivity) dominates all the body zones, the skin surface, and the sense organs in the infant's growing readiness for stimulation. The primary mode (incorporative) is taking in, sucking, or, as Erikson says, "getting what is given." The extent to which the other modes come into play during this first stage varies with the individual infant and also with the way the mother manages nursing. For example, among the Iatmul people of New Guinea, the typical nursing posture is for the mother, seated on the floor or on the ground, to rest the infant on her crossed knees and, bending over, to present the breast to the infant's mouth from above, almost like a fruit dropping into the mouth. The infant very early learns to press its lips hard in order to grasp the nipple as the mother makes slight, involuntary adjustments in her posture.

At Stage II, in which the second mode (incorporative 2) dominates, the infant becomes more active. He has teeth and bites. He learns to "grasp" with his eyes and ears, to turn his head and his whole body, and to reach out with his hands and feet and explore. At this stage, according to Erikson, the baby may have many difficulties, especially during the process of weaning and temporary separation from the mother—difficulties that also depend on the extent to which he succeeds or fails in coping with his frustrations and rage. It is in these two oral stages, Erikson postulates, that the child develops a sense of basic trust or, on the contrary, a sense of basic mistrust in relation to the world and itself.

Stage III, which Erikson calls the anal-urethral-muscular stage, has as its focus the control of retention and elimination as well as muscular control of grasping, dropping, or discarding objects. Erikson points out that in Euro-American societies, particularly in the middle class, control of the bladder and bowels has become a serious form of training for the two- to three-year-old. However, in the United States this stricture is diminishing considerably. Some form of control (minimally learning to go to the designated place) is learned in all societies, but control can be taught very gradually, not by admonition and punishment but by guidance and patient encouragement (as, for example, in Japan). At this stage there is a great deal of reciprocal regulation between mother and child in response to which the child may become resistant to pressure so that it has no alternative but to regress to an earlier stage of activity (bite or suck its thumb, for instance, or give way to infantile rages) in order to "survive." Although the modes of retention and elimination predominate, incorporative and intrusive modes are also manifested.

Stage IV, which Freud would term *phallic,* Erikson designates as a stage of infantile genitality, for he sees in it the first elaboration of intrusive and incorporative modes—a differentiation between male and female roles. In one sense both boys and girls at this stage are phallic; that is, they may be aggressive and have a variety of sexual fantasies and activities. Both boys and girls enjoy competition and strive for goals that appeal to them. But in this phallic stage some differentiation between the sexes begins. Erikson suggests that the phallic-intrusive mode begins to take on a milder quality for girls, who tease, annoy, and seek approval. During Stage V, the genital stage, boys and girls become yet more differentiated one from the other, especially in terms of genital feelings, for the modes of intrusion for the boys and incorporation for the girls become more dominant.

Interferences along the way can frustrate the psychosexual development of the child, who may become fixated at the pregenital stage or regress to an earlier stage. Several of the factors responsible for these fixations and regressions have become common knowledge since Freud expounded his psychoanalytic theory. Erikson suggests that the zonal-modal approach to development can help to clarify just where development went wrong for a disturbed child or adult. Thus, an oral-aggressive adult character functions at Stage II, a compulsive adult character at Stage III. In addition, of course, using the zonal-modal chart as a ground plan, it is somewhat easier to systematize observations on the ways child development is handled in an unfamiliar culture and to communicate the special emphases on modes or stages in different cultures—for example, mothers in one culture may encourage the continuance of the passive acceptance characteristic of Stage I or may pre-figure the control characteristic of Stage III, and so on.

Erikson (1963) showed how the psychosexual development of the child is modified by psychosocial influences and different cultural patterns. Using his schema of orifices, he recognized that different societies emphasize different modes within a stage of pregenital development. For example, he found that Sioux Indians handled oral receptivity well. Infants were treated with considerable permissiveness in suckling. Since colostrum was considered poor nourishment, the baby was first given a buffalo bladder with a breast-like shape containing berry and herb juices, which it was allowed to suck until its mother's milk came in. The child was permitted to nurse until it was three, four, or five years old. (Even at eight, if a boy had a cold, his mother would come to school to nurse him.) But biting was not tolerated, so there was little room to express pregenital aggression. The baby that bit was hit on the head. It was strapped to a cradleboard to make it strong and (according to traditional belief) to store up rage to be diverted later to enemies. Erikson noticed that neither children nor adults sucked their fingers, indicating that they had had sufficient oral receptive pleasures, but judging from the frequency with which they played with their teeth, bit their nails and snapped their chewing gum, he concluded that oral aggression had not been satisfied.

Erikson suggested that in Sioux culture there seemed to be adequate means of solving oedipal conflict, especially among boys. A boy was emancipated gradually and firmly from any fixation on the mother. There was extreme emphasis on his right to autonomy and on his duty to take initiative. He was given boundless trust and gradually, through shaming rather than guilt, learned to treat his mother with reticence and respect. In former times he was expected to direct his frustration and rage into hunting, war parties, and the seduction of loose women, and also against himself in his search for spiritual powers. His father's pride in him fostered his sense of identity. The difficulties of this training for a Plains Indian boy reared on a present-day reservation, and some of the underlying problems of adjustment, are brought out in Devereux's (1969) discussion of the psychotherapy of a Plains Indian man (see Chapter 7).

Opler's Critique of Psychoanalytic Theories

The cultural anthropologist Marvin K. Opler (1967) has criticized the attempt by psychoanalysts to explain not only adult personality but also cultural patterning on the basis of infant disciplines, such as nursing, weaning, toilet training, and the like. He is particularly critical of Erikson's use of a zonal-modal conditioning theory to account for both personality and culture. As Opler interprets Erikson's work, he derives Sioux Indian cultural patterns from early childhood experiences such as cradleboard swaddling, long nursing after the teeth have appeared, and so forth. He objects, for example, to Erikson's suggestion that swaddling restrictions lead to a need on the part of the Sioux to wander over the plains. According to Opler, Ute Indian children, like the Sioux, were swaddled on a cradleboard, were nursed even longer, but had no disposition to wander. He sees the way children are disciplined as a reflection of the social and economic life-style of a given people, not as a cause of cultural patterning.

Although Opler's critique can be applied to some attempts by psychoanalysts to come to grips with the problems of culture and personality, it is in fact a serious misrepresentation of Erikson's essential approach and viewpoint. Erikson's zonal-modal chart, which can be extended to include all the major bodily systems, is intended to provide a schematic method of ordering developmental data for purposes of comparison. As an analyst who pioneered in work with children, Erikson has contributed immensely to our understanding of child development from a psychosexual point of view and of pregenital and genital sexual behavior of adolescents and adults in relation to the emphases that are prefigured in childhood training within a given culture.

What is more serious is Opler's failure to recognize that Erikson's work on Sioux and Yurok personality development was carried out in the field in collaboration with cultural anthropologists H. Scudder Mekeel and Alfred L. Kroeber, who had themselves carried out intensive investigations of Sioux and Yurok culture, respectively. Thus Erikson's investigations were set within the framework of whole cultures, and his statements about Sioux and Yurok childhood disciplines and adult personality are relational, not (as Opler suggests) causal. Child rearing practices provide one point of entry into an understanding of adult personality in a cultural context, providing it is recognized that any single child rearing practice must be viewed in the light of the meanings it evokes in any given culture. Swaddling can develop very different feelings in infants if, in one case, the mother treats the swaddled child as weak and in need of protection (Zuni), or if, in another, the mother regards the child as so strong that, without swaddling, it might injure itself (Great Russia). The existence of a behavior pattern does not preclude individual differences in the relationship of specific mothers and their infants, but the meaning of these differences will be modified by the more general expectation. The Zuni mother who felt that her first child was unusually vigorous, and the Russian mother who recognized that she was caring for a puny, ailing infant would each, nevertheless, see her child in the context of the cultural expectation of what a child is like, and her individual handling of the unusual child would reflect the generalized expectation.

Thus it would seem that pervasive cultural expectations that give meaning to specific child rearing practices must be taken into account in interpretations of these practices in psychoanalytic terms and in attempts to assess the effects they may have on the formation of character. For example, every culture has ways of fostering sex identity as well as self-identity in the child. In some cultures sex identity is stressed from birth, and the infant's maleness or femaleness is constantly reinforced through such means as the use of names that are exclusively male or female, the expectation that boys and girls will play with certain types of toys or engage in certain kinds of games, and the performance of rituals in which boys only (or, less often, girls only) are involved. On the other hand, in contemporary American culture, parents make a considerable effort to repress sex preferences, and early differentiation between boys and girls is played down in favor of sex symmetry—in which sex identity is linked to the idea of sex equality.

Anna Freud

Psychoanalytic theory has undergone many revisions, the most outstanding of which is the shift from the topological position as first presented in 1900 by Freud in *The Interpretation of Dreams* (1953)—in which the mind or mental apparatus is divided into unconscious, preconscious, and conscious—to the structural theory he presented in 1923 in *The Ego and the Id* (1961)—in which the mental apparatus is divided into id, ego, and superego. Many psychoanalysts have accepted the newer approach, expanded it, modified it, and stressed the value of dealing with the ego and its defenses as well as with instinctual drives in psychoanalytic practice (see especially Hartmann 1958, Brenner 1982).

Recently Kohut (1975) has expanded psychoanalytic theory to include what he calls "the self." He states that this is a third psychoanalytic paradigm (self-psychology) which supplements both drive theory and ego psychology. Kohut feels that everyone has narcissistic needs and that these needs take on different forms as the person develops. These needs must be respected, and individuals with deficits in development have distorted or exaggerated narcissistic needs.

Structural theory has been employed in formulations concerning infant development that have emphasized the formation of the ego and superego and the relationship of these to the id and to each other as the child gradually enters into object relations and begins to relate differentially to significant persons in his life. Anna Freud (1965) makes quite clear the importance of observing a child's behavior (not only in the analytic session, but also, for example, in his play activities, his illnesses, his school, and in the presence of his mother and peers) so as to use these more surface manifestations in conjunction with depth probing in order to arrive at a more thorough understanding of his total personality—that is, his ego development and its conflict-free areas and the ways in which he tries to cope with his conflicting intrapsychic and interpersonal wishes and needs. The present-day family therapist would add that it is also necessary to take into account the child's position within, and relationship to, the family.

According to Anna Freud, the way a child develops, pathologically or normally, as he grows up is hard to predict in any culture. However, if there were a clearer understanding of cultural patterns, including familial ones, in relation to unpredictable events, perhaps a better prognosis of future development and later emotional disturbance could be made. Attitudes toward illness, death, and seduction, for example, take specific forms in different cultures and, therefore, have different effects on emotional development in different cultural contexts.

Actually, today, there is a greater understanding of learning and enculturation in the developmental processes of children. That is, we have a more intensive and extensive knowledge of the ways individuals growing up in different cultures systematically attain ego control and learn to handle sexual and aggressive needs, other needs such as hunger and fatigue, and the need for sensory stimulation and integration at various stages of maturation. Even Fenichel, an orthodox Freudian, discusses in *The Concept of Trauma* (1954:64) the importance of childhood sex education in what happens to children during latency and at puberty, and suggests that other societies should be studied before there is universal acceptance of certain limited ways in which latency may be handled or instincts may be warded off or encouraged.

As one illustration, Devereux (1951a) has demonstrated that the latency period is not present among Mohave Indian children, and that for them the primal scene, whether witnessed or fantasied, does not seem to have as intense an impact as it does in Western societies in which references to sex and sexual play are discouraged or prohibited entirely. Further, Devereux has repeatedly stated that the Oedipus complex is largely dependent on the way little children are handled by their parents. For example, a seductive mother and a distant and punitive father can create an intense sexual attachment to the mother. The punitive and distant father can make a child fear him but feel protected by the mother. The complex is not resolved. In a recent article, Devereux (1982) has reiterated that oedipal impulses are not universally identical and are highly responsive to familial and cultural patterns.

Hartmann, Kris, and Loewenstein (1951) have suggested that if Freud had developed his structural theory further, he would have employed it more dominantly in considering the differences between his patients and individuals in so-called "savage" societies, and would perhaps have come to somewhat different conclusions about psychosexual development, oedipal struggle, and latency. These authors deemphasize phylogenetic influences on, for example, the Oedipus complex, castration fears, and latency; they emphasize, instead, ontogenetic influences, that is, the way in which specific patterns and sequences in child rearing (such as an emphasis on oral indulgence combined with restrictions on motility and the expression of emotions) influence major personality patterns, largely through the molding of the ego and the superego, and the control these exercise on the third mental structure, the id.

Nevertheless, these psychoanalysts also have pointed out that despite the experience of similar modes of child rearing within the same cultural setting, adult behavior may be differentiated, owing to differences in later experiences. Conversely, similar adult behavior may characterize individuals whose early experiences were different but whose later experiences are alike. This phenomenon has been observed in the field by anthropologists who are trained in psychoanalytic theory.

The Oedipus Complex

The Oedipus complex forms the central core of psychoanalytic theory. Freud postulated that the oedipal struggle (including castration fears), a struggle that takes one form for males and another for females, occurs universally.[2] He did think, however, that the complex develops far more intensely in groups in which children are prevented from indulging in sex play by strong sexual taboos and the firm social repression of libidinal impulses in the young. But

Róheim (1946, 1952a), who had available not only his direct observations in several societies but also a large accumulation of field studies by other investigators, which had not been available to Freud, pointed out that in some societies, for example, among the Baiga of the Central Provinces of India (studied by Elwin [1939]), this is not the case. In this society full sex play among children is permitted even to the point of one boy saying to another, "I'll copulate with your mother." Nevertheless, these children have castration anxiety dreams in which they are killed by the father, even though in reality fathers and sons may cherish each other.

Róheim also pointed out that Baiga folklore includes stories about the destruction of the father, not by the sons but by a jealous deity, stories in which the sons are told to eat the father's flesh. On the basis of this material and evidence from other societies, Róheim concludes that even in cultures in which sex play in childhood is permitted or ignored, emotional emphases nevertheless can be organized around extremely complicated taboos and phobias regarding sex.[3]

Bronislaw Malinowski, the Polish-born and educated but British-trained social anthropologist, created a great stir among both his fellow anthropologists and early psychoanalysts—as well as among general readers on both sides of the Atlantic—by his innovative analysis and presentation of the matrilineal social structure of the Trobriand Islanders in a series of major publications that stretched over some twenty-nine years, from "Baloma: Spirits of the Dead in the Trobriands" ([1916] 1954) to *Coral Gardens and Their Magic* (1935).[4] Other anthropologists had described in formal terms the marriage customs and sexual relations of the people they had studied. Malinowski, who was deeply influenced by his reading of Freud (Fortes 1960), was the first to work closely and insistently with his informants on these subjects and to discuss in considerable detail (although without individual life histories) the formal rules and the actualities both of family and intimate kin relations and of sexual relations among experimenting young people, girls and boys, and among adults.

In Trobriand society, parents and children form a household in the village of the father, but sons are among the potential male heirs of the mother's brother. (Trobrianders denied the facts of physiological paternity, which were well known to other island groups with which they were in contact. Thus, physical contact—not impregnation—was the conscious focus of the incest taboo.) The mother's brother may be a somewhat distant authority figure in the lives of his sister's children since young men realize that, in most cases, there is little or no likelihood that they will actually be heritors.

In contrast, as Malinowski demonstrated repeatedly, father–son relationships are warm and close in childhood and later, when a young man marries (for the father must stand aside during the years of his daughters' and sons' free sexual relations). Then the father tries to give what he can in the way of control over land and knowledge of magic and ritual to his own, but technically non-kin, sons (rather than to his heirs). Very occasionally, he may attempt to arrange a marriage between his son and a sister's daughter or granddaughter to create a link to his (the father's) true kin (Weiner 1976).

Initially Malinowski accepted the theory underlying the analysis of the Oedipus complex. In the case of the matrilineally organized Trobrianders, he hypothesized a split in which negative aspects of the male's ambivalence are directed toward the (kin-related) mother's brother, while positive aspects are reflected in the lifetime relationship of (non-kin) father and son. Malinowski carried out a long and well-publicized debate with the psychoanalyst Ernest Jones (1964), who considered that emotions reflected in the mother's brother–sister's son relationship were a secondary displacement and that the matrilineal focus of this society was a defense against father–son ambivalence. Actually, the son is well aware of parental sex relations, and denial of the father's role in procreation (but not the male's role in making possible pregnancy) was tied in with his central belief in reincarnation (Malinowski 1953, 1954, 1962).[5]

One outcome of the debate was Malinowski's rejection of psychoanalysis as an explanatory model. However, Annette Weiner (1976) has demonstrated the basic accurancy of (as well as the lacunae in) Malinowski's observations, and in her sophisticated elaboration of Trobriand social structure both brings together concisely data scattered in Malinowski's publications, and contributes new and contemporary balancing material on the position of women in the society. However Malinowski's theoretical position may be judged today in the light of immensely expanded experience, what was much more important at the time (mainly in the 1920s) was the opening up of a subject, both as a new field for research and as a fresh incentive to awareness and insight. Indeed, the problem of the relation of a boy to his actual progenitor and another significant male has acquired special relevance in modern societies in which, owing to divorce as well as the break-up of other relationships, a boy so commonly grows up in a home in which his "own" father has been replaced by his mother's husband or companion, or in which there is no other significant male.

In Papua New Guinea—as in virtually every other region of the world— rites of transition from one stage of life to another are carried out and have been widely studied. Understandably, those which have excited the greatest interest are those Ruth Benedict spoke of as "making-a-man cults," that is, rites and ceremonies of initiation that mark the transition from boyhood to manhood. Earlier theorizing grew out of—and added to—very confused thinking on the subject (see Allen 1967; also Keesing 1982). Recently, as such rituals have been more systematically studied in the context of the whole culture and with careful attention to symbolism as it is interpreted by members of the culture, there has been considerable clarification. But such a study requires very long-term commitment to work within a single society.[6]

Herdt's research on the Sambia is one of a number of illuminating studies of this kind (Herdt 1982a; 1982c). The Sambia, some 2,000 people, hunters and gardeners and, until pacification in the mid-1960s, fierce warriors, live in dispersed clusters of hamlets on the formerly isolated fringes of the Eastern Highlands of Papua New Guinea. Like so many of the peoples of Papua New Guinea—and elsewhere in the world—Sambia men have deeply ambivalent attitudes toward women. In adulthood, on the one hand, a man and a woman live together with their children as a small self-sustaining household. On the other hand, from childhood boys are systematically taught that woman's blood, especially womb and menstrual blood, mother's milk, and even women's breath are dangerous pollutants that prevent boys from growing into strong warriors and that weaken and destroy strong men.

The Sambia consciously symbolically identify the male nose and the penis. By means of secret bloodletting through the nose—by measures that are at first violent and later become private and voluntary—the body is cleansed of the contaminants that are absorbed and collected in the nose, and so bloodletting promotes male growth and protects strength. Sambia men equate this bloodletting with menstruation.

Until boys are seven to ten years old they, like their sisters, are reared principally by their mothers and have (or had, before pacification) little contact with their fathers. But from this age until well after their formal marriage, they live wholly apart from women and, in the course of the rituals of six stages of initiation, are taught the dangers of feminine contact, how to become manly men, and how to maintain mastery over women. The first set of three stages are bachelorhood rites in which boys from several hamlets advance together in age-graded groups. The second set of rites are individually celebrated and are specifically related to the maturation of the girl betrothed to the boy.

At stage one the boys are removed from the women. Tied to the backs of their ritual sponsors, they are dragged through a frightening symbolic birth process; then one by one they are violently forced to nosebleed. Later they recall, "I feared they were going to kill me" (Herdt 1982b). Instead they begin to acquire semen (for they believe that men do not naturally have semen) by entering into a passive fellatio relationship with boys past the third initiatory stage.

Nosebleeding is omitted at stage two (as it also is at stage four), but at stage three, when the boys are from fourteen to sixteen years old, nosebleeding is again violent and follows after the boys, "lined up, military fashion," are attacked by warriors "hooting, shouting and feigning an ambush." Thereafter they become the active partners in fellatio, giving semen to a new group of little boys.

After stage four's secret rites the formal marriage takes place, but the couple do not come together until after stage five, which is signaled by the girl's menarche. At this stage, teaching concerns "making men responsible, autonomous warriors, by redirecting onto women some responsibility for the 'pain of nosebleeding' "—that is, for ordeals men have endured in order to become fully masculine. And as she is responsible, she must subordinate herself to him. The final rites, at stage six, take place when the wife gives birth to their first child; they are repeated, over the years, until four children have been born. With two children both are full adults. After coitus and each time the wife menstruates, the man secretly and voluntarily induces nosebleeding; he has taken charge of his own life.

Nevertheless, as Herdt points out (1982c), nearness to women is still believed to impart femaleness (pollution) to men, that is, demasculinization. Enforced nosebleeding controls behavior at critical stages in his relations with women throughout a man's life, beginning with separation from the mother. But it must be kept secret; male vulnerability is hidden from women at the same time that nosebleeding, voluntarily repeated, reinforces the man's sense that he is a man, a person. It is difficult to say whether, in the various cultures that emphasize such rituals of violence, bloodletting, masculine superiority and great secrecy, the male is in danger of becoming feminized—or unmanned (which may be something else, for women are considered to be "naturally" strong).

In Sambia culture, in which oral incorporation is given great ritual importance, oral, phallic, and oedipal phases must be intertwined. Males first incorporate mother's milk for nourishment and later incorporate male semen to obtain semen for themselves, and thereafter nourish boys and still later a wife or wives with semen. Perhaps these males do not solve the oedipal struggle but remain in a phallic sado-masochistic stage, never emerging into postoedipal life except in a defensive manner.

As has been described, Herdt has discussed the oedipal transition of boys in the Sambia tribe: the rituals of nosebleeding in order to remove female blood, and the swallowing of male semen to become fully male. More recently, Lidz and Lidz (1984) have discussed the rituals among various groups in Papua New Guinea, including the Sambia. These authors suggest that another reason for removing the boys from their mothers may well have been to avoid a possible incestuous relationship between mother and son. Women, it is said, are treated like pariahs by their husbands, so their libidinal needs can scarcely be satisfied by an adult male. Lidz and Lidz suggest it would be very tempting for these mothers to make some sexual contact with their sons.

The anthropologist Crapanzano has taken a psychoanalytic position in explaining psychodynamic processes (1982). But he takes the view that a rite of passage (Van Gennep 1960), such as a circumcision rite for boys, may not necessarily signal a change from one state to another, that is, from boyhood to recognized masculinity and manhood. Crapanzano has worked intensively with Moroccans (1973, 1980, 1982) and has studied the circumcision rite for boys in a village of illiterates near the city of Meknes—a rite that is quite at variance with others of that kind. The ritual is complicated, involving movement toward manhood and regressive shifts to babyhood as well, so that the resolution of oedipal conflicts may not occur.

Boys from the ages of seven to twelve have a circumcision rite carried out for them. There is a day of dancing and music at which a prostitute appears, perhaps symbolizing, according to Crapanzano, that circumcision is related to sexuality. The boy's hands and feet are painted with henna, a feminine pigment, as women use henna on their hair; this is supposed to protect the boy. He also wears an amulet to protect him from the evil eye, presumed to be that of a woman. Thus the boy begins to learn that women are dangerous and, according to Crapanzano, to respect the incest taboo.

The next morning, the boy's head is shaved and he wears a special tunic and a hood over his head. He rides a horse or a mule three times around a mosque (less often if he is poor). Thereafter he may enter a mosque as a man does to pray. After this, he is carried to the room where the circumcision is to be performed by a barber. The mother or another woman performs ritual acts to ease the pain: she places one foot in a basin of water in which a piece of iron also is placed; she stares into a mirror and holds some object in her hand. As she does so, mother and son are symbolically equated (oedipal attachment). The barber snips the foreskin and inserts the dung of a sheep between foreskin and glans; he then plunges the penis into a broken egg and some other liquid to ease the pain.

Musicians play and women dance outside the room. The mother dances until the boy stops crying. Then he is placed naked on his mother's bare back so that the bleeding penis presses against her. Crapanzano comments that it is difficult to decide whether this is a birth act or a sexual act. It is perhaps a birth scene, as the boy is now wrapped up, put to bed, and given sweets. The mother cares for him while he appears to regress to an infantile state. Meanwhile the prostitute dances and then has sex with the man who will give her the most money.

The whole rite, according to Crapanzano, seems to be circular. The boy is led out of the women's world to the man's world of the mosque. Thereafter he is led back to the woman's world, where the circumcision takes place and he is put to bed like an infant. The rite appears to be symbolic neither of incestuous desires nor only of castration anxieties. It is disjunctive and carries contradictory messages: "You are a man" and "You are not actually a man." Crapanzano concludes that this circumcision rite is not, in fact, a rite of passage, but, instead, a rite of return—to babyhood, to a fear of women. He concludes that perhaps the oedipal conflict is not resolved. The pain of circumcision seems to remain forever in the Moroccan male's memory; he is not circumcised early enough to forget the painful event.

In the experiences one of the coauthors (Abel 1962) has had in treating China-born Chinese patients, as well as from information gathered from colleagues, it appears that the oedipal struggle, castration fears, and sibling rivalry are as strong for Chinese males as for American males. Chinese patients had intense feelings of desire for and also hatred and fear of their biological parents. These feelings were aroused, in addition, in the child's relationships to various parental figures and siblings: a boy's libidinal and aggressive impulses would be induced by mother and father representatives as well as by sisters, brothers, cousins, uncles, or aunts as sibling surrogates.

One patient, Lee, had not resolved his oedipal conflict and his identification with a male figure when he came for therapy. Lee had sexual longings for his mother, felt separation anxiety for his paternal grandmother (who had died when he was four) and consciously hated his paternal grandfather's concubine while unconsciously having libidinal fantasies about her (for he had frequently slept in bed with her and his grandfather). Moreover, Lee developed strong sibling rivalry with a younger brother (his father's favorite) and two uncles, six and eight years older than he, who Lee felt were given preferential treatment by the grandfather. Certainly, the oedipal struggle was fierce, although the objects of love and hate varied. These objects, of course, could be considered as displacements from the original triangle, but un-doubtedly they influenced the total configuration.

The anthropologist Melville Herskovits (Herskovits and Herskovits 1957), while accepting the idea that the oedipal conflict of child and parents is one aspect of their interpersonal hostilities and desires, has added another dimen-sion: sibling rivalry, of which Freud was well aware. But sibling rivalry, as Herskovits envisioned it, could be conceptualized as including the father's jealousy of the son in a sense that goes beyond direct competition for the wife's attention, for this jealousy through projection can reactivate the fa-ther's own infantile competition for his mother. Herskovits found evidence of this in his study of Dahomey (Herskovits 1938), where there are myths concerning rivalry between the creator's sons and his multiple wives. He shows that in Dahomey sanctions are provided in ritual and nonritual forms for the resolution of parental anxieties in the face of certain categories of challenge from their offspring.

The social anthropologist Yehudi Cohen (1964) has made an interesting suggestion of two bases for the incest taboo, one stemming from a need for individual privacy and the other related to the structure of the society, that is, the matrilineal or patrilineal emphasis of the social structure. In common with most anthropologists, he also distinguishes three core sexual taboos: the parent, the child, and the brother–sister pair (pp. 159–96). Additionally, Devereux (1962) has suggested that an important element in the incest taboo is the need of the child to separate two aspects of the mother—as a nurturing object and as a sexual object.[7]

Ann Parsons (1969b) has proposed that the term *nuclear complex* would be more appropriate to the total affective patterns found in family relation-ships—triangles in particular. In her view, the Oedipus complex is only one of a series of such patterns, each of which is influenced by the characteristic structures of the culture that determine the direction taken by libidinal and aggressive drives. Parsons called the brother-sister-and-sister's-son relation-ship among the Trobriand Islanders their nuclear complex.

In her study of working-class families in Naples, Italy, Parsons (1969c) found what she regarded as a nuclear complex that is characteristic in the Latin world, but in exaggerated form. The essentials for creating this com-plex, as Parsons phrases it, are that the husband does not command prestige within the house. Even though fathers and sons can demand whatever they want (for example, food at their own convenience), factually the father is equally as subordinate as his children.

As for little girls, parents are aware of their seductive effect (potential and actual) on their fathers, an effect which is countered by the ritual of first communion: the girl, dressed in white (purity), is expected to delay her libidinal wishes until she marries, again dressed in white. The boy, on the other hand, has no ritual status. On the contrary, open admiration of his sexual attributes is shown, especially by the mother (who favors him) since the father is normally absent from the house. Although the son is permitted to go out, as is his father, he continues to occupy a subordinate position in the sense that authority, stemming from the mother, is fully internalized and any violation causes guilt. Open rebellion and expressed hostility toward the father are allowed. But the mother–son relationship is different from that stipulated by Freud, for the son is expected to remain orally dependent (a pregenital manifestation), continually expecting maternal comfort and giving. Sex wishes toward the mother are sublimated in the Madonna, who displaces the father as the superego figure. She is also the one who forgives. Hence the mother, who is an internalized tabooed object, is represented as the Madonna who plays the role of conscience, but who also condones and pardons.

We find that in the American family, as well, aspects of the oedipal struggle differ from the description given by Freud. Freud based his concepts on a family structure within an authoritarian state, in which the emperor, the father, the priest, the schoolmaster, and others were awe-inspiring figures whose authority was absolute and who could command blind obedience. The role of the woman, including that of the wife and mother, was subordinate and submissive. In contrast, in American culture as among Southern Italians, the superego may to an appreciable degree be an introject from a feminine source. It is largely the mother who sets the tone of the home, establishes the rules of conduct, and demands proper behavior. She defines the circumstances in which her son should stand up for himself and fight, and the situations in which he should refrain from sex, liquor, and so forth. She expects him to succeed and defines his success as in some way excelling his father. The father also anticipates that his sons—and even his daughters—will do better than he does and may surpass him financially, educationally, occupationally, and socially.

The son in American culture does not identify with the mother sexually (except in disturbed cases), for his father does play a significant role in his life. He teaches him male activities (hunting, fishing, sports, and so on), and the boy learns that there is a male world outside the home which is serious and important—the world of work, the business and professional world. Nevertheless, the son introjects ethical standards set by the mother, and he does so at a young age, when his superego is emerging.[8]

Today, with the advent of the feminist movement, there is less emphasis on differentiating the activities of boys and girls, particularly in middle-class America. Girls now demand to play baseball in boys' Little Leagues. Women are entering fields previously more or less limited to men: engineering, computer science, even construction work and mining.

Thus we can say that the oedipal triangle differs in focus, depending on the cultural patterns of approved behavior inculcated by parents as well as by other significant persons in a society at a given historical period. All these different emphases—in some cases, displacements—in the triangular relationship of father, mother, and son (or daughter) can still be treated as variations of an oedipal struggle (rather than a nuclear one, as Parsons suggested) in which a male or female child learns to give up the pregenital sex object (the mother) and the genital sex object (the parent of the opposite sex) and to identify more rather than less with the parent of the same sex. The "parent" may be a parent surrogate or a series of parent displacements, as among the Chinese.

Within any given culture, of course, there may be many variations in the way the oedipal conflict is resolved or continues into the adult life of the individual. Depending on the circumstances, there may be regressions to pregenital behavior, fixations, inverted oedipals, or identification with the sex role of the opposite-sex parent or with various roles assigned by parents (particularly parents who are themselves disturbed). The fate of the oedipal struggle depends on many things—the individual's constitution, existing pathologies within his family, traumas, and significant persons the individual meets in early life. But the framework is provided by the structure of the family in a given society at a particular period in history and, on a larger scale, by regularities in the patterning of authority in the society as a whole (Bateson 1953). Thus, as Gorer also has pointed out (1964), the father models his behavior on roles that are significant in his culture and the child interprets the various representations of authority in the surrounding world in the light of his attitude toward his father and that of his father toward him.

In the present day in the United States there are a great many single-parent families, only in part owing to divorce. It has been estimated that in

1980, 25 percent of all children seventeen or under were living in a one-parent home; 17 percent of these were white children, 58 percent black. The kind of male models children develop in such families has yet to be investigated intensively. There are many variations, presumably depending on how often the real father is seen, how he treats his offspring, the role of the stepfather or lover (or succession of lovers) of the mother who live part-time in the home.

Psychoanalysts who have come to understand the necessity of studying the patterning of culture have been able to interpret child and adult behavior in psychodynamic terms commensurate with earlier and later Freudian formulations and with the modifications appropriate to a specific culture. But they sometimes forget, as Yehudi Cohen (1966) has pointed out, that in addition to the childhood experiences and traumas that mold the personality and the institutionalized ways in which such traumas are handled in the culture, there is, within the society, a specific social structure with articulating principles that accounts for such various practices as initiation, marriage, and death ceremonies. That is, the individual has to learn to adapt to the social institutions of his society, institutions that developed in various historical circumstances, not merely as counter-cathexes to infantile traumas, important as these may be for the individual.

Five

The Interview

Ways of conducting interviews with patients, clients, students, parents, and others have been widely discussed by authorities in the mental health disciplines. The clinical interview, particularly in psychiatric practice, has been the focus of special attention (Deutsch and Murphy 1955; Wolberg 1967). But whatever the main goal of the interview may be, the mental health professional tries to make the questioning as meaningful as possible by helping the person to feel comfortable so that he can express as best he can his problems, his views of his interpersonal relations, and something of his developmental history.

Dynamically oriented psychologists look for various communications on the part of the subject as conveyed by his manifest behavior, his subtle gestures and reactions (such as scratching his ear, pointing his index finger, or flushing) and his verbalizations that seem to have latent meanings, such as "I hate my job. I'll give it three months"—a statement that may well mean "I hate coming for help, but I'll give it a three-month trial." This interpretation will be corroborated if, for instance, the patient later says, "Well, if Dr. So-and-So sees me, he'd better be sharp and work on me in a hurry."

In other words, the interview is geared not only to fact-finding—age at which tonsillectomy was performed, time of father's death and so on—but to finding out what lies behind specific statements. Often the mental health professional evokes some associative material in the interview. For example, in giving his current history, a young man who came to seek psychotherapy said that he was working for his doctorate in English literature. When asked, "What have you chosen as your dissertation topic?" the patient gave a man's name and described him as "a minor English poet" of a certain period. In answer to the question "Why did you choose this poet?" (for the psychologist wondered whether or not the patient identified with the term "minor" and felt inferior to a sibling), the patient said he had chosen the poet because he had not been the subject of a dissertation; it was a new topic. He added that the poet was simple on the surface but very complex underneath. When the psychologist commented, "Maybe that's how you feel about yourself," the patient answered with a smile, "It won't be easy to fathom me. I can't fathom myself." Later in analysis the patient in his associations found many similarities between the poet and himself (they each, for example, had a mistress with the same first name). He also wanted to identify with this English poet since he himself was striving to be "English and have gentlemanly manners" and to deny what he felt to be his "poor" Jewish background.

Cultural Differences

Now the question arises: How can an understanding of the cultural implications of dyadic (or multiple) interview relationships provide more insight into a particular problem? Cultural anthropologists have learned to guide open-ended interviews and discussions along pathways understood by informants in the culture in which they are working. But for each new culture on which they do research, anthropologists must learn what the information-getting devices are, how a man, a woman, a child, an old person, or an expert on some subject is expected to handle different kinds of matter, what avoidances are culturally expected, as well as how to deal with problems of initiative and response, with timing, and with the rhythms of discussion.

At times, some sociologists and social psychologists have neglected to take into account relevant aspects of the particular culture, even when they are adept at keeping constant certain factors such as rural or urban background, age, socioeconomic level, amount of education, and so forth. However, others have well understood how cultural patterning may be crucial for a correct interpretation of an interview. According to Kingsley Davis (1949), "In sociology every effort must be made to overcome the tendency toward exclusion, to appreciate the fact of cultural relativity." One difficulty is that many social scientists believe that in order to obtain a good sample of the attitudes of individuals in a given group, interviews must be carried on with a standardized set of questions and with minimum emotional participation on the part of the interviewer. The assumption is that different individuals and different groups will interpret the questions in approximately the same way.

This is particularly the case in opinion polls. The techniques of opinion polling were developed for work within a single culture, in which it is taken for granted that interviewers and informants share the expectations expressed in the questions. The purpose of opinion polls is not to generate new questions, but to find out what the divisions of opinion are on subjects of general interest. The same questions asked in a different cultural setting may evoke very different—and unexpected—responses.

It is, of course, recognized that individuals of different backgrounds will respond differently to questions on a variety of topics—for example, recreation or childrearing practices. It is also recognized by many research workers that alternative phrasing of questions may be necessary, depending on the economic status, educational level, rural or urban background, vocational interest, religious convictions, or ethnic orientation of the subjects. The identity of the interviewer in relation to the subjects, patients, or clients being counseled also may be taken into account. Clearly it is important to know whether or not the interviewer is someone who has had background experiences in some respects similar to those of the person who is interviewed (who is, for example, a black American from the Deep South, or the only son in a well-to-do academic family, or who grew up in an ethnic community in an urban ghetto, or who was reared in a practicing Catholic family, and so on); whether the interviewer is of the same or opposite sex as the subject; and whether he speaks—or at least understands—the subject's native language. Nondirective interviewing, which gives the individual leeway to express himself, has also been practiced with success.

But there is one element that is often disregarded: the culture in which the subject was reared and the way in which his cultural expectations influence his understanding of the interview, his attitudes toward the interviewer, the way he responds, what he feels is expected of him, and how he chooses (consciously or unconsciously) to phrase what he has to say. In other words, what he reveals or conceals is determined not only by his own personal style but also by regularities in the cultural patterning of thought, feeling, and behavior in the group to which he belongs. Such information, gathered by cultural anthropologists, can be invaluable to mental health professionals who do not have time to find out about modes of living, attitudes toward education and training for different kinds of work and skills, family patterns, attitudes toward sexual experience, and so forth. Some are not even aware that such information should be known; however, professionals who deal with mental illness and emotional disturbances are becoming more aware of the significance of cultural patterning.

The psychologist adjusts automatically and without any special awareness in judging the responses of a patient or client whose background is similar to his own; his ear is tuned to hear the discrepancies, the contradictions, and other indicators of trouble. On the other hand, a clinical psychologist, when interviewing, may need to take into account the cultural attitudes and beliefs of a patient who comes from a background different from his own, who expresses cultural conflict about his background or his aims, or who has been shaken by the experience of too-rapid and intense change.

The psychologist may be puzzled, but he will also catch on to gross manifestations of maladaption in a person who feels significantly different from those around him—a foreign student trying to get along in an American middle-class family or to adapt himself to the unfamiliar American style of teacher-student relationships; or a Puerto Rican man who, in his own country, worked while his wife stayed at home but who, in New York, is unemployed while his wife has become the family breadwinner; or a young girl from a conservative Latin American family who has never before moved out of the closed social circle of relatives and family friends and is bewildered by the difficulties of living alone in a large American city—all these are cases in point. It is the less evident manifestations, the culture conflicts that are latent in the individual and are not understood by the interviewer, that may create a block during an interview.

A sixteen-year-old girl in a senior high school in New York was sent to the clinical psychologist of the school because, according to her teachers, she had been "very obstinate," having refused to participate in a ceremony in the auditorium. She was to carry the flag in a procession down the aisle. Instead, she remained silent and insisted on sitting on a bench in the hall during the ceremony. Her teacher assumed that the girl, who came from a very poor family, was ashamed of her clothes, but in fact she looked well dressed in a white blouse and pleated skirt. The psychologist's job was to find out what was upsetting the girl and to make a decision as to how she could be helped. The girl answered a number of questions. No, she was not feeling sick. No, she had no trouble at home. She liked school and planned to graduate. She did like her teachers. No, she had no trouble with the other girls. When at one point she said, "I can't carry the flag today," it occurred to the psychologist that there was something wrong with the girl on that particular day. When asked, "Could you carry the flag on another day?" the girl said she could. The psychologist, realizing that the girl was Jewish, asked whether or not her parents were strict in their religious observances, to which the girl replied in the affirmative. Now the psychologist guessed the cultural point: the girl was menstruating and in her unclean state she believed she would contaminate the flag. In her house, the girl said, she was always given a special stool to sit on when she ate her meals during her menstrual period. Since the girl shared many ideas predominant in American culture, she was quickly able to accept the idea that in America menstruation and carrying the flag were not incompatible. After a little more conversation, the girl went off to the ceremony. Her conflict had not been severe, but she had been pushed into a scared and defiant position. This does not mean that, at another level of intrapsychic conflict, she was not struggling with a problem of sex identification and with ways of handling aggressive impulses. But in this particular interview, exploration of such problems was not indicated. The girl had not presented any signs of deep-lying difficulties in her school setting.

In another case, a seventeen-year-old, second-generation Italian girl, in her senior year in high school, one day seemed unable to do her work. When she was questioned, she at first remained silent and then burst into tears. Given her continuing agitation, she was sent for an interview to the psychologist, who was able to calm her down enough so that she could talk about her problem. She said that her mother had told her that morning how ashamed she was of her behavior: the girl had been allowed to go out with a boyfriend to a church dance and had come home an hour later than she was supposed to. When the psychologist, in order to discover the extent of her guilt, asked whether she had been scolded by her mother or punished by her father, the girl replied, "It's not me they're ashamed of—it's my father; he didn't beat me." The psychologist wondered whether the reason the girl felt rejected by her father was that in her fantasy she longed for him and might have enjoyed any contact with him, even a beating. When she was asked how her father reacted, she replied, "He asked me if I had a good time!" Thereupon she cried again. According to the girl's mother, such permissiveness was not acceptable to the Italian neighbors, who would criticize the family. This is what she meant when she reprimanded her daughter that morning.

There were other factors, of course. The mother saw her husband as weak, not strong—or as American, not Italian. Nevertheless, the father's culturally unexpected response added to the girl's conflict about enjoying herself in a situation in which, according to her Italian upbringing, she expected punishment by both parents. From the psychologist's point of view, this girl was struggling perhaps with an unsolved oedipal conflict; had she been more seriously maladjusted—or in danger of becoming so—a different emphasis would have been needed in counseling or therapy. As it was, by clarifying her views about what makes a good father in America, the girl was able to accept the situation to the extent that she understood it.

A knowledge of cultural patterning is also important to clinical psychologists in the counseling of parents of children they see in therapy. They may, for example, find themselves running into conflict with the parents' attitudes and expectations. Although they learn to listen to parents and try to explain the goals of therapy to them, they may miss some of the implications of the statements made by a parent in an interview and find themselves trying to impose their own values in an arbitrary way. Dolto (1955), a French psychiatrist who has worked with both French and American children, has shown how differently the interview goes with mothers in the two cultures. The French mother wants a diagnosis, and when this is given she will take the responsibility for treating her child. The American mother, as Dolto sees it, wants to shift the responsibility onto the therapist; "You do it," is her attitude.

Thus the initial interview in each case has to start with the angle from which the situation is understood by the parent, and procedures must be worked out from there. Sometimes the interviewer may get a cultural shock from a parent and misinterpret what he has heard. For example, an Eastern European Jewish mother who has not taken up Dr. Spock and the American view of how a mother should talk about a child may say, "This boy killed me. His birth killed me, and I suffered so." Or she may say of an adolescent boy who is going out with a Gentile girl, "He's killing me. If he marries her, I'll go blind." These statements are traditional. A mother suffers, sacrifices, and "dies" when she gives birth, and she suffers again when a child does wrong. Coming from an American mother with a cultural outlook different from that of an Eastern European Jewish mother, such statements would indicate rejection, immaturity, or a greater need of being nurtured. In this case, the interviewer has to make a different estimate of the actual individual role the mother has played vis-à-vis the child who has come for help. The most, as well as the least, responsible mothers of this specific cultural background say—and feel—that they have sacrificed and suffered for their children. The statements have to be placed in context and interpreted then in the light of actual behavior.

Studies of Culture at a Distance

A better understanding of the ways in which cultural expectations (not only on the part of the subject, but also on the part of the interviewer) may help the mental health professional improve his interviewing skills. For this reason we shall briefly report on some investigations of various interviewing techniques developed in work with persons from different cultures. Although much of the systematized material is not concerned with patients in clinics or hospital settings, professionals in the mental health disciplines may find that the general approach is helpful.

In the late 1940s, working under the direction of Ruth Benedict and, later, Margaret Mead, a cross-disciplinary research group (cultural anthropologists, sociologists, social and clinical psychologists, historians, political scientists, artists, and other specialists) investigated the patterning of behavior in seven cultures: Chinese, Czech, Eastern European Jewish, French, Great Russian, Polish, and Syrian.[1]

Intensive open-ended interviewing was one of the principal methods of investigation. Interviews consisted sometimes of one session, more often of a series of sessions with an individual or, at times, with a family or a small group. The interviewers themselves came from different cultural backgrounds. For each group studied, interviewers included members of that culture, some of whom were American-born while others had lived in the United States for varying lengths of time. Most researchers had training as interviewers and all were aware of systematic differences in the cultural patterning of behavior, their own and that of others. The research was exploratory, but the internal consistency of the findings on each culture was marked.

EASTERN EUROPEAN JEWS

Interviewers who worked with Eastern European Jews reported that it was not possible to use set questions, for informants were unwilling to follow them. Having started on a particular line, an informant saw no reason to deviate from it merely because the interviewer introduced a different topic. Actually, it was found that the number of direct questions that could be asked and answered depended largely on the individual interviewer and informant. Questions were used least of all with informants in a Jewish home for the aged; once a person started talking it was as if the interviewer had vanished. But a questionnaire elicited only yes-no responses and too many direct questions, especially with children, created a test situation. In spite of having had the nature of the interview explained to them in advance, children were apt to consider the interview a test and their parents hoped they would do well on it.

Moreover, informants resented questions whose answers could be found in books. The informants' attitude was: "You want to know about this? Why don't you look it up?" They felt that knowledge is more easily obtained from books and that scholars consult books to get information. The interviewer who asked too many questions was considered ignorant, but if he asked a question to confirm what he already knew, it was acceptable.

This attitude on the part of informants—and what may happen when it is not recognized—is well illustrated by a situation that arose in a clinic when a prominent psychiatrist questioned a young male patient of Eastern European Jewish parentage about his problems. The young man had been in therapy for a year and had agreed to be interviewed by the psychiatrist in a one-way vision room. The therapist felt that the patient would be flattered by being interviewed by a prominent "learned" man. The procedure was part of a workshop on interviewing techniques and techniques of appraising personality.

At first, the patient answered questions well and seemed to be willing to cooperate. But gradually his behavior shifted, and he responded much less openly and in monosyllables or short phrases. The psychiatrist had begun to repeat some questions, phrasing them differently each time, and repeatedly asked about the young man's developmental history. The patient's lack of response was put down to resistance to therapy, to his habitual way of defending himself against closeness, and to his reaction against a possible homosexual threat. He seemed to back away. He showed obvious resentment and even hostility. Certainly, he did feel threatened, but it also seemed that he would have liked to say, "You could have looked up a lot of this information in my case history. I've been talking about myself and my past life for a year," or "Why do you repeat foolish questions? You asked me this once before!" These points shaped his perception of the interviewer. It is not certain how much weight they carried, but they should have been taken into account. It is possible that with less questioning the young man would have talked more freely, or that if he had been told, "I am verifying so that we can do more to help you," the procedure would have had a different meaning for him.

Generally, the Jewish informant is strikingly fluent. He describes his experiences with ease and has no trouble remembering past events, although sometimes he seems not to be giving details out of his own experiences, but rather reconstructing a pattern—such as that of the Passover meal, of which he remembers the whole ceremony—giving a composite picture of Jewish life. The interviewer cannot always tell whether the person is relating his own experiences or communicating a picture of Jewish childhood he has read about and has been told about by his father. Moreover, the Jewish informant will use many examples to prove a point—illustrations from the lives of people he knows—which are meant to round out the total or composite picture he wishes to present.

Reciprocally, the Jewish informant may take an extreme interest in the personal life of the interviewer, ask questions, and give advice. The interviewer who establishes himself as a Jew may then be open to the free advice-giving which is such an important part of Jewish interpersonal relationships. In fact, it may happen that the roles are reversed, so that the interviewer comes away not knowing whether he was the interviewer or the informant—an important point to look out for in therapy.

Interviewers found that sex was not discussed cross-sexually or between the married and the unmarried. Unlike, for example, an Italian husband and wife, Jewish couples did not openly discuss their marital relations. However, much depended on the relationship established between interviewer and informant. For example, an interview might start rather impersonally with a discussion of the informant's opinions about aspects of Jewish life and then, if the interchange proceeded favorably, other topics of a more personal nature, including sex, could be brought in.

Group interviewing worked well, especially when a whole Jewish family acted as informants. They stimulated one another and often argued over points. When a husband was being interviewed, his wife readily chimed in. Willingness to communicate is an important point in selecting families for therapy.

THE CHINESE

Initial establishment of a relationship of trust is critical in work with Chinese informants who are expected to discuss their own life experiences and personal views. In a research program on culture change and health, where members of the Chinese community in New York took part as volunteers, support of the aims of the research by a highly regarded member of that community (who offered himself as one of the first informants as well) did a great deal to provide an initial atmosphere of confidence—which grew as informants exchanged information with one another about their interview experience.[2]

When two or three Chinese informants joined an interviewer (or some-times two interviewers) for a restaurant meal, they often began to exchange experiences, including childhood memories, quite freely. In these circum-stances, the best thing interviewers could do was to sit quietly and listen. Both Chinese and American interviewers found that two or three congenial informants worked well together. But the real bonus came later in separate interviews, when the same informants, commenting on the earlier discus-sion, produced much more personal information.

Interviews with Chinese subjects may be more or less structured and focused on a particular topic. One useful technique was to propose a set of topics for discussion, leaving a margin of freedom as to whether one or an-other should be taken up immediately or postponed until later in the inter-view or until another hour. Actually, both Chinese and American inter-viewers felt that there were great individual differences both in the kind and richness of material informants offered. An informant might be very commu-nicative over a long period of time, yet remain evasive in handling certain personal material. In part this seemed to be a matter of confidence in the indi-vidual interviewer, a difficulty that could be accentuated in cross-sex inter-viewing. For example, on Rorschachs given by women examiners, the males regularly showed greater evasiveness than did the females. But, in part, pointed evasiveness was a more or less conscious technique of signaling unreadiness to take up some subject or some aspect of a subject under discussion. Maneuvering of this kind served as a form of distantiation. But informants often dropped clues indicating to the alert interviewer that signifi-cant material had been omitted—as when an informant mentioned an incor-rect date that indicated either an error in sequence or (as often turned out to be the case) the omission of a very important period in his life, about which he was not yet ready to talk.

Informants did not like being pushed by questions. They preferred a fairly unstructured interview that allowed them to reminisce and draw on their own associations. On the other hand, left to their own devices, some informants turned the interview into a teacher-pupil situation in which the informant as teacher pontificated or, as student, sought information. From time to time, most informants philosophized. To avoid too much phi-losophizing, interviews had to be guided, for some informants could not readily be brought out of a philosophizing mood.

Some informants were less resentful of the interview—and talked more freely—when the topic was one they regarded as an elementary subject. They felt that the Westerner who was ignorant about Chinese life had a right to ask as a way of learning, particularly on matters about which they believed any Chinese would be well informed. They also felt, on occasion, that it was possible to discuss with an outsider things they would never tell another Chinese. They would say, "I don't know why I told you that—please don't tell anyone!"

Reciprocity is a central theme in Chinese relationships, and a sense of mutual benefit was essential to a successful interview relationship. The informant who felt that granting an interview was a favor expected something in return. Similarly, Chinese interviewers often felt that they must make some return—give some present—to the informant. The feeling was so strong that Chinese interviewers sometimes cut off the interview relationship rather than carry the load of unfulfilled obligation. Informants asked American interviewers for help of many different kinds—help in entering a university, advice on how to deal with American authorities, instruction in the niceties of American customs, even assistance in arranging a marriage.

Not speaking Chinese, the American interviewers had to work out some order of meaning, some bridge of understanding. Part of interview skill consists in developing techniques for getting ideas across to the particular informant and of understanding what the informant says; each interviewer has to develop his own techniques. In work with Chinese informants, some interviewers used drawings, kinship diagrams, picture interpretations, Rorschach blots, or resorted to verbal analogies; from time to time, informants reciprocated by providing pictures, analyzing the elements included in the Chinese ideogram for a complex idea and so on—all of them techniques that can be used in interviews by mental health professionals.

The translation of certain concepts from one language to the other can present a great deal of difficulty. There is no way of rendering directly in Chinese the automatic American "sorry"—sorry I am late or sorry I stepped on your toe. On the other hand, it is difficult for a French or German speaker (also, though to a lesser extent, for a speaker of English) to realize that Chinese is a language without gender, so that, where the information is necessary, a special element indicating male or female must be added.

In some cultures the slightest stumbling effort to speak a phrase or two in the native language is welcomed with enthusiasm. But the French think it is disgraceful to speak poor French, the English laugh at poor English, and American children of immigrants often feel deeply embarrassed when their parents speak their native language in public. For the Chinese, the problem was more complex. Few Chinese felt embarrassed by their own difficulties in English, but a foreigner's misuse of Chinese (for example, the use of one dialect to a Chinese of another dialect or language group) embarrassed them. One useful technique was to ask an informant what word he would use to describe something—a situation, a mood, a key idea—discuss its possible meanings and then, later, use the word as a point of reference for informant and interviewer, but always subject to further discussion.

THE FRENCH

The French living in the United States do not form compact communities as some other groups prefer to do, but as individuals even those French men and women who have entered wholeheartedly into the stream of American life tend to preserve their cultural identity.[3] Many maintain ties with France and own property there or hope someday to buy some. No matter how long they have been in the United States, they do not "forget" how to speak French; it remains a living language spoken in the home, even with Americanized children, and with French friends. Visitors from France sometimes laugh at or are horrified by the Americanized words or grammatical constructions that have crept into the speech of long-time residents, but aside from such shifts in idiom and the loss of certain grammatical constructions, the language seems to remain intact.

In their home life, families of French background are inclined to cling to familiar habits and values. Children of French parents or of mixed marriages (of the French informants with whom we worked, most had French mothers and American fathers) may be so explicitly instructed in certain rules of conduct that, as adults, they are quite able to fit into a French milieu or, at least, are able to discuss French as well as American attitudes and ways with a certain clarity. The explicitness and the lack of carry-over from one culture to the other are about equally evident. The French—and their children—remain clear about what is French in a formal sense; indeed, about some things they are clearer than are the French of France—a special distortion in itself.[4]

In work with any foreign-born group and their descendants who still form an ethnic community, it is necessary to be alert to the possibility of various kinds of distortion (in relation to the parent culture). These may result, for example, from the absence of important social institutions, or shifts in emphasis resulting from the contact situation, or the demands of new activities, or a freezing of behavior forms or values that would normally have changed (and in the parent culture may have changed) in response to new life situations.

Since the inquirer is invariably considered an outsider by his French informants, he must make of this as advantageous a position as he can. Actually, it is a good position from which to work with the French because of their basic assumption that outsiders are likely to be interested in French life, and because of the belief that French ways are logical and applicable and, therefore, communicable. It is assumed that what is French is human— that is, universal at a high level—and optimally comprehensible to all civilized people. According to a favorite French aphorism, "Intelligent people all the world over are the same; it is only in their stupidities (*bêtises*) that nationalities differ."

When French informants, particularly men, related their life history, they tended to begin with early adolescence instead of childhood, saying, "When I was twelve or thirteen or fourteen"—as the case might be. Pressed to talk about their childhood, they were apt to recall what older people, parents or teachers, expected of them rather than their own versions of events. This is in keeping with the French sense that the child is an apprentice human being. Most information about the more spontaneous games and pastimes of childhood was given by foreigners who had spent part or all of their childhood in France, or by foreign observers of French children. This accords with the rarity of books about childhood by French writers—and with the fame of the few that have been written. French films about childhood have explored the child's world with extraordinary imaginative effect as a lost world or as a counterpoint to the adult world; it is worth noting that these films, which are so often concerned with the inner, imaginative life of the child, frequently have as their central figures children in the latency years. Truffaut's film version of Itard's *The Wild Boy of Aveyron* (1932), which is based on an actual experiment with a so-called wolf child, epitomizes the struggle to establish communication between the child and the adult world—a struggle that most French people tend to minimize in accounts of childhood. Since the main emphasis on the adult world is in keeping with the value placed on a life of reason (which is thought to begin more or less at adolescence), there is, in discussing personal life history, a tendency to stress those elements in childhood and adolescence that lead to adult life.

Sometimes, when French informants were speaking about themselves, they would turn back in time and speak of the marriages, the family life and so on of their parents and grandparents: how their grandparents brought up their parents, how grandfather was a black sheep and was disinherited by his mother and the like. In much the same way, in a study of infancy based on French, English, and American case materials (Soddy 1955), French researchers tended to emphasize how the parents of the infants under observation had been reared by their parents. When the projective test material began to show the importance of distantiation, the tendency to move back in time took on new significance beyond the obvious one of knowing financial, marital, and other details of the lives of two or three generations.

Some subjects, such as quarrels, were very difficult for French informants to deal with. The hedging and discomfort shown when French men and women were asked to deal with contemporary infighting in the family (rather than with episodes removed a generation or two in the past, which had been in some way resolved) highlighted the problem of controls. The most important material on such subjects was obtained by means of projective tests and through the examination of other fantasy materials.

Observations of French mothers and small children brought out another point of distantiation. In moments of anger over disobedience, mothers called their two- and three-year-olds by the names of the same mythological monsters and fright-figures that some adults "saw" in the Rorschach blots. These they described as figures, existing outside the home, with which adults frightened children—though, they also said, they assured the children they were not real. Thus, in effect, the disobedient child was identified with the monster, which was frightening, outside, and unreal.

Once a type of relationship had been established with a French informant, it tended to remain stable. When interviewers attempted to introduce some change (such as, for example, a shift from a very formal to a very informal relationship, in keeping with an American style of handling acquaintanceship), informants were apt to retreat or to insist on retaining the earlier structure. This does not mean that there was no progression, but that there was a strong preference for progression within a well-defined framework. This fact was an important clue to French relationships in general and, in therapy, might be important in considering transference phenomena.

Lerner (1961), who organized a large sociological research project in France involving 1,500 leaders in business, politics, social service, the church, labor, the military, and so on, worked out ways of conducting interviews between a Frenchman and, for example, an American. Although some points made by Lerner have already been considered in substance, others may be helpful. He speaks, first of all, about the distance and formality maintained by the French as a defense against intimacy in an initial encounter. For example, answering the telephone, the Frenchman says, *"J'écoute"*; or when someone asks, *"Comment ça va?"* ("How's everything?") he will reply, *"On se defend"* ("I'm managing").

It was difficult to convince the French to be interviewed, for they set up a wall that was hard to penetrate. They did not like their privacy to be challenged (for example, by provocative questions). Lerner's subjects insisted that they were not typical, as did French informants interviewed in the United States. However, once the barricades came down—that is, once the informants were convinced that they had something special to contribute and were given to understand that the interviewer was obliged to ask questions, but that they need answer only those that interested them—they were willing to talk for hours and clearly enjoyed the exchange of ideas.

The material reported on by Lerner was obtained in 1954. When he reinterviewed a group of subjects in 1959, he found that they responded more easily and far less evasively. He wondered whether this was owing to changing conditions in France or whether his subjects remembered the earlier setting and felt reassured. The question is one that will have to be explored.

SYRIANS: CHRISTIANS AND MUSLIMS

The problem of cross-sex interviewing is an important consideration in work with Syrians (this includes the Lebanese), whatever their religious affiliation. However, in the research that was carried out (Mead and Metraux 1953), the problem was discussed only with regard to the disadvantages of having a woman interview a man. The general opinion, especially among Muslim Syrians, was that an unmarried woman interviewer was preferable to a married woman, who ought not to be alone with a man. Male informants were willing to cooperate with an interviewer who was an unmarried professional woman and who spoke with some authority, but it was felt that sooner or later he would cease to see her as "neutral"; then the fact of her eligibility as a woman would interfere with the interview situation. For this reason interviews between an unmarried woman interviewer and a male informant seldom continued beyond a few sessions. One young Turkish-American professional woman, a Muslim, became an excellent interviewer in cross-class relationships with male informants who honored her as a scholar belonging to a milieu quite different from their own. (Similarly, in working with Native American families, one of the authors found that Native American men accepted her as a family therapist because she was a professional and "not a woman.")

The complex problems of cross-religious and cross-cultural interviewing were also considered. A Muslim interviewing a Muslim immediately made her religious position known and had no difficulty. However, it would be more difficult for a *Shiite* Muslim to interview a *Sunnite* Muslim than for a

Christian Syrian to do so. In interviewing Muslim Syrians one Muslim interviewer, a Turkish national who was Russian by birth, emphasized her Turkish position, which had prestige value for her informants. Since up to 1914 the ruling class in Syria was largely Turkish, it was said that many Muslim Syrians claimed to have Turkish blood as a way of enhancing their social position. Moreover, since all Turks belong to the Sunnite Muslim sect, a person with this background was said to be doubly acceptable to Muslim Syrians.

Interviewers reported that with Syrian Christians it was preferable to avoid discussion of religion in the initial stages of work. A Syrian interviewer was more acceptable than a non-Syrian. A Syrian who also belonged to the Orthodox church or who came from the same part of Damascus was even more acceptable.

In Syrian eyes both religious affiliation and nationality were important considerations for the establishment of good rapport; each group, however, had its own hierarchy of preferences that included other factors, such as wealth or good family. At the present time, when political tensions are running high, the question of whether an individual is friendly toward Israel or the Arab states is likely to outweigh most other considerations.

In New York, Syrian Christians preferred to discuss personal matters in English, even with an Arabic-speaking interviewer. They used English, for example, to complain about other people, their own hard lives, or money. It was suggested that in such situations they felt they were Americans talking with other Americans. A language shift also could be used to bring about a change of pace; when an interviewer, speaking in one language, added, "You know what I mean," in the other language, the shift gave informants a jolt that led to improved communication. Even fourth-generation Syrian Christians continued to curse in Arabic. Moreover, American wives complained that their husbands spoke Arabic when they were angry. It is also said that Syrian Christians pick up Arabic phrases from Egyptian films—phrases that may have love or sex as their theme and that would not be used in Syrian Arabic—and young people use them freely, since the Egyptian terminology lends distance and safety.

Finally, there was evidence to suggest that focusing on a topic made for a successful interview, providing the subject matter was satisfactory to the particular informant; otherwise the interview tended to become stereotyped. The use of kinship terms was a successful topic with Muslim Syrians, who enjoyed the subject. The topic of circumcision had to be broached carefully, for the idea of it made them feel inferior. However, if one first talked about money, a topic they found interesting, circumcision could be discussed later.

Among Syrian Christians the basic areas of resistance were those regarded as highly personal, such as money, what each person was doing, sickness (which was kept secret), and sex (a tabooed subject). When someone speaks about illness to Syrian Christians, they murmur certain words to prevent the idea of sickness from circulating. In one family, when a daughter came home from the movies during an interview, she was not introduced but sat back in a corner. When the interviewer asked, "Who is she?" the reply was "She isn't well." That closed the question.

Interviewers were clear that Syrians would only talk about what they themselves wanted to talk about. Too many visits to an informant, whatever the conditions, were a hindrance. The relationship progressed to a certain point—and then stopped.

Persons belonging to divergent cultures have very different ways of entering into a dyadic interview relationship. Informants responded in characteristic—though distinct—ways to the nationality, religion, age, and sex of the interviewer. They differed in their feeling about language use in the interview; in their approach to the interview—in the kind of relationship with an interviewer that was meaningful and inspired confidence; in the kinds of topics they felt they could discuss freely (or only with difficulty, or not at all); in the kind and amount of direction they demanded or would accept from the interviewer; and in what, if anything, they expected to gain. Directly or indirectly, the interviewer has to be sensitive to nuances of meaning and feeling in the individual that reflect his intrapsychic conflicts, his relations with others (parents, peers, and "bosses" at work) and his overt attitudes, all of which—as well as his expectations about medical care, reasons for seeking help, and so forth—are shaped by regularities in cultural patterning.

Of course, the focus of an interview differs greatly according to its purpose, whether it is research dealing with child rearing practices, for example, or with attitudes toward health and illness in an ethnic community, or the physical illness or emotional problems and maladjustments of an individual who comes voluntarily or is sent. The manner of conducting an interview and the areas touched upon depend on the professional training of the interviewer, whether he is an anthropologist, a social worker, a clinical psychologist, a psychiatrist, or a psychoanalyst. Each one, with his different background and training, will focus on different aspects of the individual's total situation, including his background, his expectations about help, his physical condition and "mental status," and his suitability for treatment of one kind or another. The orientation of the interviewer will also largely determine how an interview is conducted—whether few or many questions are asked, whether the individual is given a psychological test, and whether he is free to talk on any topic he chooses or to associate without interference.

Yet despite all such purposes and variations in the interview situation, some understanding of specific cultural expectations—or at least some sensitivity to their effect on how the interview proceeds—is essential in evaluating the individual's personality, in diagnosing his case, in deciding what is to be done about helping him, and in determining the method of treatment. If the purpose is research, that same awareness of the role of cultural patterning will make for a more accurate and complete evaluation of the problem under investigation.

The interpretation of how an interview is conducted, particularly the kinds of questions asked, among individuals from different cultures, may vary extremely from what the psychologist, for example, expects. The psychologist is aware that the way he phrases his questions must depend on whether his subject is naïve or sophisticated, male or female, and on how conversant he is with the English language. The psychologist also is sensitive to the kinds of questions he can ask, and to the caution he must exercise in asking personal questions, such as those concerning sexual behavior. If possible, he is guided by the person's ongoing responses. But the person interviewed may find subtle means to avoid responding or he may well respond in a way the interviewer did not expect, for his responses depend not only on his idiosyncratic ways of coping with a situation but also on very basic, culturally determined attitudes.

The expectation on the part of Eastern European Jewish men and women that the learned man—the interviewer or the doctor, as the case may be— will ask intelligent questions; and their rejection of those who ask what they regard as "foolish questions" is a case in point. The preference of Chinese subjects for relatively unstructured interview situations and their sense of being able to talk more freely—on some subjects—with non-Chinese (that is, American) interviewers than with Chinese interviewers presents a very different set of problems in the management of an interview.

Of course, an American pyschologist who is unfamiliar with Eastern European Jewish culture or with Chinese culture has some difficulty in establishing rapport and may be led astray by situations of mutual misunderstanding. But in the course of working with his patient, he can establish some order of meaning, providing he takes into account the unexpected ways in which therapist and patient, coming from different cultures, may interpret each other's words and behavior. A working relationship depends on achieving—on both sides—some grasp of these differences in the way experience is organized, perceived, and responded to.

Carstairs (1961), a British psychiatrist—a Scot by birth who was reared in India—had had considerable experience with patients both in England and in the field in India. He has made valuable observations in addition to those already discussed. First of all, he indicates that the *interviewer's* experience varies according to the place of interview—whether it be a Westernized setting (such as a "Western" college in Bombay or Singapore) or the cultural setting of the one interviewed. Carstairs also mentions the difficulty of interviewing a patient from the same cultural background but a different economic level, stressing differences in the value systems of the interviewer and the one interviewed.

In any contact with a patient from a different cultural group, two immediate difficulties may arise. One is language. Difficulties in communication where there is a language barrier are understandable. As Carstairs points out, the problem may be complicated if the patient gives the impression that he understands a second language better than he actually does, which leads to distortions that can well interfere with the interviewer's evaluations. Secondly, the patient may give the impression that he understands "Western" ways of life, for he does not want to appear ignorant in the eyes of the interviewer. In this case, Carstairs says, distortions can be avoided if the interviewer knows something about the patient's cultural background and his expectations. If he does not know, he can, of course, find out to some extent during the interview.

One very puzzling thing in interviews with Chinese informants (some of whom were advanced graduate students) was the utter lack of concern some of them felt about their very limited capacity to understand or use English. Discussion of the problem with informants revealed that, in China, when children moved from one language area to another, no one was disturbed by the fact that the new pupil in school could neither express himself nor understand the teacher's spoken instructions. It was taken for granted that mutual understanding would come—and it did. There was no need to push or to be pushed or to be fearful of the outcome. In the interim, written communication was available to both teacher and pupil.

Carstairs judges that some problems of patients should be regarded not as neurotic but rather as the emotional disturbances of the young person who feels his lack of identity with the adult world and is thus insecure. Often the difficulty has to do with problems of adjustment to new situations which the patient will not—or cannot—acknowledge.

For example, the patient of one coauthor (Abel), a Hindu student, was sent to a clinic in New York because he had become fearful of failing examinations. The initial interview revealed that he was trying to be like an American student in every way which, among other things, meant eating in the automat or the college cafeteria, eating hamburgers, hot dogs, and potato chips, drinking a great deal of coffee, and being as independent as possible (looking after his own clothes, laundry and so on). Actually, he was miserable, was not sleeping well, felt lonely for the companionship of fellow Hindus and, most especially, missed Hindu food. Often difficulties such as these are symptomatic of deeper conflicts stemming from the patient's earlier life, as Carstairs correctly states. In the case of the Hindu student, it turned out later that he had many deep-seated conflicts. But the point here is that some of his difficulties had to be surmised during the interview, since the student was guarded and reluctant to admit his longings and dependency needs, many of which were patterned by his culture—in India he had never had to look after his own personal needs, for he had lived in an extended family in which many women, including his wife, had looked after him.

Carstairs also made a number of points about doing psychiatric interviewing in a culture different from one's own. For one thing, the interviewer has to be conscious of his ignorance about cultural patterns, and should not give the subject (informant or patient) to understand that he knows more than he actually does about such matters. Carstairs speaks of the importance of being sensitive to the kinds of subjects that can be broached and to the phrasing of questions. Even such techniques as taking notes (including writing down names) may be viewed with suspicion in certain groups (as may also be true for a paranoid American). Carstairs also warns against a too-rapid interpretation of material offered by the subject, in order to avoid such mistakes as making a "diagnosis" based on modes of behavior that are considered pathological in European or American society, but that may be accepted or expected of a member of some other society.

In the last ten years or so, a great deal more information about cultural variables in interviewing clients and patients at the onset of therapy has been brought out. In later chapters we shall discuss problems of communication during therapy with groups from different societies as well as the ways in which communications become distorted under the influence of transference and countertransference.

As we have already indicated, different cultural groups respond in various ways, depending on who is interviewing them, the conditions under which they are interviewed, and the kinds of questions they are being asked.

During the last twenty-five years, family therapy has become more and more commonly employed by mental health professionals, but cultural variables in family therapy have been taken into account only in recent years. A family from a different cultural background may come to an initial interview bringing with it customs, ideas, and attitudes that seem foreign to the mental health professional. Furthermore, there is the pressure of having several individuals focused on one therapist. In addition, a family generally consists of at least two generations, often three, where the younger generation has become more or less acculturated to American cultural patterns. So the therapist must deal with difficulties among family members and between the generations concerning attitudes and modes of behavior. The conflict may spread through three generations, where parents are torn between the views of their parents and those of their children. Welts (1982), for example, states that it is unusual for Greek-Americans to seek therapy.[5] When they do come for help as a family, it is hard for the therapist to understand the whole problem, for the family assumes the therapist will not talk freely before a child or a "sick relative" (the identified patient). To discover exactly why the family comes for help, the therapist may need to have an interview first with a single responsible member of the family. Second, it is important for the therapist not to try to join the family, for this is unacceptable. Among Americans the therapist can enter the family system to a degree from the start. In talking to a Greek-American family, a male therapist must ask questions that are authoritative and formal, while a female therapist can gear her questions more in the direction of nurturing needs and function as a mediator.

Portuguese-Americans (Moitoza 1982) usually come for help when referred by others. In fact, they prefer family therapy to individual therapy, for they may feel that a dyadic relationship in therapy is intended to break up the cohesiveness of the family. These families are very reluctant to go to an office or clinic because of their fear of the outsider, the therapist. They are much more comfortable if the therapy is done in the home. The therapist coming to the home arrives as a visitor and is expected to dress professionally (ties for men, stockings for women). The initial interview begins with comments by the therapist about the house and decorations, as well as questions about the family history, who the children are, the grandparents, and so on. All questions must be directed to the father as a sign of respect. The father tells about the family and their problems at first. Progress toward therapy must be slow.

With Mexican or Spanish-American families the initial encounter with a therapist must be very polite and formal. Adults must be addressed by their last names only, not as in America where a teenager may start calling a therapist, old enough to be her grandmother, by her first name after the first session. Falicov (1982) adds, however, that as Mexican families move along in the therapeutic process, they become very friendly with the therapist. They hug and show a good deal of warmth, much more so than do American families.

At an early stage, Falicov indicates, the therapist needs to realize that with Mexican families the focus of questions must be on the parent–child dyad. Mexican women do not worry so much about being good wives as they do about being good mothers. Marital problems can come up only in long-term therapy after a considerable period of work. But any time Mexican wives are seen alone, they complain about their husbands. They do not do this when the spouse is present.

In the Polish family, according to Thomas and Znaniecki (1927), respect—not love—is the binding tie. The father is the real power figure. According to Mondykowski (1982), Polish-Americans maintain these attitudes and beliefs from their native land.[6] They have strict rules about sex; however, sex is considered good, not bad. A husband may become sexually playful with his wife in front of the children. As expected among Roman Catholics, many children are desirable.

Polish-Americans rarely go to a mental health clinic or to a private professional for help. Only after failing to work out a problem in the family or the extended family will a family seek help. The problem, however, must be one that threatens the family's integrity, such as alcoholism, money, or conflict over who is to care for a sick parent.

A therapist seeing a Polish-American family for the first time must be aware of certain characteristics, such as a great show of emotion which appears as warmth and a desire for therapy, but actually is a defense mechanism to hide a need to be taken care of, a need that is forbidden by the culture. Individuals must be independent. The therapist has to communicate to the family that what they will try to do together will be practical (action-oriented therapy). Furthermore, the therapist must immediately let the family know that he respects and understands—or expects to understand—Polish values.

In any setting, an initial interview—whether carried out by a psychiatrist, a psychologist, a psychiatric social worker, or some other member of the mental health disciplines— can be upsetting to members of a family as well as to individual clients or patients, even if they have come voluntarily.

Questions having to do with feelings, attitudes, and aspects of their life history can create anxiety and provoke a variety of defenses that may interfere with the progress of the interview. As we have said, insensitivity to the factors that disturb patients—including those of cultural origin which the interviewer has not understood, thereby "putting his foot into it" as it were—can make for a difficult situation, leading to distorted interpretations and discouragement of patients, who are then unwilling to seek further help.

Yet the initial interview, which both prospective patients and the therapist enter with a certain tentativeness, can also convey to the individual patient, to the couple or to the family members, that this can be the beginning of an experience of gradually acquired mutual confidence and of learning. In such an experience the therapist and the clients or patients are all participants.

Six

Attitudes Toward Treatment of Mental Illness

As shown earlier, cultural factors can play a distinct role in the kinds of mental illness and emotional disturbance that occur and in the forms they take. Studies have been made in the United States (see, for example, Srole et al. 1962) on sociocultural patterns that can affect etiology and epidemiology. Who goes for treatment, why he goes, where he goes, who treats him, and what kind of treatment he will accept, all may be influenced by manifest and covert cultural patterns that determine an individual's attitudes, feelings, modes of behavior, and intrapsychic pressures. Sanua (1966) has covered this topic quite comprehensively. Furthermore, the kind of treatment itself reflects the viewpoint of the innovator, a member of a particular society at a particular time. Psychoanalytic and psychotherapeutic theories and practices have been developed by individuals from specific cultures and have been influenced also by the culture of the patients who have been treated.

It was Freud himself who first drew attention to the impact of non-psychological factors in psychotherapy. Freud had formulated some ideas as to the kinds of patients he believed were suitable for psychoanalysis. He felt that patients needed to have acquired a fair degree of education and also to have a quite reliable character structure to be able to profit from psycho-analysis. He also believed that individuals over fifty years of age were too inflexible to work with in psychoanalysis (1950a). However, this referred only to psychoanalysis and not necessarily to psychotherapy. Freud was aware of the need to provide psychotherapy for a broad range of people, independent of age, intelligence, and character development. He went so far as to recommend that such services should be offered without charge (Freud 1950b).

It may well be that attitudes toward treatment in different social classes and cultures are related in part to attitudes of mental health professionals themselves. Freud's working hypothesis that certain kinds of people are not suitable for psychoanalysis may have led to a rejection of psychological treatment by those very people. Roll, Millen and Martinez (1980) trace the low participation of Spanish-Americans in psychotherapy to attitudes on the part of therapists rather than of patients. Hence the authors caution that glib generalizations, such as that members of one or another cultural group or social class are not suitable for psychotherapy, need to be explored and greatly modified.

Until recently in Europe, an individual was likely to seek help (usually from a psychiatrist) because he had a symptom, and the focus was primarily on symptom removal. But currently in Europe, outside the Eastern bloc, psychotherapeutic and psychoanalytic movements have experienced considerable expansion and growing popularity. An example of this is the attention and controversy that surround the work of the French psychoanalyst Lacan (1966, 1971). Throughout Latin America, especially in Mexico and Argentina, both psychoanalysis and psychotherapy are practiced in large urban centers.

In the United States, as in Europe and Latin America at the present time, the predominant focus has long been on the individual's problems. A patient who has a symptom (an ulcer, a phobia, anxiety, or sleeplessness) is thought of as having a problem, rather than a disease that may require only medication. A patient may, however, be given tranquilizers or energizers (or both) as an adjunct to working out his difficulties.

In the United States and some other Western societies individuals who enter psychotherapy voluntarily are likely to be highly educated and to have sufficient income to pay for treatment. Moreover, patients turn voluntarily to psychotherapy (including psychoanalysis) when it is readily available. The less-well-educated and those of meager income are more likely to receive treatment only when they are referred to a therapist by a physician, clergyman, social worker or another professional. But this is changing; today more individuals at various socioeconomic levels have begun themselves to seek specialized help for their emotional disturbances.

In the various forms of dynamic psychotherapy the patient is encouraged to think about himself and to evaluate his own needs (that is, to question authority in its various forms) and to reveal his feelings, even though these seem contrary to his upbringing or to the prevalent modes of conduct in the society in which he lives or in which he was reared.

However, the idea of psychotherapy is not equally acceptable to all cultural groups. For example, Chinese and Greeks in the United States, regardless of their socioeconomic status, are less likely to seek therapy or to send members of their family for therapeutic help than are members of some other ethnic groups. Chinese are relatively tolerant toward nonviolent deviant behavior. On the other hand, psychoanalysis and psychotherapy are likely to be considered acceptable forms of treatment among educated Jews in large urban centers. Their willingness may well be owing, on the one hand, to the large number of Jewish therapists and, on the other hand, to Jewish reverence for the learned man—the doctor and the psychotherapist.

Various attempts have been made to explain the reasons that the idea of psychotherapy has taken a much stronger hold in some countries than in others. This is particularly the case with psychoanalysis and with dynamically oriented forms of treatment that include helping the patient to gain insight into the nature of his conflicts and the difficulties he has in interpersonal relationships. It has been pointed out that certain countries have not been receptive to the free development of dynamic therapy. Examples are the Soviet Union, where individual rights and privileges are subject to the control of the state, and countries like Japan and Germany, with predominantly hierarchical social structures. Small enclaves of psychoanalysis have appeared in Japan and Germany and other countries with similar social structures, but not yet in the Soviet Union. Some forms of psychotherapy are emerging there; treatment, however, may be slanted away from the rights and privileges of the patient.

Until recently in the Soviet Union, psychotherapy had to conform to activities that could be made to fit a Pavlovian model (Winn 1962). But now, according to a recent report (Daniloff 1984), even though Freud's works are still virtually unavailable in the Soviet Union, there is an emerging recognition of unconscious psychological factors and a reduced focus on Pavlovian methods.

Papiasvili (1984) presented a first hand account of psychotherapy in the Soviet Union at the 1984 meetings of the International Congress of Group Psychotherapy in Mexico City. He reported also on his work in mental hospitals in East Germany, Czechoslovakia, and Poland. In his training and practice, Freud's writings, as well as those of most Western psychologists (including Skinner), were strictly forbidden, but in East Germany, Poland, Russia, and Czechoslovakia there was some interest in psychodrama. In the

Bechterev Institute of Leningrad, for example, psychodrama was practiced along with discussion of images and ideas culled from Russian literature and the cinema. These sessions were interspersed with lectures on Marxism and Leninism. In Poland there was some dynamically oriented group therapy in hospitals and some was even being done privately. The latter, especially, was conducted without sanction and, Papiasvili felt, at considerable personal risk.

According to Redlich (1958), Americans were willing to admit that they are afraid and anxious and that they suffer without physical cause, and so are willing to seek help. Lasswell (1948) suggested that dynamic psychotherapy meets the needs of Americans, who welcome a way of getting relief from guilt and anxiety about sexuality—guilt that has its origins (as they see it) in a puritanical morality. It should be pointed out, however, that this willingness is in keeping with the much more basic American emphasis on self-improvement—the belief that it is the individual's responsibility to take corrective measures to improve himself—and with the optimistic belief that efforts at self-improvement can succeed and make possible a better life. In France, where there is less guilt over sex, aggression, and dependency, attitudes toward psychotherapy are not the same. An adult Frenchman who asks his father's advice about major changes in his life, such as selling or buying property or entering a new business venture, does not consider himself dependent or weak, as an American might. (The American, instead, consults an "expert.") This does not mean that the French do not suffer from guilt over sex, aggression (especially physical fighting in contrast to verbal vituperation), and dependency, but only that the contexts are not the same.

In spite of the growth of psychodynamic methods of treatment in Europe, their popularity is still relatively limited. Perhaps this is because a great deal of stress is laid on medicine as a way of reducing mental illness. Moreover, on the Continent, endocrinology plays a major role in efforts to alleviate mental disorders. This is less prevalent in the United States, although there are variations from one region of the country to another. The recent focus on chemical treatment in the United States is beginning to bring about a shift toward the organic point of view in American psychiatry. In Europe, on the other hand, in addition to various forms of organic treatment, there is a philosophical orientation, and a number of psychiatrists and psychologists have been influenced by the ideas of phenomenology and existentialism (developed by Husserl, Jaspers, Heidegger, Buber, and others) to develop new theories in psychoanalysis and therapy (see Lacan, especially 1966, 1971).

Several studies in the United States have attempted to sort out the various attitudes toward treatment and toward patients, particularly in the north-eastern states. In a study of upper Manhattan, Srole and his associates (Srole et al. 1962) investigated the prevalence of mental illness in the area (number of cases in outpatient or inpatient installations or in treatment with private therapists). Socioeconomic level, as well as cultural and religious back-ground, was found to play a role. In the area studied, about one-half the mentally ill patients were seen by private practitioners; these patients were well-off people who could pay fees. Yet among lower socioeconomic groups, more emotional difficulties and mental impairment were reported than among the well-to-do. Hence it seems that the relationship between socio-economic group and treatment was inverse to the degree of impairment. The investigators also found that more non-Jews than Jews were being cared for in state mental hospitals, and that more Jews than non-Jews were being treated by private therapists, either in their offices or in private psychiatric hospitals. Moreover, in outpatient clinics in New York City there was a larger proportion of Jewish patients than of non-Jewish ones. The investigators suggested that Jewish patients have milder disturbances and are more ready to seek help, whether in an outpatient clinic or privately. They also suggested that certain cultural attitudes are relevant; for example, among Jewish groups historically realistic anxiety, kept alive through tradition, and strong in-group pressures may have a positive effect in overcoming severe disturbances but may add to milder disorders.

In this investigation an open-ended questionnaire was used. One ques-tion presented a problem about a family, one of whose members was men-tally ill. The respondent was asked what he considered the proper thing to do in the case. Jewish informants suggested psychiatric consultation more often than did Catholics and Protestants; here, of course, the different cultural background of the Catholic and Protestant respondents may have played some role.

Treatment and Socioeconomic Level

The well-known investigations of Redlich and Hollingshead (Redlich, Hol-lingshead, and Bellis 1955) in New Haven, Connecticut, have revealed that persons of lower-class background (Class V on their socioeconomic scale) were less inclined to seek treatment voluntarily than middle- and upper-class persons (Class I and II) and were least likely to change their attitudes during treatment. Lower-class patients were more apt to be treated by medical students and to be sent to mental hospitals. In therapy, lower-class patients

(Class IV and V) averaged eleven interviews, whereas middle-class patients (Class II and III) averaged about twenty-five sessions. Moreover, lower-class patients tended to be given organic treatment or custodial care, while those who were more well-to-do (Class I and II) were much more likely to receive psychotherapy and were not placed in custodial care.

In a follow-up investigation of the hospitalized patients reported on in the New Haven study, Myers, Bean, and Pepper (1968) found that social class was the most important variable in determining a patient's chances of being released from a psychiatric hospital.

Among patients still hospitalized over a period of a decade, 39 per cent were members of Class I and II, and 57 per cent were members of Class V; 31 per cent of patients coming from the more well-to-do groups (Class I and II) were living in the community, but only 10 per cent of the poorest group (Class V) did so.

In a more recent study Meltzoff and Kornreich (1970) conclude: In the United States the more money a patient has, the more likely the patient is to receive psychotherapy. The more economically deprived a patient is, the more likely the patient will receive medication and physical treatment.

The question is not merely one of the form of treatment members of different socioeconomic groups in the United States are likely to receive, but also one of what patients understand and expect with regard to treatment and the role of the therapist. Jones and Kahn (1964) employed an attitude scale (worked out by Kahn et al. 1963) to investigate this problem through a comparison of the responses of lower, middle, and upper socioeconomic groups of institutionalized patients. The questionnaire contained fifty-five statements that were to be evaluated on a four-point rating scale. Out of a patient population of sixty-four, 87 per cent responded to the scale. The themes dealt with in the questionnaire were: (1) authoritarian control and nonpsychological orientation; (2) negative hospital point of view; (3) external control, cause and treatment are seen as external to oneself (illness attributed to others; treatment as physical, such as shock); (4) mental illness viewed as physiological; and (5) letdown of control for therapeutic gain or acceptance of arbitrary restrictions (patient needs to be built up, needs nursing care and so on).

Jones and Kahn predicted that patients belonging to the lower socioeconomic group would give high ratings to topics in item (1); patients belonging to the upper socioeconomic group would assign high values to topics in item (5), the release of tension and control for therapeutic gains during hospitalization; and patients belonging to the middle socioeconomic group would give the highest ratings to topics in item (3), external control. The results confirmed Jones and Kahn's predictions. Neither religion nor occupation alone seemed to be related to the ratings on the questionnaire. Education appeared to be somewhat more related insofar as patients with more education tended to shift their emphasis from topics in item (1) to those in item (5). However, occupation and education, taken together, showed a high correlation with socioeconomic status, judging from the ways in which the patients responded. Generally, it was found that patients of lower socioeconomic status with negative attitudes toward hospitalization made a social recovery with somatic treatment, whereas patients of upper socioeconomic status with far more positive attitudes toward hospitalization were treated more satisfactorily by psychotherapeutic techniques. Hence the investigators concluded that the patients' values were crucial to their responses to various types of treatment. This study did not take into account, however, the attitudes of hospital personnel or therapists to patients coming from different socioeconomic groups.

Attitudes Toward Therapy in Different Societies

Attitudes toward psychiatric care in a hospital have been investigated in other parts of the world. In Israel, for example, Hes (1966–1967) compared the attitudes of Moroccan and Yemenite men (fifty men in each group) with those of Polish men (fifty-one men) all of whose wives were hospitalized. (The Moroccans and Yemenites had migrated to Israel within five to fifteen years of the study. They were grouped together because their responses, as revealed by the study, were quite similar.) About half of the Moroccan and Yemenite husbands had consulted a native healer or a rabbi about their wives while their wives were hospitalized. The Polish husbands did not do this.

Contrasting attitudes were found in answers to such questions as whether hospitals treat patients or just detain them, whether other patients are believed to be dangerous and whether hospitalization is concealed from family members, neighbors or coworkers. The Yemenites and Moroccans had far more doubts than the Poles about whether the hospital could offer treatment. The fact that most of the Poles were middle-class whereas many of the Yemenites and Moroccans came from a lower socioeconomic group may have accounted for some of the differences in attitude. But cultural attitudes were also involved. For example, Yemenite and Moroccan husbands complained about the strange food given their wives and the lack of contact with professional personnel (especially physicians); in particular, they complained that the hospital did not take over the care of the family at home. The husbands expected the hospital to provide substitutes for their wives, an attitude, Hes suggests, in keeping with that of the Yemenite or Moroccan father who hands his daughter over to the care of her prospective husband and his family. Polish husbands were able to cope with their family needs themselves.

In Korea a study was carried out by Kahn et al. (1966–1967) on attitudes of patients toward mental illness and hospitalization. This investigation used the scale employed by Jones and Kahn (1964) in the research reported earlier. Jones and Kahn's questionnaire, translated into Korean, was given to 202 patients, the entire population of a psychiatric hospital in Seoul. The patients' responses were then compared (using computer techniques) with those of the American patients in the Jones and Kahn study.

A number of differences were found. For one thing, the Korean attitudes were largely presented in five rotated factors, the American in seventeen. There were differences in attitudes and in emphases as well. The Koreans found the hospital a pleasant, cheerful place in which to relax and viewed other patients and the hospital personnel positively. The Americans who took a positive view emphasized their enjoyment of dependence and being looked after. Some Koreans and Americans were negatively oriented to the hospital. The American responses, however, emphasized the restrictive penal aspects of hospitalization more strongly than the Korean responses did. The most negative American responses had to do with authority, restriction, victimization and external control, reflecting the American insistence on individual freedom and personal autonomy, and their refusal to submit arbitrarily to authority figures. The Koreans, on the other hand, accepted authority relatively easily. They found the hospital more supportive and agreeable than they had expected, and their negative orientation to the hospital had more to do with fear of other patients and feelings of general pessimism than with attitudes toward authority figures.

Unlike the American patient group, about half the Koreans had had other forms of treatment (herbal medicine, "superstitious" remedies, religious measures) before entering the hospital. Moreover, the Koreans ascribed their illnesses largely to external forces (including heredity). The Koreans did not see illness as having its source in intrapsychic or interpersonal conflict, a view held by many Americans, particularly those in the upper socioeconomic group. Some Americans, particularly those in the lower socioeconomic group, held views similar to those of the Koreans.

Overall, the Americans presented a much more complicated series of attitudes toward mental illness and hospitalization than did the Koreans. Kahn and his collaborators were aware, however, that the Koreans formed a much more homogeneous group than the Americans, who came from various cultural and socioeconomic groups. The Americans were also much more familiar than the Koreans with testing procedures as well as with the particular rating methods used. Moreover, the questions were originally designed for Americans and drew far less on Korean beliefs and attitudes.

This last observation points up a common failing of tests and questionnaires that incorporate the prevailing attitudes and values of the culture in which they originated. In research with Chinese volunteers at New York Hospital-Cornell Medical Center (in which the anthropologist coauthor participated), the subjects were routinely asked to fill out a very lengthy, medically-oriented questionnaire. The few answers given, other than a simple Yes or No (often in long series), appeared bizarre to the American physicians interviewed. The Chinese informants themselves either politely avoided discussion of the questionnaire, even with interviewers with whom they had good rapport, or explained that they did not understand the questions or the reasons for asking them. The answers they genuinely attempted to give (the "bizarre" ones) made good sense once they were discussed; but had seemed bizarre because they were based on premises that were not in the minds of those who had designed the questionnaire.

Outside the United States, students' attitudes toward counseling and therapy also vary considerably from those of American students, who are generally aware of the opportunities for counseling at colleges and universities. For example, in 1967 Levon Melikian, a professor and clinical psychologist at the American University at Beirut, Lebanon, discussed the problems he had had setting up a counseling service for students. Melikian, a native of Lebanon from the Armenian community, had received his doctoral training in the United States. He found that counseling and psychotherapy were practices unfamiliar to Arab university students, especially those from traditional villages in Syria, Jordan, Egypt, Lebanon and elsewhere. In contrast to urbanized students, who took a relatively liberal position, many of these students from rural areas developed major conflicts about their traditional views of religion and social conduct. Quite a few became severely emotionally disturbed; they were unable to study and had doubts about their ability to carry on. This conflict was exacerbated by economic problems.[1]

Under such emotional pressures, these students were willing to listen to the dean (an authority they respected) when he suggested that they talk over their academic program with a member of the psychology department. The phrasing "academic program" was used because they otherwise would not have understood or would have been reluctant to seek a consultation about their worries. Although the students who availed themselves of this counseling discovered that they were able to unburden themselves and express their feelings about conflicts that did not necessarily pertain to their course work, they were also concerned with finding a philosophy that did not conflict too much with their orthodox religious beliefs and yet was more "modern." Quite a number of students remained for approximately twenty sessions and experienced relief after brief psychotherapy with a psychologist who understood their problems, spoke their language, and was sensitive to the values of their society.[2]

The relevance of cultural patterning is evident in the most cursory examination of the complex problems involved in the individual's search for treatment. It is evident in the way he sees his problems, the kind of treatment he is offered and the kind of therapy he can accept (or feels he will not benefit from), the expectations he has about the outcome of therapy and his interpretation of the experience, as well as in the views of mental health professionals about the different kinds of people who seek help or whom they encounter as clients, students, and patients in clinics, schools, hospitals and other settings.

There is some work available on the subject of variations in psychopathology and attitudes toward treatment in different cultural and socioeconomic settings.[3] However, there is no compendium designed to alert the mental health professional to the relevant aspects of all the world's cultures in all their ethnic and social variation. It is, therefore, incumbent upon the therapist who works in a variety of cultural and socioeconomic settings to discover for himself, from the scientific literature and from community resources, what he needs to know, particularly about the prevailing attitudes toward mental illness, psychotherapy, and therapists, both among those who are to be treated and those who recommend or provide treatment. To this end, the psychotherapist may have to visit the setting in which the prospective patient lives—his home and neighbors, his school and church, and possibly place of work, as well as places where he finds entertainment— if only to remind himself that he, too, as therapist, has something to learn if treatment is to be effective.

Equally valuable to successful therapy is the therapist's own self-discovery and reevaluation of his own ethnic, cultural, and socioeconomic commitments. In growing up, each therapist absorbs, to some degree, specific attitudes toward treatment and psychopathology. These attitudes may consciously and unconsciously influence the treatment the therapist can offer the patient. As Boszormeny-Nagy and Spark (1973) state, an individual's loyalty commitments may be latent, cognitively unformulated, and preconscious; and, we would add, often unconscious. Boszormeny-Nagy and Spark indicate over and over how invisible loyalties slow the progress of therapy (in their case, family therapy). This invisible loyalty, as well as invisible cultural attitudes and attitudes related to socioeconomic background, can unconsciously, latently, or preconsciously influence the course of treatment. The following example illustrates this problem.

One of the authors (Abel) had a Pakistani psychologist in therapy. G. could understand intellectually the concept of varying standards in sexual behavior. G. worked mainly in therapy with Jewish patients, although he himself was a Muslim; but he stated that religious differences never came up because the patients thought he was a Hindu, toward whom they felt no prejudice. Nevertheless G. could make no progress with a few women patients. The therapist felt that G. must have had "invisible loyalties" toward his religion that blocked progress. One day G. commented that these patients were having too many sexual affairs and that they should be ashamed, since they were not married. He felt that these young women were no better than whores, for in Pakistan no respectable girl so much as kissed a man before she married. He had repressed his feeling of disgust to show how flexible and modern he was. By degrees, as he worked this conflict out, G. began to do much better work.

In his book *Culture, Behavior and Personality* (1982), LeVine stresses an important variable in working with individuals from any cultural group: the range of variation in attitudes, beliefs, and feelings toward the predominant cultural patterns of behavior of members of a given group. Characteristic patterns of behavior in a culture, or a version of that culture, are unlikely to be adhered to universally. These variations, of course, are based on many factors, including personality differences and the specific experiences of members of the society or even of individual members of a family, but such variations are nevertheless related to the accepted modes of behavior. For instance, Italians from southern Italy living now in America may express a whole range of different attitudes toward seeking treatment. One Italian-American may easily accept the American preference for turning to mental health clinics or individual counselors and psychotherapists. Another may refuse the help of professionals, even though he comes from the same part of Italy and is the same age and sex as the one seeking professional help. The person who refuses help—as well as his whole family—may never have heard of mental health centers, or, if he has, may think it sheer nonsense to ask for assistance from others than family members or the parish priest.

Thus LeVine emphasizes the possibility of fundamental variations in different individuals' acceptance and interpretation of the cultural forms of their own society or ethnic group. In the same way, there may be wide differences of personality—and cultural acceptance—among members of any organized religious or political group. In a family constellation, individual differences are in part an expression of personal intra- and interpsychic conflicts as well. This is the case not only for the therapist's patients, but also for the therapist himself.

The following chapters will explore further the cultural factors that affect the psychotherapeutic processes; the transactions between therapist and patient; the patients' relationships to one another (in family and group situations); the kinds of communication—verbal and nonverbal, covert and overt—that take place; and the transference and countertransference phenomena that arise as therapy proceeds.

Intracultural variability has also been addressed by Pelto and Pelto (1975) and by Swartz (1982). Sapir (1951) has pointed out that our understanding of culture is based on information from hundreds of persons, but these do not share equally in the totality of knowledge, beliefs and meanings that characterize the culture.

Choosing a Therapist

It is worth pointing out that the mental health professional in his consultations and in therapeutic practice has to deal with the problem of his clients' and patients' attitudes toward him as a person; that is, he has to cope with their attitudes toward a person of his sex, age, training, and analytic orientation, and with his personal idiosyncracies and, above all, his cultural background. Patients sometimes explain that they have chosen a particular therapist because of his background—because, as they often say, "He will understand me and my problems." However, other patients may deliberately choose a therapist with a background different from their own because they feel that he will permit them to do and think and feel things that would be disapproved of within their own cultural group. This is particularly the case with sexual behavior. But even in those situations in which people do not raise questions about the consultant's or the therapist's background (or in which they are given no opportunity to do so), they will still respond to him as someone like or unlike themselves in certain respects.

Although clients and patients eventually discover that the particular background of the consultant or therapist, whether similar to or different from their own, is not very important, they do respond to an understanding of what their own background means in terms of their life experience. For example, psychotherapists are many times obliged to interpret religious values and to understand religious affiliations in all their implications. The complex position of a minority group in the United States today also raises problems of understanding and interpreting ethical values as well as the day-to-day intergroup relationships. The therapist, in particular, must be aware of the extent to which the patient makes use of cultural attitudes to resist change in therapy. But the therapist should also be sensitive to cultural attitudes that may support and strengthen the therapeutic process. Inevitably, this includes attitudes toward the therapist himself or herself.

In sum, many factors enter into the individual's decision to seek help. The age of the individual, his cultural and socioeconomic background, his particular disorder, the type of clinic or hospital he enters (and whether voluntarily or under pressure), all play a role in assignment and disposition, once he enters a treatment setting, and influence how he functions in a patient-therapist relationship. Many factors also enter into the therapist's choice of patients, the kind of treatment they will receive, the length of time they will remain in treatment, and the extent to which they are helped. Therapists have their own goals for therapy and feelings about their own abilities and their relationships with different kinds of patients. They, too, are influenced (to a great extent unconsciously) by value systems that stem from their own cultural backgrounds, as well as by their conscious, learned attitudes about the nature of psychotherapy and the meaning of a working relationship.

Thus the outcome of therapy, like the outcome of a great many professional consultant-client relationships, depends to a greater extent than is usually recognized on a mutual understanding of the process of change.[4]

Seven

Communication in Therapy

In the past, psychoanalysts and psychotherapists did not necessarily concern themselves with a patient's culturally oriented attitudes toward treatment and the therapist. Within the last decade, however, more attention has been paid by therapists to cultural aspects of psychodynamic functioning (Roll, Millen, and Martinez 1980). In a recent article, Satow (1983) discusses the case of a young Puerto Rican girl who suffered severely from penis envy. In his discussion Satow demonstrates how cultural and individual intrapsychic factors converge. In Puerto Rican culture, the male enjoys the privileges of *machismo,* while the female is considered either a mother (saint) or a whore. Boys are encouraged to have sexual experiences, but girls are kept under strict surveillance. In the case described by Satow, the girl had felt penis envy for as long as she could remember. She stated that, on the one hand, her mother had protected her from knowledge of sex, but, on the other hand, her mother as well as her grandmother, her aunts, and other women relatives laughed at her when she began to develop secondary sex characteristics. They touched her breasts and pubic area teasingly and suggestively. The girl became deeply ambivalent. Feeling herself to be like a man with a penis, she became a lesbian.

Freud himself was well aware that social, as well as biological, factors play a role in human development. Even when he began to formulate his structural theory, Freud indicated how the superego, an introject from parental pressures based on concepts of right and wrong, was affected by cultural values accepted by the parents. More recently, those analysts who have further developed and emphasized structural theory have also investigated ways in which ego functions reflect cultural patterning, that is, the more—or less—integrated beliefs, values, and modes of thought and behavior characteristic of a culture at a certain period of time.

Nowadays, psychoanalysts and psychotherapists have become more aware of the ways in which the needs of an individual are modified, intensified, or muted, not only by the idiosyncratic interactions of parent and child, but also by the ways in which cultural expectations affect maternal and infant interactions. These interactions reinforce mutual modes of response through which the child learns to adapt in culturally approved ways evoked by the mother.

Today, difficulties experienced by a child reared by parents whose behavior deviates markedly from culturally expected modes of parent-child interaction are well known. For example, the American father is expected to be strong but not authoritarian in his relationships within the family. An American boy who is brought up by a rigid, authoritarian father—and, conversely, a boy who is brought up by a father who is incapable of asserting himself in the home and in the world outside the home—will have difficulty later in life in assuming appropriate masculine roles and in responding appropriately to masculine authority figures. These difficulties are even greater for boys reared in a period when older cultural values and modes of behavior are changing, as they were in America in the 1960s (Keniston 1967; Mead 1978).

A contemporary psychotherapist, H. E. Lerner (1983), writes on the theme of what she calls "hidden" culture as an aspect of the changing role of women in present-day American society. Thus she describes situations in which therapists believe that certain woman patients are responding to therapy with resistance. According to therapists, these are women who consciously wish to develop greater autonomy but who resist taking the necessary action to do so. The therapist pushes the patient to act and then, annoyed by the patient's inaction, probes the patient's resistance. In reality, according to Lerner, the difficulty lies in the "hidden," unconscious, culturally accepted belief that it is the woman's role to be submissive. This belief controls the behavior—the hesitation to become autonomous—of these woman patients. The problem, then, is not one of resistance, but rather of a strong unconscious pressure to maintain a valued mode of behavior.

Difficulties of this kind are almost inevitable when therapist and patient are members of different generations in a period of change. Such difficulties are compounded when therapist and patient are members of different societies, and quite different "hidden" unconscious cultural pressures may be affecting the interactions of both therapist and patient.

Discrepant unconscious pressures undoubtedly affect men and women in our society as they attempt to incorporate newer cultural conceptions of male and female roles that have slowly taken shape in our society over the past sixty or more years. The contemporary feminist movement has heightened the awareness of change in both women and men, but this has been only one of the many influences directing human relationships in the modern world toward equality and a more positive recognition of both personal and ethnic identities (DeVos and Romanucci-Ross 1982). There are, of course, those who consciously and resolutely resist role change. Thus there is a continuing need for empirical exploration of the depth and consistency of cultural change in role expectancy as it is reflected both in social institutions and in individual lives.

Treatment Goals and Cultural Factors

Psychotherapists and psychoanalysts have taken various approaches to treatment goals.[1] One view is to disregard cultural patterns; the goal may be to make conscious the unconscious and to lead the individual to a greater awareness and understanding of his or her attitudes and modes of behavior and to work through only understood conflicts. An alternative view is to recognize cultural patterns; the goal may be to help the patient make adjustments to fit more or less easily into the cultural value system and modes of behavior of the society in which the therapist and the patient live (Fromm 1949).

Jerome Frank (1961) has indicated that therapy may become dogmatic, placing too much emphasis on intellectual comprehension (despite the ideal goal of emotional release) and the fine points of interpretation. Frank also questions whether the characteristic American "do it yourself" attitude (in other words, do the work yourself in therapy), will actually be effective in cases where value systems different from the predominant American one enter into the therapeutic transaction.

Generally speaking, culturally based attitudes may be more significant in earlier than in later stages of treatment. Still, the therapist does have to remain sensitive to cultural factors that may be part of the patient's communications at any stage during the therapeutic process. Often these communications are covert, unknown to the patient and scarcely detectable by the therapist. For example, a patient may approve overtly of masturbation but covertly think it is a "dirty habit." He may have accepted the covert belief because that was the approved view of his parents. This is a well-known theme in therapy.

In some cultures, more complicated beliefs affect emotional attitudes toward masturbation. Among some Indian Muslims, for example, loss of semen, either through intercourse or masturbation, is considered debilitating (it weakens the semen, in particular). This belief may be consciously retained or repressed. For instance, a Muslim Indian patient in America had masturbated and felt guilty, since he had formerly belonged to a religious sect that demanded abstinence of its members (except in marriage). He believed he was getting over his guilt because of his present conscious view, but he still felt very tired after masturbating. He could not understand why he felt such lassitude. The therapist, an American, had never heard that in this particular culture loss of semen was believed to be debilitating. The patient himself was not aware of this. But one day, when he arrived at his session, he reported that he had had a wet dream and had woken tired, crying, and telling himself that he had lost something. As he talked, he remembered the Muslim-Indian belief that loss of semen is debilitating. The therapist had felt that the patient's weariness was still due to guilt despite his avowed acceptance of masturbation. The therapist was correct in essence, but the patient's conflict was due not only to guilt over sexual activity, but also to fear of weakening his semen. (See the work of Edwards referred to in Chapter 3.)

Around the world in various different societies, therapeutic practices connected with rituals and ceremonies of a religious nature, as well as with traditional healing practices and rituals carried out by so-called medicine men and others, coexist with the practice of contemporary medicine. In newly developing nations and in areas where preliterate peoples are entering the modern world, mental health practices by professionals from industrialized countries or by persons trained by such professionals influence the kinds of treatment given the mentally ill and the emotionally disturbed.[2] Therapists in general are cognizant of the different kinds of medical treatment given to the mentally ill (electric shock and medications)—methods used only by members of the medical profession trained in Western medicine—but they are much more familiar with the kinds of therapy in which they themselves have been trained (psychotherapy and psychoanalysis). These therapies are currently employed in the United States, England, France, and other Western nations, and to some degree in non-Western countries such as Japan, but it may be helpful for therapists to understand that trained therapists in other societies have developed new modes or have modified Western modes of therapy to meet the needs of a particular cultural group.

Therapy in Japan

A description of a method of therapy used in one country, Japan, will demonstrate how this method deviates from the more familiar Western therapies. It will also show how it may be necessary to take into account the fact that techniques, even in America, may occasionally need to be adapted not only to the type of patient (paranoid, depressed, psychotic or neurotic) but also to his cultural background.

Modern Japanese have introduced many Western cultural practices into their lives. But adaptive changes are taking place, as invariably happens when the institutions and techniques of one culture are transferred to another. Psychiatric treatment in Japan may be based on Western organic practices, psychoanalysis, psychoanalytically oriented psychotherapy, or other psychological methods developed in Europe and the United States. Treatment may also take the form of a therapy of Japanese origin, such as Morita therapy, which emphasizes suppression and work.

Japanese psychoanalysts trained in the West have had some difficulty in using purely psychoanalytical procedures. Moloney (1953) has described some of the problems the Japanese face in practicing psychoanalysis. He points out that in Japan it may be hard to sustain the goal of psychoanalysis: to free the individual from strict authority so that he can make his own choices, not only on a rational but also on an emotional level. Moreover, even though the analyst may have this goal, the patient does not always understand it. In many ways, the Japanese consider the nation a single unit, and each individual feels strongly that he is part of that unit. They still live in a highly structured society, with the emperor (superego) at the head, even though this structure is beginning to change. Within the total structure, certain principles must be followed—the cardinal principles of the entity of Japan. While some of the writings of Japanese analysts seem to preach the doctrine of Freud, they also, to a degree, follow principles which in Japanese are called *Kokutai no Honji*, (i.e., belief that the Japanese nation is an entity, like a family, with the head, the emperor with absolute control).

Doi (1963) points out another characteristic of the Japanese which creates an approach to psychotherapy different from that usually practiced in the West. This characteristic is the expression of dependency wishes that are expected and responded to in Japan. In Western societies these dependency wishes are highly discouraged and generally are repressed. Doi indicates that when Japanese patients accept therapy, they tend to develop dependent feelings called *amae* toward the therapist in the transference situation. In Western society, these deep-seated dependency feelings generally appear in the last phase of psychoanalysis. According to Doi, these feelings are consciously expressed early in therapy in Japan. Still, Tatara (1974) found it very difficult for his patients to terminate therapy because of this dependency.

Amae are those feelings the infant has in the later phase of his oral development when he recognizes the mother as an object separate from himself; these feelings are conscious and are fostered by society. Two adults can have these feelings about each other, and such feelings are accepted. Doi believes that another reason the Japanese do not accept psychoanalysis is that they want to continue their dependency, or *amae*. However, he does say that they are becoming more modern under the influence of the West. Hence Doi feels that the Japanese will accept more and more Western modes of therapy in treatment.

MORITA THERAPY

A therapy peculiar to Japan was developed for neurotics by Morita of the Jikeikai School of Medicine in Tokyo nearly seventy years ago (Morita 1917),[3] and still exerts considerable influence in Japan.

In the Sansei Hospital in Kyoto (which one of the psychologist coauthors visited six times between 1963 and 1983), fifty neurotic patients are given Morita therapy at one time. Treatment in this hospital lasts approximately forty days. During the first week of treatment, the patient must lie on his bedmat and remain there silently. He is given his meals and taken to the toilet. If he appears too anxious, an attendant fans him or places a wet towel on his head. He may speak only to the psychiatrist when he makes his rounds. No medication is given. After a week, the patient is expected to move about and meditate, usually in the garden. He is required to keep a diary describing what he is experiencing. At Sansei, patients have a few group therapy sessions. In this second stage the patient also begins to do light housework. In stage three, manual labor increases: there is more housework, and more time is spent in a workroom carrying out specific tasks, such as assembling and pasting boxes for industry. In the fourth stage (the last week or so), the patient may leave the hospital during the day to go to his regular work or to school.

The purpose of Morita therapy is not to effect a cure but to have the individual accept himself and his troubles. A patient is given to understand that it is perfectly normal to have certain feelings—to feel tired or dizzy, or to have stomachaches—since all normal people experience such sensations. The idea is that there is a reduction in the intensity of the symptoms because they are accepted and not opposed. For example, a patient might write in his diary: "I am feeling dizzy." The doctor comments in red ink at the side of the page: "Don't try to stop it." Or in a group session a patient might state: "My heart pounds fast." The answer would be: "Everyone's heart pounds when he runs."

The expressed intent of this treatment is to have the patient accept his true nature. This is a basic Zen tenet. Morita therapy sounds quite authoritarian, and it seems to favor suppression on the part of the patient quite in opposition to the principles of psychoanalytic techniques.

Communication Between Patient and Therapist

Obviously, modes of communication between patient and therapist vary from patient to patient, from therapist to therapist and from culture to culture. Acculturation may play a large role in the way a patient expresses himself. The sophisticated Japanese patient who has had some American education, has read widely about the United States or has lived for a while in a large American city may not be so obviously "Japanese" in his modes of thought and behavior as the less sophisticated Japanese who has had only casual contacts with the West. Therefore, two Japanese with different experiences who come to a clinic in New York or Los Angeles, for instance, may appear very different.

A Japanese graduate student once came to one of the psychologist co-authors for therapy. The young man had read Fenichel and was ready to discuss what he called his conflicts. He was prepared to "expose his pathology and analyze it." Like most Japanese he talked freely, but he surprised the therapist by revealing rather intimate details during the third and fourth sessions—memories (from about the age of six) of seeing his mother's menstrual blood in the toilet and some of his fantasies about it. The therapist realized that the patient was doing what he thought was expected of him, that is, associating with ideas as they came to mind. Having read about psychiatry in Japan and about the openness of the patients, the therapist at first felt the patient was doing well, but it soon became clear that some of what the student was saying was actually a form of resistance to therapy because it was not spoken with any emotion. This behavior was treated as resistance. Later, the patient repeated some of the material about his mother, this time in connection with his fears and his anger.

Nonverbal Communication

Communication between individuals takes place at different levels, in verbal and nonverbal, in direct and indirect, and in overt and latent ways. For example, tactile communication varies from culture to culture. It may easily be overlooked by the therapist, even though he is alert to the way in which a patient approaches or touches him and to some of the ways in which he himself may relate tactilely to a patient (for example, shaking the patient's hand or putting his hand on the patient's shoulder). L. K. Frank (1956) has discussed how tactile experiences vary between an individual child and his mother and that they depend largely on the culturally determined ways in which mothers handle their children. Swaddling, tucking in, exposing, patting, cuddling, and bathing by a mother or a mother substitute are performed differently in different cultural groups.[4]

In China, for example, a baby is held in an upright position and encouraged to look rather than touch—but it is given a great many things to look at, since it is carried from place to place during most of its waking hours. In America, even the small infant is laid in a large crib, with a good deal of space around it, but as soon as possible it is encouraged to touch and feel objects and persons. In Japan, a baby is likely to be carried in a sack on the mother's or grandmother's back and has continuous tactile as well as kinesthetic sensations as the mother moves about her daily chores. This is particularly true in rural districts and villages today, but it can still be seen in larger cities.

As Frank points out, tactile experiences are crucial to learning and provide a good deal of the basic stimulation for developing symbolic recognition and response. If a child is neglected, or at least left alone much and allowed only a few early tactile experiences during the first months of his life, he has to wait until his capacity for auditory and visual recognition and reception have developed before he can communicate.[5] Instead of "feeling" for himself the meaning of different objects, the child may have to wait for others to tell him. A child who holds and rolls a ball experiences the meaning of rolling a ball in a different way from the one who only looks and is told that it rolls. The small child who can feel objects gains more autonomy earlier, a trait valued by Americans. Presumably, an early emphasis on exploration underlies the American's willingness—even insistence—to try things out for himself in later life. But "grasping" with the eyes may also be effective: a number of upper-class Chinese men, who were very skilled amateurs in the difficult art of Chinese cookery, claimed that they had not been taught and had never practiced cooking, but that, as children in China, they had watched expert cooks prepare meals in their homes.

Different cultures focus on developing different kinds of thresholds for tactile contact and stimulation so that the child's own characteristics—his constitution, body build, and temperament—may be accentuated or inhibited. According to L. K. Frank, each culture builds upon the early tactile experience of the infant. Many series of developmental patterns of conduct from childhood to adulthood develop, and tactile surrogates and symbolic fulfillments are provided. In other words, certain patterns of greeting, bidding farewell, playing games, taking part in sexual activities, and caring for the sick and the dead become, to some extent, regularities of conduct in a given society even though individual variations and deviations, of course, occur.

In psychotherapy, tactile and other forms of nonverbal communication (such as flirting or gesturing) are not encouraged as part of the treatment process, although they are taken into account as modes of communication with overt and latent meanings that may be dealt with and analyzed at appropriate times. Ruesch (1955) has shown how, in the cultural patterning of psychotherapy set up in Western society, verbal communication is encouraged and nonverbal communication (dancing around the room, as a gross example) is discouraged among neurotics and prepsychotic patients, but is encouraged among psychotics, especially in hospitals. Psychotic patients are given many more means of nonverbal communication, such as music therapy, psychodrama, dance, and painting; they are also given baths and massages. Moreover, psychotics are given tasks that may develop their "analogic codifications" (a term employed by Ruesch to describe psychotic language) into a language that can be shared. While it is assumed that neurotics, or at least adult neurotics, can represent analogically codified events by giving verbal accounts of their experiences, this may or may not be true or it may be more or less possible for different individuals and in different cultures. Children, of course, have more nonverbal interchanges with therapists than do adults.

Although verbal communication is generally considered the most sensitive tool in analysis, this is not always the case in understanding and in interpreting, for while individuals in one society may have long been accustomed to verbalizing situations and events, others in a different society may not have. Action therapy, or therapy that encourages nonverbal communication (as in ritual dances and festivals), may have the kind of cathartic effect that is helpful before verbal communication can take place among adult neurotics in or from different cultural groups. A good deal of research will have to be done, however, before a fuller understanding of the value for different cultures of therapeutic techniques that emphasize verbal or nonverbal communication can be ascertained.

Time and Space: Aspects of Communication

Conflicts arising from different cultural attitudes toward time and space can interfere with the communication process in psychotherapy. Arriving punctually for sessions, accepting the prescribed time limit for a session, and expecting a rapid "cure" are concepts that are interpreted differently by different individuals, both because of their own idiosyncratic attitudes and because of culturally learned attitudes toward time. Hall and Whyte (1966) have described the contrasting attitudes of North American and Latin American businessmen toward time. For the Latin American, there is nothing unusual in waiting forty-five minutes for an appointment, whereas five minutes is about the limit for a North American. The North American who is always late is considered a "risk" in the United States, but not the Latin American in his own country. Such attitudes may spill over into the therapeutic session and be misunderstood unless they are dealt with both in terms of their cultural significance and in terms of possible "acting out." The therapist has to differentiate between the two behaviors.

Similar problems arise in connection with space. The use of a couch, the position of the therapist's chair, the size of the room, the distance between the therapist and the patient, all may have culturally determined meanings. The distance between two individuals, that is, the distance at which two people feel comfortable, varies according to the society. Hall uses the term *proxemics* for the study of the way human beings unconsciously structure space: the way two people, for example, place themselves in relation to each other in different contexts, the ways in which people live together in space, and the ways in which people perceive the arrangement of space within and around buildings, in towns, in industrial parks, in recreation areas, and so forth. Hall (1963) has shown that members of different cultures attach different meanings to the space they live in and the distances persons maintain in relation to one another. Hall and Whyte (1966) also discuss the characteristic attitudes of different cultures regarding the correct distance people should maintain between them when they meet and talk.

In North America, two adult men usually stand about two feet apart when talking over a business deal (at cocktail parties, the distance may shrink to about one foot). To Latin Americans, however, standing two feet apart would be rude, a sign of coldness and distance. In an interchange with a North American, the Latin American would move in closer and the North American, feeling that the Latin American was being pushy, would back away.

Hall reported that Americans and Arabs also felt uncomfortable in conversation. The Americans felt that the Arab came too close, looked straight at him, breathed on him, and talked too loudly, and the American tried to back out of the olfactory zone. But the situation was no less unpleasant for the Arab; he felt that the American, who talked too softly, turned his face aside and continually moved out of range, was being deliberately unfriendly.[6]

Psychotherapists and others who work closely with individuals in interview situations know a good deal, intuitively and by observation, about variations in nonverbal behavior, but they may need to become more aware of the cultural consistencies in this behavior. The therapist should be sensitive to what constitutes withdrawal, acting out and resistance in different contexts; to the ways in which attitudes and actions are influenced by the patient's (and the therapist's own) conceptions of time and space; and especially to the fact that in large measure the interchange of nonverbal messages tends to take place below the level of ordinary awareness.

Cross-Cultural Values in Communication

A patient who seeks or is sent for some kind of help—counseling, psychotherapy, or psychoanalysis—is a representative of a particular cultural group. His therapist is also a representative of a cultural group. Each has a set of beliefs, goals, and values expressed in his personality, modes of thought, attitudes, and ways of acting and interacting; he is aware of some of these, but not of others. The patient arrives with a problem that bothers him or that annoys others with whom he associates. When therapist and patient come from different cultural backgrounds—or from widely different versions of the same culture—and so understand the problems in different ways—the values and expectations involved in therapy, as well as what constitutes improvement—there can be difficulties, especially in the initial stages. Social workers have dealt with cross-cultural problems and difficulties in acculturation among immigrants and refugees—uprooted and transplanted individuals—longer and more extensively than have psychologists and psychiatrists. Most social workers have understood, to some degree, the value of knowing about cultural patterns. One social work agency, for example, did not try to understand the reasons for cultural patterning; they simply knew that people from different countries had to be handled differently. For example, when an Irish mother was hospitalized, the agency on the case considered the father capable of looking after the family. But when a Sicilian or southern Italian mother was hospitalized, the agency provided a housekeeper in a home in which there was a young girl as the Italian father—it was believed—could not be relied upon not to make sexual advances to his daughter. In American society, this behavior is taboo; it is also considered by analytically oriented professionals to be a trauma to the girl owing to her oedipal conflicts. In the Sicilian family, incest is also wrong, but it somehow must be accepted if the father so chooses. This attitude is covert. A therapist treating such a case would need to get a feeling for whether a Sicilian girl would feel the same degree of guilt and trauma as an American girl.

More sophisticated case workers have tried to explore and understand anthropological research, and they have taken a psychocultural approach to their work. Social workers in a mental health center in Jerusalem were able to cope with both Israeli-born clients and those from Eastern or Western Europe, but they needed help in understanding how the basic needs of disturbed children and adults uprooted from Yemen and Morocco could be satisfied. In America, Pollak and his associates (1952) emphasize that social workers involved in treating children and their parents need to understand cultural factors. But they also point out how too much emphasis on such factors may obscure dynamic considerations (including symptoms). As Pollack says, the clinician needs to be aware of normal expressions of culture and whether, when an individual deviates from this norm, he does so because he is defiant or because he is too accepting and submissive. Behavior that is labeled either rebellious or submissive in one culture may not be considered so in another. Pollack also suggests that the misbehavior of a Jewish child who rebels against orthodoxy by lighting lights, riding the subway, and so forth on the Sabbath, may be the expression of an unresolved Oedipal conflict. On the other hand, a Jewish boy who appears to be "good" about following customs may actually be conforming to them in order to annoy and punish his parents. Pollack gives the example of a boy, Eli, whose Hassidic parents went daily to the rabbi for advice and inspiration. Eli, too, insisted on doing this, but he insisted on going in the early morning before school, thereby causing a commotion in the household. The family came to the agency for help because they could not control their son. Eli was, in fact, seeking attention and attempting to communicate to his parents how little warmth and understanding they gave him. In the course of psychotherapy these dynamic factors came to the fore.[7]

In an excellent example of sophisticated cross-cultural work, the psychoanalyst Boyer (1979) was able to communicate meaningfully and conduct therapeutic work with psychiatric patients on the Mescalero Apache reservation in south-central New Mexico (see Chapter 3, p. 68 for a detailed discussion of Boyer's work). Boyer had learned the Apache language and had become familiar with the Mescalero Apache's belief in ghosts, witches, and supernatural creatures such as the coyote, owl, and bat. This belief could cause great fear, but it could also be used as a defense by the patients. Boyer was accepted as a shaman and thus gained the confidence of the patients, including the psychotic ones.

Problems arising from cultural factors do not necessarily occur in the early stages of therapy. After two years in therapy, a patient of one of the psychologist coauthors was helped over a final hump in his recovery by an interpretation centering on a cultural point. This patient was a thirty-year-old man who had been unable to get a job and who had led a restricted social life because of his anxieties. After two years his difficulties were largely over: he had started to work in a good job, he had gone to quite a few parties, and he was "going steady" with a girl whom he was thinking seriously of marrying. One day he told the therapist that the girl had told him what her financial assets were and had asked about his. "It took me a year to tell you about my income," he said, "although I have never told you specifically [he had inherited quite a lot of money], but somehow I was shocked by Nancy." The patient even contemplated breaking off the engagement. The therapist was aware that the patient was still somewhat shaky in his relationship with a girl; he still felt that his mother might disapprove, and he still felt, to a degree, attracted to his mother. But the therapist also considered the patient's cultural background—how he had been brought up in a Protestant, puritanical home by a mother who was overshadowed by two nineteenth-century maiden aunts who ruled the home, and by a father who was distant. "So Nancy isn't a lady," the therapist said. "She talks about money." The patient laughed and replied, "Gee, I thought I had shed those old girls long ago. I've got to watch my step or they'll creep up on me. In fact, today, I expected you to be shocked by Nancy's disclosures." This experience helped the patient to overcome more of his separation anxieties concerning his ancestral home.

Americans are very conscious of physical appearance. We have certain expectations about fat and thin people, and about short and tall men and women. As Jules Henry (1963) indicates, Americans have ideas about how people should look at certain ages, but we also pay attention to how people look and act regardless of age. Both a therapist and a patient reared in America are influenced by these cultural attitudes toward the body, as well as by the more idiosyncratic difficulties that affect their self-image: the patient may be somewhat shorter or taller than average or "a little" over-weight; he may let his hair grow long in an attempt to identify with a particular social group or in rebellion against family values; a therapist may grow a beard in order to create the image of a seasoned professional, a "Freud."

But actual physique varies in different stocks (population groups), for example, range of height or shade of skin color. What is tall for one group is average or short for another; similarly skin color defined as dark by one group may be average or even fair as defined by another. The cultural idea, of course, varies also. This affects, for instance, the judgment made by members of one group of the style of speech characteristic of a different group. Although there are many regional variations, Americans do have certain expectations of how a voice should sound. In general, the voice should not be shrill, speech should not be fast and a man's voice should differ from a woman's. By American standards, a very fast-speaking Italian man with a high-pitched voice may well be considered hypermanic, perhaps feminine identified; yet by Italian standards, he may be in balance, not particularly excited and behaving in a masculine manner. When a therapist begins to understand his own responses to a patient's appearance, mode of speaking, and manner of gesturing, he will get clues also as to how others respond to the patient and to a problem he may not have faced or known he had to face (not only because of the patient's personal conflicts but because of his deviance from the cultural norms of appearance and manner of the group in which he was raised or to which he has been assimilated). Obviously, all these differences between the patient and the therapist can be better understood when a working relationship gets under way; yet they may influence the therapist's judgment unless he is attuned to the communication possibilities of appearance.

Henry (1963) gives many illustrations of regularities in American behavior. For instance, Americans assume that a person will warm up by degrees to a new situation and will not talk all the time. If a child never stops talking when he comes for play therapy, he may be judged more disturbed than a silent child, for in our society there is a greater stigma attached to garrulousness than to silence (except at bars, cocktail parties, and the like). Generally, the trained professional understands the underlying dynamics of the quiet child or the very talkative one; he nevertheless, must take different cultural backgrounds into account. Henry also observed that generally in America, when a child or an adult behaves in a predictable way, he is supposed healthy, although there is a trend among the educated to admire unpredictability. The relationship between these different expectations and emotional disturbances may be quite complex.

Resistances in Cultural Contexts

Resistance, another form of communication, can also baffle the therapist. This type of communication may emphasize specific cultural points that can be missed or misinterpreted by the therapist. Devereux (1951b) points out that when a therapist uses his concrete familiarity with a patient's culture, he may catch on more quickly than he otherwise might to the meaning of a communication. For example, a male Plains Indian patient dreamed that he left his mother at the bottom of a hill and then went up the hill, where he met his father and mother. We might understand this dream as one in which the patient left his mother to go up the hill to look for his father (to make up with his father for being with his mother) and then met his father and mother (oedipal barrier). What Devereux did was ask the patient whether or not the woman at the top of the hill was the same mother as the one at the bottom of the hill. The patient replied that the one at the bottom was a different mother, his aunt. In this culture, a mother's sisters are called mother. Thus a familiarity with the culture—in this case, knowledge of the kinship system and nomenclature—is helpful in therapy.

Devereux states that material should be understood in a specific cultural context, even though at a later stage in therapy a deeper psychodynamic meaning (perhaps less influenced by the particular culture) may be explored. He gave the illustration of a near-psychotic hospitalized Plains Indian woman he was treating, who hid her face under a blanket and would not talk to him. The therapist first told her that she was playing dead; he also suggested that she wanted to be a baby. These comments produced no response. But when he suggested that she must be an Indian maiden hiding under a buffalo robe while her suitor courted her, she popped out from beneath the blanket. This (culturally flattering) interpretation worked, although Devereux felt that at a deeper level the patient was playing dead because the confrontation with the therapist was too threatening. The point here is that the nonverbal communication of the patient and the verbal communication of the therapist both drew on culturally relevant material that helped establish a relationship between the therapist and the patient.

Devereux gives another example of Indian cowboy patients who indirectly convey messages about castration fears and incestuous impulses. It is possible to interpret the material on castration fears quite early in therapy (as the cowboys are used to castrating livestock), but it is not possible to touch on themes dealing with incestuous impulses for some time.

An American therapist in a clinic treated a young Mexican man who kept talking about his testicles (called *huevos* or eggs by Mexicans), saying that they did not have much in them and that he felt his father and brothers had more in their testicles. The therapist wondered whether the patient had an undescended testicle or might be sterile. After quite some time it occurred to the therapist that the patient was discussing feelings of sexual inadequacy since he kept reporting how inadequate he felt on the job. Had the therapist realized that Mexicans locate virility in the testicles rather than in the penis, he might have been less perplexed and able to help the patient sooner. As it was, it was hard for this somewhat inexperienced therapist to understand why the patient was not preoccupied with the size of his penis.[8]

In play therapy, children in different cultures may be able to communicate more or less freely and clearly through play, depending on the kinds of relationships they customarily form with adults and on their willingness to play as well as talk in the presence of adults. Françoise Dolto (1955) reported on differences in carrying out play therapy with French and American children in Paris. The American child is more successful in playing with the doctor and enjoying himself in the presence of an adult, whereas the French child is much more on his guard with adults, especially with doctors, and plays more easily and enjoys himself more with other children. This difference is comprehensible in terms of the different attitudes toward childhood in the two cultures. For Americans, childhood should be enjoyable, and adults not only encourage children to play but they also play with children. In contrast, the French regard childhood as the period in which the child learns how to become an adult, that is, as a period of preparation for the future, and they believe that adult enjoyment depends on first correctly learning the rules of living. Retrospectively, fictional accounts in the two cultures are reversed: in American fiction, childhood, as a theme, is treated as a period of hard learning, whereas in French fiction, childhood is treated thematically as a life apart, with its special pleasures and fantasies, but also its special dangers. This reversal suggests the complexity of both of these culturally differentiated views of the developmental process.[9]

Limitations on the Goals of Therapy

When a patient is selected for psychoanalysis, it is assumed that he understands (or can learn to understand) its purposes and goals, that he has some ability to communicate verbally, and that he has some ego strength and potential for growth, tolerance of frustration, and enough motivation to follow certain rules. This treatment may be carried out cross-culturally and certainly has been in various Western societies. Cultural points do arise and can be worked through if they seem to be employed as resistance to change in particular. But analysts need to be aware that any individual's idiosyncratic functioning reflects the culture in which he was brought up. Hallowell (1956) makes it clear that one cannot entirely understand the motivational patterning and the roles played by individuals without looking into the goals, values, and beliefs of their society. This holds true for the patient entering analysis. Some of the values he clings to (unconsciously) may have been communicated to him by his parents and may be inappropriate to his present adult way of life. This is most likely to be the case of a person whose parents were reared in a different culture (or a different version of the same culture) and, only partly acculturated, communicated conflicting values and goals to their children. Generally, the analysand's difficulties of latent communication are finally worked out. We have shown, however, how members of some cultures—the Japanese, for instance—are not able to understand and accept the analytic goal of making the individual free and independent.

Moreover, in cross-cultural therapy (or therapy involving cross-versions of a culture), as in different personality constellations (neurotic, borderline, weak ego), therapeutic goals can often be limited to and, to a degree, tailored to the individual patient. Bishop and Winokur (1956) discuss cross-cultural therapy, particularly in connection with Bishop's treatment of a fifty-six-year-old hospitalized, depressed Japanese male, Issei, in the Midwest. Bishop was familiar with Japanese culture, and she took the patient's background into account by relating his problems to Japanese character structure and expectations rather than to expected American behavior. This patient was very depressed and having a great deal of trouble getting along in America, much more so than his Japanese wife who had adapted fairly easily. His father had died early and his life had been dominated by women (his mother and wife). Although he managed for a time to get along passively, he was extremely bothered by the fact that he was never able to assume the role of the master of the home. The psychiatrist was aware that considerable conformity, compulsiveness, and perfectionism were expected of the Japanese, and that they did not take up these modes of defense (or adaptations) unless the defenses became particularly incapacitating (as they could well do with a mentally ill individual). Bishop also avoided dealing with the man's suppressed hostility, since this mode of conscious control is important for a Japanese; instead, she encouraged and accepted the patient's verbal resentments (as much as he could tolerate) against his wife and against the therapist (who was also a woman). The patient was also critical of certain American characteristics, such as their generosity (most likely, he wanted their generosity in his deep longing to be cared for). When the patient left the hospital, he went to live with a nephew for a while (as if in a halfway house) and continued in outpatient treatment. Although the nephew was quite Americanized, he understood some of his uncle's problems and also the worries his uncle might have about his obligations to his host (the nephew). The patient was gradually able to cope with his feelings and get along more successfully.

Certainly, the goals of therapy and the selection of a particular form or technique of treatment for a patient may have to be modified in cross-cultural therapy. Devereux (1951b) has shown that one difficult problem in therapy with Plains Indians is therapeutic objectives. He pointed out how it was possible to make fairly accurate cross-cultural diagnostic evaluations (such as differentiating between the characteristic reserve of a Plains Indian and schizophrenia or between delusion and "superstition"), but just what the goal of treatment should be was not always clear. In the case of his Plains Indian patients, Devereux suggested that goals should not be incompatible with the kind of external environment patients would have to live in after leaving the hospital (a reservation or an American setting in which they could expect to meet considerable discrimination). It would not only be unreasonable to expect to turn these individuals into upwardly striving Americans, but such a goal would further complicate their already difficult lives.

Devereux also suggested that the patient's striving toward emotional maturity and rational behavior should be encouraged without taking away from him some of his particular values (unless, of course, these values are irrational and obsolete). For example, he felt strongly that American Indian patients (and this would be the case for any adult moving from one cultural setting to another) should be helped to get along in American culture by integrating, as far as possible, American cultural patterns and the patterns of their own Indian culture. As Devereux points out, this is precisely what Plains Indians in our society have attempted to do spontaneously. As an example Devereux spoke of a Plains Indian mother who took her son to a bus terminal on his way to boarding school and sang the songs to him on the way that Indian women had sung in the past when their menfolk went off on a war party. He added that the therapist must be attuned to what constitutes recovery and health on the part of the patient. The Indian patient who decides to become a medicine man after he leaves the hospital may be making an adaptive choice that is appropriate in his own society and not, as some therapists might feel, one that indicates he is still "sick" and "irrational."

The situation in which some special adaptation must be made in the methods of treatment or the goals of therapy is repeated many times over in the therapy of patients who come from a culture different form the one in which they are now living (for example, immigrants or refugees) and to which some may, perhaps, return (for example, foreign students or the employees of international corporations). Parallel problems arise also for the individual who is trying to adapt to a different version of the culture in which he was reared, particularly when that adaptation involves coping with very real social difficulties, as it does for many members of ethnic groups in America and elsewhere. Certainly, black American patients can learn to work out many of their intrapsychic conflicts in therapy, but those who do still have to face discrimination and, today, the question of where they stand in regard to separatism or integration. These same problems arise when members of a social group—the women in the feminist movement in the United States, for example—attempt to bring about changes in their own cultural values that will alter their place in the society.

What, then, are realistic goals in therapy? Restoring a person to himself— the therapeutic goal suggested by Frieda Fromm-Reichman—is perhaps the best goal, provided that therapist and patient are able to communicate and understand just what this might mean.

Group and Family Therapy

When therapists work with groups or families, taking the culture into account is even more necessary than when they treat an individual patient. The therapist must be continually aware of cultural points that are being made, often covertly, by the several members of the group or family. The therapist may not be cognizant of the more subtle cultural points or of the underlying value system of a society with which he himself is unfamiliar. There are additional problems when the therapist—or cotherapist—works with an ethnic group of which he himself is a member. In this situation, he may perhaps identify too closely with the patients and overlook some intrapsychic factors masked by the cultural value system.

Similar problems arise when a therapist works with members of an ethnic group or version of the national culture not familiar to him (for example,

French Canadians or black Americans), with members of a subculture (for example, Zuni Indians), or with members of an unfamiliar religious sect (for example, Jehovah's Witnesses). Groups in treatment may include members of several different ethnic groups. In New Mexico, for example, Americans and Hispanic-Americans often come together for group therapy. These Hispanic-Americans, mainly from cities, are quite sophisticated and likely to choose a well-trained professional over a *curandero* or a priest to solve their difficulties. But in rural areas and in northern New Mexico they are more likely to seek help in the traditional manner from a *curandero* or a priest.

Tylim (1982) reports on a three-year study he carried out with Hispanic patients at a day hospital in New York City. These patients came mostly from Puerto Rico, Cuba, and Colombia, but from time to time the group included at least one person from another Latin American country. Thus, the group lacked unity, but they had a common language, Spanish—although spoken with many idiomatic and symbolic variations. Groups were open-ended and averaged twelve persons at a time, ranging in age from sixteen to seventy; patients remained for six to ten months. The chief therapist was an Argentinian who had lived for many years in the United States. The cotherapist was a female Cuban psychiatric nurse. Spanish was spoken throughout treatment.

According to Tylim, a prominent characteristic of the group was the almost immediate rapport established between the therapists and other members of the group. This led rather quickly to regression: the members became "siblings," for it is customary for Hispanic siblings to confide a good deal in one another. Tylim also felt that there was an easy, narcissistic transference to the authority figures. Group members also had difficulty in integrating physical complaints with their emotional troubles and feelings. This split took time to overcome because the members continually sympathized with remarks about a physical condition made by any other member. There were also difficulties in working out the reality, namely, that the therapists were human beings, not omnipotent spirits or *curanderos*. In addition, there were obstacles to working out some of the cultural differences between the therapists and among the group members from different countries.

The Puerto Ricans were often looked upon as a favored group because they could leave when they felt threatened and return to Puerto Rico. Other group members envied the Puerto Ricans because it cost more for any of them to return to their native land.

According to Tylim, Hispanic patients look to the therapist as the "omnipotent parental object." Hispanics have great respect for older people, especially those in authority. The therapist reported that initially he felt uncomfortable having to bear the brunt of so much omnipotent idealizing transference. At first Tylim thought that, as he spoke Spanish, he could handle countertransferences, but he soon discovered that it took time for each patient to realize that the members from other countries had distinctive characteristics. Tylim also looked behind their fantasies of his omnipotence and their feelings of isolation, and he himself got in touch with his own feelings of isolation and homesickness. Over time, the therapist and cotherapist discovered their own cultural differences and discussed them. This led the way for each patient to face the others and the therapists in an individual manner, as well as to accept one another's cultural differences.

Many of the problems reported in this study may occur, of course, in any group therapy, but a description of this group's attitudes highlights the way distortions can take place in transference and countertransference under the influence of cultural variables.

One of the authors (Abel) worked on a short-term basis with several Indian families, mainly from Jemez Pueblo, but also from Santo Domingo, Santa Ana, and Isleta pueblos. Her cotherapist, also a non-Indian, non-Hispanic American (called an "Anglo" in this region) was especially helpful because she went once a week to two of these pueblos as a consultant and was familiar with some aspects of the culture. When an unmarried pregnant girl was referred by a social agency to the clinic for both individual and family therapy, the family came very reluctantly.

The people of Jemez Pueblo do not consider an adolescent, unmarried girl's pregnancy the traumatic event it would almost certainly be for an Anglo family. The young Jemez girl could have had her baby without censure, and she could have chosen to bring up the child herself or give it to her parents, grandparents, or some other relatives to rear.

Much more disruptive for Jemez families than an illegitimate pregnancy would be a show of anger, especially one directed at the father. As head of the household, the father expects to be obeyed. Expressions of anger are against the code of the pueblo. No one should express hostile feelings openly: a wife may not speak angrily to her husband nor may the husband express anger. Thus bringing out hostile feelings in a family therapy session cannot be a therapeutic goal.

At times the identified patient—the pregnant girl—did come out and speak angrily to her father and her mother after she had had some individual therapy, but this could happen only during a family session away from home. Another girl complained frequently that her father did not allow her to say how she felt about him for curtailing what she considered to be her rights. Although siblings were usually present during the family sessions, they made few contributions; instead, they talked softly to one another in their own language.

The Indians of these pueblos seem to respect Anglos, especially professionals (including women professionals), as they do agree to come for help. They are pleased when a therapist comes to their home for a visit and accepts a meal—this adds to their trust. But at times an underlying resentment emerges, particularly on the part of the father (a mother usually does not speak much in the presence of the father). On one occasion, a Jemez father said to the therapist, "Well, I see you locked the front door of the clinic. We never lock doors in our village." Meetings took place at night and the family therapy room was at the far end of the clinic. One of the therapists explained that unfortunately here in the city someone could come in and steal something. Another expression of outright resentment was made in a later session. The therapist stated that she was somewhat puzzled about what to suggest as a solution to a problem. The father immediately remarked, "You're a professional, you should know everything!"

These Pueblo Indian families generally have no desire to change, but family members are sensitive to the opinions of neighbors and outsiders. Perhaps for this reason they hope to find a more appropriate way of handling problems.

Koss and Canive (1982) have discussed in particular the characteristics of traditional Hispanic-Americans in New Mexico. Family roles are strictly defined and sex roles are clearly outlined. Men "wear the pants" and speak for the family outside the home—and in therapy in early sessions. Women are expected to be submissive. Parental control is firm, and adolescent rebellion is considered to be very disrespectful. However, the mother may protect her children from the extreme strictness and punitive behavior of the father. Discussion of sex is not permitted between the marital couple, across generations, or with more distant family members or strangers. Family members do not mention money matters in the presence of the therapist nor do they easily disclose cases of chronic illness.

In family treatment, the therapist must be patient in order to develop the confidence necessary for a good working relationship. Hispanics in New Mexico expect the therapist to share some of his or her own experiences from time to time. In general, they prefer to maintain a certain formality, but they enjoy listening to cotherapists as they discuss some of their own problems. This approach helps to break down barriers while maintaining the basic atmosphere of mild formality.

One of the psychologist coauthors (Abel) worked for a time with a married couple. The husband was a New Mexican Hispanic-American, the wife an Anglo from a northwestern state. Both had been married before and had children from these marriages. Conflicts about rearing the wife's children—how to punish them, whether to give them an allowance, and so on—turned out to be almost insurmountable. The husband's children were already adults. They had worked from the age of thirteen, after school, and unlike the wife's children had never been given an allowance or special privileges.

Other Ethnic Groups

As cultural factors are probably most clearly revealed and worked out in family psychotherapy, it is not surprising that family therapy and cross-cultural psychotherapy have enjoyed a parallel development. Sufficient work has been done that therapists who have worked out a viable approach to the problems of cross-cultural psychotherapy can now approach with confidence therapy with families whose cultural backgrounds may not be familiar to the therapist.

Moitoza (1982), for example, reports on the mental-health attitudes, beliefs, and practices of Portuguese-Americans. Based on research on Portuguese families in Cambridge, Massachusetts, Moitoza and his colleagues report that the first and crucial step for the family therapist is to "join" the Portuguese family; that is, the therapist should tactfully and respectfully become engaged in the linear power hierarchy and the closed family system. Further, they point out that the inclusion in the therapeutic group of extended family members, especially godparents, is not only acceptable but perhaps crucial in family therapy with Portuguese-Americans.

The researchers suggest that the therapist exercise caution about cross-generation alliances and interpretations of body language. Furthermore, the therapist who turns down invitations to special family events (baptisms or funerals, for example) seriously risks dishonoring the family, particularly the father. As a result, the position and power of the therapist is seriously weakened.

Jalali's work (1982) in the Family Therapy Unit of the Yale University Department of Psychiatry, has yielded a guide to family therapy with Iranian families. One of the authors (Abel 1978) was teaching family therapy in Iran, at the Neurological Institute in Shiraz, at an early stage of the Iranian revolution. Her experience, like that of Jalali, demonstrates that the Iranian patient is reluctant to enter individual therapy, but will respond with greater ease to a call for family meetings in a therapeutic setting, because the identified patient is de-emphasized in a family group.

In family therapy with Iranians, it is important to address the father first and to recognize him as the head of the family; failure to do so will alienate an Iranian family. Moreover, it is important to avoid discussions of sexual matters with members of the opposite sex. The close and permissive tie between a mother and her sons must also be recognized.

Welts (1982) and Abel and Major (1981), who have worked with Greek–American families, agree that these people have a strong sense of identity and pride in being Greek. Recognition of this national pride is important in communicating with Greek families in therapy. In work with Greeks, therapists must also be aware of a mode of behavior that Holden (1972) describes as a constant oscillation between opposites:

> Spirit and flesh, ideal and reality, triumph and despair—you name them and the Greeks suffer or enjoy them as constant poles of their being, swing repeatedly from one to the other and back again, often contriving to embrace both poles simultaneously, but above all never reconciled, never contented and never still (p. 33).

According to Welts, this oscillation is combined with pride in individual achievement. Within the family, there are rigid role definitions and a strong focus on honor. These are all characteristics that therapists must take into account in approaching Greeks and Greek families.

Therapists who work with patients and families who are members of cultures other than their own add a double task to the principal task of therapy. First, the therapist must become sensitive to, and aware of, cultural beliefs and modes of behavior (of which the patient may or may not be conscious) and recognize their impact on the various aspects of psychotherapy. Indeed, the principal aim of this book is to provide a basic orientation to this problem. Second, the therapist must become familiar with the literature on the cultures that are represented in their patient population. New journals and texts related to cross-cultural psychology may make the search for pertinent information somewhat less difficult (see, for example, McGoldrick, Pearce and Giordano 1982; Spiegel and Papajohn 1983). However, as such treatments are seldom holistic in their approach, the therapist who hopes to gain a deeper understanding of a patient's culture will wisely also turn to published ethnological research for organized information.

Eight

Transference and Countertransference

In psychotherapy, patient-therapist interaction may take various forms. Perhaps the most important form of communication is transference from the patient to therapist and countertransference from the therapist to the patient. The notions of transference and countertransference introduced by Freud are seen as the central point of psychoanalysis (Wallerstein 1969), and these concepts, or very similar ones, have been adopted by most schools of psychotherapy. Our use of the concepts here includes conscious and unconscious feelings determined not by the reality of what is going on in the session but by external factors, including unresolved childhood feelings and detours in communication stemming from the personalities and backgrounds of the two persons involved. Cultural patterns reflected in the communication between the patient and therapist also add to transference and countertransference. These patterns may play a major role or a relatively minor one in the relationship, but it is important that the therapist be aware of the influence of cultural patterns on transference and countertransference.

It is important to note that cultural factors do not by themselves create transference and countertransference—the conditions of treatment do that. Rather, any issue from the patient's past (for example, being continually misunderstood as a child) can be exacerbated by a cultural factor (for example, having a therapist from a different culture who does not understand the influence of a particular cultural factor on the patient's life). Cultural factors, then, are pertinent issues in transference and countertransference. Language, religion, time orientation, even styles of greeting may become ways in which the patient's conflicts surface or disguise themselves to help or hinder the therapeutic task.

In a paper on values, Mildred Burgum (1957) gives an excellent instance of transference in which a patient used a cultural point to attack the therapist. The attack was a defense against feelings of worthlessness. A non-Jewish patient hummed a bit of a tune from a Jewish ritual in a mocking tone to her Jewish therapist, who took up the point and questioned the patient. The patient said she had been thinking "Jew." As it turned out, the patient had been alone in the therapist's room earlier and had read a personal letter she had seen on the desk. The patient felt guilty and thought the therapist would be displeased with her (as other authority figures in her life presumably had been). Here the cultural point played only a minor role in the patient's therapy. However, by taking up the cultural point, the therapist showed the patient that she was aware of what the patient was doing, and that she wanted to explore her thoughts and feelings with the patient to help her discover the root of her hostility.

Misunderstanding of Transference

A particularly striking instance of a failure in child therapy is presented by Pollack and associates (1952). A little Jewish girl was unable to get into a positive transference relationship with her therapist for three yeras, because the therapist did not understand the point the child was trying to communicate. For example, the child wanted to play mother and wished the therapist to be the bad child who insisted on drinking milk with meat sandwiches. The therapist did not understand the meaning of what the child was suggesting and tried to bring in other forms of activity. Finally, a second therapist got the idea that the child came from an Orthodox Jewish home. (Combining meat and dairy products is forbidden to Orthodox Jews.) The child was trying to work out her difficulty through Jewish practices—the only practices she knew. Once this was recognized the child was able to relate to the therapist, and together they could work out the meaning of the child's difficulties—how the little girl could not honor her mother and father as a good child should, because this would mean accepting their hitting and yelling.

One of the psychologist coauthors slowed up analytic therapy with a Chinese patient because she misunderstood, for a while, the patient's communications in English. Often, she could not understand the patient even when he was asked to talk more slowly, and she assumed that this was owing to his difficulties in speaking English. It was the therapist's impression that the Chinese patient talked as she remembered a Chinese laundryman talking to her in her childhood. This was certainly an instance of countertransference, for, as it turned out, the patient spoke like the stereotypical Chinese laundryman to annoy the therapist. Fortunately, the therapist soon woke up to the possibility that the patient was using garbled speech as a resistance device. When she asked him whether his Chinese friends had trouble understanding him when they conversed in Chinese, he laughed and said they often complained that when he talked excitedly he could not be understood at all.

Transferential Variables in Cultural Communications

Spiegel (Spiegel 1959; Spiegel and Papajohn 1983) undertook an investigation of cultural aspects of transference and countertransference phenomena in both emotionally disturbed and well families. Spiegel's analysis was based on research carried out with the collaboration of Florence Kluckhohn and several other investigators on three groups living in the Boston area: Southern-Italian Americans, Irish-Americans and Old Americans. The emotionally disturbed families in each group were selected from the patient population of an outpatient psychiatric clinic; the well families were chosen by public health and social agencies. The well families were chosen on the basis of their not having a broken home and, as far as could be ascertained, not having a psychotic family member or child in need of treatment. The parents in all the groups were born in the United States. In each case the grandparents were born in their native lands. The investigators hypothesized that variations in value orientations characteristic of each family group would make for differences in both the types of problems found in family relations and in the motivations for treatment (among the "sick" families). The value orientations were assumed to be unconscious.

The value orientations for each group were classified according to a system of categorization worked out by Kluckhohn (1958) and Kluckhohn and Strodtbeck (1961), in which certain assumptions are made about universal human problems and the range of possible solutions. The first assumption was that there are a limited number of problems common to all human beings for which solutions must be found in all societies. The second assumption was that although solutions vary, they are not limitless or random. The third assumption was that although variations of all solutions are present in every society, certain ones will be preferred in different societies.

The value orientations were classified in terms of the five problems that Kluckhohn regarded as common to all human groups: (1) *time focus* (main orientation to the past, the present, or the future); (2) *modality of human activity* (mode of self-expression in activity with emphasis on being, being-in-becoming, or doing); (3) *relational* (main emphasis on individualism or autonomy, on collaterality or the laterally extended group, or on lineality or relationships through time); (4) *relationship to nature and the supernatural* (subjugation to, harmony with, or mastery over nature and the supernatural); (5) *the character of innate human nature* (good or evil, good and evil, or mutable or immutable).[1] Spiegel and Papajohn (1983) use the following table to summarize how these foci can be used to compare cultural groups.

The three groups studied were categorized in terms of the ways in which their modes of thought and behavior expressed value orientations, that is, their culturally preferred solutions to the set of problems outlined above. For example, the middle-class Old American families were future-oriented, believed that man should dominate nature and emphasized achievement (that is, success). In contrast, the Irish-American families were present-oriented, felt that man is subordinate to the nature/supernatural world, and emphasized being (that is, spontaneity of expression). The Southern-Italian-American families also differed from Old Americans. For example, they emphasized collaterality, expressed above all in the interdependence of the kin group, while Old Americans placed individual relationships first, lineal relationships (that is, generations in time) second, and collateral relation-

Table 1 Comparison of Value Orientation Profiles

	American Middle Class	Italian	Irish
TIME	Future > Present > Past	Present > Past > Future	Present > Past > Future
ACTIVITY	Doing > Being > Being-In-Becoming	Being > Being-In-Becoming > Doing	Being > Being-In-Becoming > Doing
RELATIONAL	Individual > Collateral > Lineal	Collateral > Lineal > Individual	Lineal > Collateral > Individual
MAN-NATURE	Dominant Over > Subjugated > Harmony	Subjugated > Harmony > Dominant Over	Subjugated > Harmony > Dominant Over
BASIC NATURE OF MAN	Neutral > Evil > Good	Mixed > Evil > Good	Evil > Mixed > Good

ships third. Given the fact that Southern-Italian-Americans reverse this ordering of relationships, their difficulties in adapting to the predominant American life-style were understandable.

It was found that collateral relational ties were still strong in healthy Southern-Italian-American families, whereas in the sick families these ties had often broken down. These families were trying to function as isolated nuclear families. Southern-Italian-American families also had difficulties in understanding solutions to problems that seemed to them to isolate the individual. For example, when an American physician suggested that a child who was sick with rheumatic fever should have a room to herself, and special care and privileges, her Southern-Italian family did not understand why.

Spiegel attempts to relate these differences in cultural patterning to the ways in which transferential and countertransferential phenomena show up in psychotherapy. He first deals with the concept of reality as it is used in relation to the patient's functioning. Certain goals are set for the patient by the American therapist—for example, requiring the patient to report as much about himself as possible, to tell about whatever ideas and associations come into his head, and to take responsibility for himself and not depend too much on his family. The therapist also has expectations that the patient will want to have a future different from his past, that he will view the therapist as a professional who knows his business, that he will gradually become able to talk about his thoughts, memories, and feelings, and that, eventually, he will be able to cope appropriately with his expressions of emotion. As Spiegel says, these are certainly American middle-class values.

The therapist also has certain expectations about himself: to be responsible, to help the patient do reality testing, to maintain a neutral attitude and not impose his own values on the patient, to uncover the patient's present and past in order to better his future, and so forth.

When patient and therapist come from the same cultural background and class, the difficulties may be minimized. But what happens when patients and therapists come from different cultural backgrounds? The therapist is expected to have freed himself of his family ties (particularly to his strong superego) and to be flexible in the presence of many values that are different from those he absorbed as a child. According to Spiegel, quite a strain may develop when there is a conflict between the original values of the patient and the original values of the therapist, or when the therapist may still have an unresolved conflict between his archaic superego and his new identity as a professional (despite his own analysis).

As an illustration, Spiegel gives the case of an Irish-American father who maintains his Irish value orientations. This man would not tell everything he knew about himself because, in Ireland, intimate details of one's life are not revealed to family members, and certainly not to strangers. If the things an Irishman has to say about himself are guilt-ridden or shameful, he may hide them from himself by denial and repression, or he may confess to a priest; the therapist is not considered the proper authority for such revelations. Moreover, the Irishman perceives the neutrality of the therapist as hypocrisy and condescension. Because the Irishman's values are present- and being-oriented, he is little motivated to work on his problems for the future good of his child and family; and, because in his system of beliefs human nature is intrinsically evil, he believes he must hold on to the concepts of evil and punishment at all costs.

The therapist with a different constellation of value orientations may well feel frustrated in his efforts to solve the problems of treating his patient: he feels he must stick to his techniques and feels guilty if he lets the patient go before he has made some progress. In this situation, the therapist can make no progress, but he keeps on trying.

In the course of their research, Spiegel and his collaborators found a way to help their Irish-American patients. Although they maintained their American belief that man is the master of his fate (so clearly expressed in American attitudes toward self-improvement), they abandoned the therapeutic emphasis on past-time orientation (that is, on recollecting the past, especially childhood). Their approach took in the extended family and even, to some degree, the community. The therapists became acquainted with many of the patient's relatives and became somewhat assimilated into the linear family chain of influence that is so important to Irish-Americans. The therapists saw family members when and where they were available (emphasizing present-time and being orientations). They relaxed on the matter of nonreciprocity and answered questions about themselves. The therapists also let the patients know they were ashamed of some of the patients' impulses when those impulses would also have made them feel ashamed. Various modifications of this kind were found to be valuable in work with the cultural groups studied; This technique also improved their understanding of transference and countertransference communications.

Ticho (1971), a psychoanalyst who has worked in three countries (Austria, Brazil, and the United States) makes some very keen observations about the role played by culture in transference and countertransference during analysis. She discusses the stereotypes and prejudices of both patient and therapist and the need for the therapist to be aware of what is going on. She points out how hard it sometimes is to decide what is cultural and what is symptomatic. For example, when a South American patient is constantly late for his appointments, the therapist must determine if this is resistance or the characteristic behavior of South Americans, who do not hold the same views about punctuality as North Americans.

Ticho mentions a mistake she made with a black girl patient who expressed hatred for white people. One day this girl told the therapist that the year before there had been a German girl in her class whom she had begun to like. Without thinking, the therapist replied that she herself was not a German but an Austrian. She realized immediately that she considered Germans racists just as the patient considered white people racists. As a safeguard, Ticho suggested that therapists undergo intensive, continuous self-analysis, and that they obtain as much information as possible about the culture of the patients with whom they work. According to Ticho, these efforts will make the therapist more tolerant. Wolberg (1967) also underscores the need for continuous self-evaluation throughout therapy. Countertransference, like transference, is a double-edged sword: unanalyzed and undetected, it can hinder or halt therapy, but used as a key to the patient's conflict, the therapist's difficulties with the patient, and their mutual or conflicting cultural "baggage," transference and countertransference can become points of leverage for therapeutic advantage.

Therapy Between Black and White Americans

Much has been written about the difficulties white therapists encounter working with black Americans. Chess, Clark, and Thomas (1953) were among the earliest professionals to point out the misapprehensions of white therapists treating black children of lower socioeconomic backgrounds.[2] The therapists could not understand the full implications of the versions of American culture in which these disturbed children were reared. One little girl was diagnosed as psychopathic because she was "fresh" to her therapist; actually, she was trying to get closer to the therapist. Therapists were also shocked by the apparent indifference of black children to acts of violence they witnessed in their homes. Misconceptions of this kind can result in a variety of transferences on the part of the therapists, such as a need to do good and make radical changes in patterns of behavior, as well as countertransferring their own feelings about certain behavior.

Viola Bernard (1953) discusses how important it is for white therapists to become aware of their motives for selecting black patients for treatment (in cases where this was a choice), or for favoring the selection of patients from any ethnic group in particular. She suggests, for example, that a white therapist might want to treat a black patient out of feelings of guilt about his own prejudices. One psychologist coauthor (Abel), who began therapy with Chinese patients, apparently presented herself to herself and her colleagues as a therapist who was interested in and could work well with individuals from different cultural groups. This image had to be worked out to the point of awareness that such an image or attitude might be detrimental to the formation of effective therapeutic relationships.

A therapist may have various attitudes and feelings toward any patient— whether the patient comes from a similar or a different socioeconomic background, from an unfamiliar ethnic group or from a different culture. Such attitudes may be conscious and realistic, or they may arise from prejudices of which the therapist is unaware, or they may come about as countertransferential phenomena in response to a patient's transferences to the therapist.

One young therapist, who felt that he was very open-minded about marriage between blacks and whites, took on in therapy a white woman who had married a black medical student. The therapist also knew that an older psychoanalyst had refused to treat the woman because he disapproved of interracial marriage. The young therapist started out well with the woman, and she became attached to him in a transferential way: he was a father figure who was understanding and toward whom the woman felt some sexual attraction. One day the woman said, "I hate my husband. I want to leave him. I only married him to defy my father." The therapist found himself getting angry; he wanted to tell the woman that he was ashamed of her for being prejudiced and narrow-minded. For a while, the patient stalled in therapy. The therapist could not find a new approach to the difficulty. One day, his supervisor asked the therapist how he really felt about marriages between blacks and whites. He quickly replied, "They could work out in other countries, say in France, but not in the United States." This was the first time he was aware of his own prejudice, and he became sensitive to his countertransference feelings. The woman, in saying that she hated her husband, implied that she loved the therapist (her father); the therapist responded to this communication by seeing it, on the one hand, as a threat (countertransference to sexual advances on the part of the woman) and, on the other hand, as a reaction against his underlying prejudice toward a woman who was married to a black man. There are other implications, but these are enough to illustrate some aspects of the effects of cultural patterning on patient-thera-pist relationships.

The white American therapist may become overinvested in working with a patient of another "race," ethnic group, or different version of American culture. This can cause difficulties when it is done to prove that the therapist is not prejudiced, to assuage guilt, or to show that he or she has the ability to withstand hostility, or simply out of curiosity. Devereux (1951b) has discussed this topic in connection with the therapist who is motivated chiefly by research interests. He cites the case of a Native American patient who dreamed that when she met the therapist, he did not even call her by her name, implying that the therapist was interested only in finding out about a particular Native American tribe and not about the particular pa-tient.

Schachter and Butts (1968) discuss at length some of the difficulties and attitudes revealed in analysis with a black therapist and a white patient or a white therapist and a black patient. They report the case of a white patient who chose a black analyst because he believed that all black men are excep-tionally virile (an American stereotype), and he hoped he could become virile like the analyst. The patient failed to recognize the possibility that he himself might have some damaging prejudices toward a black person, and that the black analyst might conceivably have some prejudicial feelings to-ward him.

In 1962, when one of the psychologist coauthors (Abel) worked with her first Chinese patient, she asked quite a few questions early in therapy about the patient's family. Soon thereafter the patient had a dream in which he was arrested in Peking and was questioned by a Communist general. The patient had to pay some money, and the general asked too many questions, all about America. This dream clearly reflected the patient's feeling that the therapist had asked too many questions. She suddenly realized that her research interests were interfering with the therapy, as Devereux had sug-gested in his own case. Any involvement that only serves the particular needs of the *therapist* (research, narcissistic needs and so on) can interfere drastically with therapeutic progress. Freud himself is said to have trans-ferred an Egyptologist patient of his because he, Freud, became too en-grossed in what the patient had to say about ancient Egypt.

Kardiner and Ovesey (1951) spoke about the difficulties that arose in the course of psychotherapy with twenty-five black patients. They felt that the main problems were frustrated hostility toward whites and confusion be-tween the roles played by men and women. Black women generally feel more economically secure than black men. Furthermore, the black American woman is often the sole parent in the home. Indeed these analysts discovered that there were many problems between the sexes among black Americans.

Barbarin (1984) summarizes transference themes affecting the treatment of black patients. Relying on his own experiences and on the existing literature (for example, Jackson 1973; Griffith and Jones 1979), he points out that black American patients are likely to see the neutral stance of the therapist as a lack of interest. Black patients are also more likely to see the white therapist as all good (a savior or a saint) or all bad (an exploiter or a persecutor). The expression of aggression among black Americans is often repressed, and the possibility of its expression leads to heightened anxiety. Such conflicts get played out in the therapy in subtle ways, ways that can be destructive to the process of therapy. This, in turn, is a possible factor in the tendency of black patients to terminate treatment early.

Barbarin also outlines countertransference issues affecting the treatment of blacks. Most striking are prejudicial issues about blacks not being suitable for dynamic therapy or being too passive or resistant, or too little motivated. Infantalization of blacks in the dominant American culture may also predispose the white therapist to expect the black patient to live out the stereotype of a primitive, child-like creature. Barbarin also points out that the white therapist's guilt makes him reluctant to address or even admit the black patient's hostility toward him.

Unfortunately, we do not have guides for each culture in which a therapist is likely to work. Therapists therefore have to extrapolate information from the general literature on transference and the literature available on the specific culture of the patient with whom they are working.

Some Effects of the Caste System on Blacks

Using a projective test, Karon (1958) made a careful study of the effects of the caste system on the personality of black Americans. He used the Tomkins-Horn Picture Arrangement Test (PAT), which consists of twenty-five plates. On each plate there are three rather simple line drawings arranged in a circle so that the plate must be turned to view a picture in the upright position. The circular arrangement is intended to equalize the pictures. Each drawing on the plate has a symbol attached to it; the three symbols are arranged in random order on the different plates. As he looks at each plate, the subject is asked to decide on the order in which the three drawings should be placed to make an intelligible sequence. He is then asked to write the symbols for each plate one beneath the other on a page in the order he has decided upon and on one line beside each symbol to write a description of the picture. The three-picture sequence forms a story.

The analysis of the results revealed a number of differences between southern and northern blacks and between those living in rural small towns and those living in large industrial centers. The differences were especially striking with regard to such feelings as fear of facing aggression alone (unconscious) and conscious suppression of anger and weak affect. These fears were most conspicuous in the responses of rural, small-town southern blacks.

Clearly, where the black patient comes from—the North or the South, the country or the city—and how long he has lived in the North (if he has migrated) affect some aspects of his relationship to himself, to others, and to his therapist. It should also be clear that blacks who were born and reared in other societies (in Africa, in the Caribbean, or in Latin America), as well as the children of immigrants from these societies, will establish different patient-therapist relationships, depending on the cultural patterns of that particular society, including the patterning of black-white relations in that society. Thus a black man from Martinique, who is a French citizen and has a French education, or a black Trinidadian, who has grown up in a very complex pluralistic society, or a Ghanaian citizen, the carrier of an old and proud African heritage—each of these, coming to the United States, would have a very different emotional response to the alien, so-called "racial" prejudices prevalent in this country.

It has already been pointed out that black Americans often consciously suppress aggressive impulses toward whites, especially those in authority, such as the therapist. Powdermaker (1953) suggests that although blacks may take a masochistic position and "enjoy" suffering, their suffering is not necessarily brought on by unconscious neurotic needs, but may be the outcome of actual punitive social experiences. It should be added that blacks can be masochistic, as well as sadistic, depending on their own intrapsychic conflicts (independent of black-white conflicts). In recent years, in a radical reversal among many black American groups, (which may or may not involve permanent intrapsychic change) there have been open and at times violent expressions of aggressive impulses.

Adams (1950) indicates that black patients may use "race" as an unconscious defense to conceal more basic conflicts. He feels that they, like other Americans, can make good patients, since they generally want to improve themselves and strive for upward mobility (basic American values). Adams

states, though, that blacks present a complex problem, for they had difficulties before becoming aware of the prejudices that so deeply affect their
lives. He discusses the need to get beyond the patient's particular resis-
tances, which include the feeling that it would be impossible to be accepted
as an equal among white Americans. A black patient may say that death is
preferable to life as a black in this country, but he generally has a white ego-
ideal. On the other hand, many black Americans, especially among the
younger generation, have a conscious Afro-American ego-ideal and are con-
temptuous of blacks who strive for social integration. Both of these stances
are forms of resistance and must be considered in the light of deeply en-
grained American attitudes toward equality. But if the therapist breaks
through this resistance and can establish a positive transference, he discovers
that the basic problem, for some male black patients, may not be a feeling of
inferiority (status) but rather of wounded pride because of their inability to
repress passive feminine wishes and their lack of masculine attributes. The
fantasied castrating agent is not the white community, as the patient believes, but his castrating father and seductive and dominant mother—his
anxiety has been displaced from his parents to the white community.

Dynamically, of course, this situation is no different from that of a white
patient (or, indeed, any patient) who displaces anxiety onto a castrating
God, dictator, boss, or social group. A black patient can blame prejudice
and discrimination for thwarting his oral requirements. In intensive therapy, he may be unhappy to discover that he is treated without prejudice.
This frustrates him, because he needs to feel discriminated against in order
to hide from himself the realization that his oral demands may never be met.
In his dreams he may still direct discrimination against himself. (Unfortunately, discrimination is also a real pressure with which, along with his other
frustrations, he has to cope.) Moreover, in solving oedipal conflicts, a black
patient with a white therapist may have transferential blocks because of the
strong social taboo against sexual interaction between the races (this is
particularly true if the patient is a man and the therapist is a woman).

Adams suggests that goals for therapy should be realistic, and that although some of the dynamics of the oedipal conflict should be recognized,
they should not be explored intensively. However, it is the psychologist
coauthors' feeling that a point can be reached in intensive therapy (and in
psychoanalysis) where the problem of so-called color differences (used as a
defense both by the patient and the therapist) can be overcome and the
patient's unresolved oedipal, as well as pregenital, conflicts and real or
imagined deprivations become the focus of therapy. An analyzed therapist is

fairly well aware of his "archaic guilt" and his own partially unresolved intrapsychic conflicts, and he can handle them appropriately. If he can overcome other obstacles to his functioning as a therapist, certainly he can overcome cultural differences as well. If not, he should not treat any patient who comes from a social setting or a cultural group about which he has reservations that may affect his relationship to the patient or his ability to deal with feelings he may develop. On the other hand, Adams makes a good point in saying that the great danger in dealing with a black patient (or, as we might better say, any patient who stands in some special, culturally defined relationship to the society in which he lives) is the tendency to oversimplify problems and ascribe them to cultural conflicts. We have observed, for example, that some Jewish therapists have a tendency to attribute the problems of some of their practicing Catholic patients to the Catholic church. The Church is the castrating father for the therapist, whether or not it is for the patient.

Some black therapists working with white patients may also have problems. In supervising black therapists, one of the psychologist coauthors found that they were generally quite able to maintain a good therapeutic relationship, since they had been analyzed or were in the process of analysis. Their major difficulties had to do with a lack of technical knowledge, as well as countertransferential feelings caused by a patient targeting some of their own unsolved intrapsychic difficulties, including, of course, feelings of discrimination. Some therapists were better than others at coping with the transferences of their patients and listening for latent communications in cases where there was a suggestion of discrimination. Some at first seemed too eager to bring up the subject of black-white relations with their white patients and asked the patient at inappropriate times, "How do you feel about me?" But, generally, these feelings were overcome. These difficulties can arise from therapists' biases toward patients from their own cultural group also. For example, a Turkish Muslim psychiatrist worked quite well with Jewish patients. His difficulties lay in his relationship to his supervisor, a woman and a psychologist who, as he saw it, was his inferior on two counts.

Bosch-Kohrer (1984), a Swedish psychoanalyst, reports on the difficulties she has working with immigrants living far from their native lands. She states that because the analyst is not familiar with the child-rearing practices of the patient's homeland, she cannot know the quality of his early experiences. Bosch-Kohrer is most concerned about discovering whether childhood practices are syntonic or dystonic to the patient. She also discusses what she considers to be the two main problems in working cross-culturally. The first is the feeling of estrangement that arises during transference and countertransference between patient and analyst. The second is that nonverbal cues are frequently misunderstood by either the patient or the analyst. This problem seemed especially acute in therapy with patients from African nations.

Finally, Bosch-Kohrer describes in detail the special difficulties involved in interpreting developmental levels (using Erikson's model) and in making accurate diagnoses across cultural boundaries.

Socioeconomic Problems

Attitudes toward treatment may vary among members of different socioeconomic groups. The attitudes of middle-class American therapists toward patients who come from different socioeconomic groups may also vary considerably. At times, middle-class therapists are repulsed by the language of some of their lower-class patients, by their "lack" of values, for instance, the parents' lack of interest in their children's schooling or in establishing "regular" work habits, or by their "crude" sexual practices, that is, sex that does not include courting, foreplay, or any apparent concern for the partner. Sanua (1966) questions whether a lower-class therapist with extended training would not be more effective than a middle-class therapist with lower-class patients. However, the strong motivation that carried many successful therapists from lower-middle-class or even lower-class families through years of training and practice has inevitably altered their original values, and, while they may be more sensitive to poverty and to patients from a poverty-stricken background, they may also be blind to certain kinds of problems which they, the therapists, have wished to forget. A good analyst should be aware of his unconscious feelings of resentment toward or liking for his earlier life experiences. He can only make positive use of these feelings if he has learned to become aware of them.

A therapist must be able to meet the particular needs of a patient so that he can help him cope with his situation in a more effective manner. For example, the families in what Lewis (1966) calls the "culture of poverty" in Mexico, Puerto Rico, and New York would not be likely to seek psychotherapy or assistance from social agencies or health centers. But situations do arise in which they may be brought into contact with a psychotherapist, who then needs to use his skills as a mental-health consultant to decide the kind of relationship, if any, he might effectively have with such a patient, his family, and his community.[3]

Georgene Seward, in her book *Psychotherapy and Culture Conflict* (1956, Chapter 5), describes problems of treatment and status, particularly in connection with patients from poor backgrounds who are social climbers or social decliners. Seward presents in detail the case of a man (treated by Judd Marmor) who was a social climber.

This man had spent his early life in squalor but became a lawyer. Though successful, he had problems adapting to the middle-class version of American culture. He remembered his early life as one of great deprivation and neglect, both material and affective: he had lived in dirt, he had been ashamed of his shabby clothes (about which he was teased), and he had been exposed to continual discussions about lack of money. His strong motivation to escape poverty led him not only to get a professional education but to learn new forms of behavior, speech, and dress, to hide from others and himself his poverty-stricken background. Since he had had sexual difficulties with rich girls, he married a less well-educated and poorer girl, but she was more at home than he with middle-class values. In therapy, the patient complained about his wife because he felt that she reserved her affection for their son—he saw her unconsciously both as his uncouth father and his unloving mother. He also believed that the therapist favored other patients over him (the patient had a number of siblings). He associated his terror dreams with being trapped in marriage as, earlier, he had been trapped in poverty. Over the two-and-a-half years during which the patient was seen in therapy three to four times a week, the reasons for his feelings gradually emerged. His major intrapsychic conflict had to do with his repression of passive, dependent, "feminine" fantasies that contrasted with the responsibilities he had assumed in his career and his marriage. He was able to express his wish for a rich, strong man to look after him. He would have liked to be a girl; he felt like a girl trapped in a man's body. These conflicts were eventually worked out.

Such psychodynamics can be found, of course, in many patients who do not come from backgrounds of poverty. On the other hand, the many who do are better able to cope with residual fears of being poor and do not need to repress longings to be looked after. They may have been fortified by greater emotional support and understanding from a parent, a stronger constitution, a more adequate ego, or an ability to dominate id impulses and superego prohibitions more successfully. Though poverty may be a factor in trauma, many well-to-do patients also have anxieties about loss of money (love) or fears of going to the poorhouse (rejection and punishment). These problems are caused by unresolved oedipal and pregenital conflicts and represent masochistic and aggressive trends.

Transference Problems among Plains Indians

In his discussion of the psychotherapy of Plains Indian patients, Devereux (1951b) takes up two topics—transference and the handling of dreams—which will be discussed here in connection with the problems of patients whose cultural orientation differs from that of the therapist and hence may not be well understood.[4]

Devereux worked in analysis with a professional woman and in therapy with a college-educated professional man and a fairly well-educated, semi-skilled worker, all of whom had a Plains Indian background. Although these patients were more or less acculturated individuals, Devereux was aware that they had been reared in a Plains Indian setting and that their cultural orientation played a role in their emotional illnesses and in the therapeutic relationship. Like Laura Thompson (1948), Devereux took the position that culturally determined attitudes and personality types may survive the cultural practices to which they were originally related.

A very real problem arises in connection with transference when a patient misdefines the relationship and arbitrarily assigns inappropriate roles to the therapist and himself. Devereux points out that a difficulty of this kind can be overcome if the therapist understands (as he would in his own culture) the familial roles and basic patterns of social interaction characteristic of the patient's areal culture as well as his more specific tribal culture.

In Plains Indian societies, the family is male-centered. Since the men were away a great deal on hunts and on the warpath, they were not the frustrators of children. The women, although they were permissive mothers, were the principal punishers and frustrators. Moreover, men could not afford to be openly aggressive toward other men, because their lives were dependent on them for status and security, but they could be aggressive toward women, on whom they were less obviously dependent.

One of Devereux's male patients had a dream in which a supposedly friendly woman pressured him into the company of a seductive, syphilitic, aggressive woman. The patient himself realized that this dream expressed his anger toward the therapist, who often had to send him to his administrative physician. Since the patient's Plains Indian background did not allow him to express his anger toward a man, he transformed the therapist into a woman in his dream.

Devereux raises a question about the kind of transference that should be encouraged in therapy with Plains Indians in view of their attitude toward women and, in view of the fact that today the father's role is extremely diminished—living on reservations, men are no longer warriors or hunters and have few, if any, occupations through which they can gain prestige.

Devereux conceived the idea of how to handle transference phenomena from the dreams of the first Plains Indian he had in therapy. This patient dreamed about the therapist as his adviser, guide, and philosopher, and as a person who could uncover the subterfuges of other people and correct their mistakes. In one dream, for example, an Indian gambler was persuading another Indian that he had magical powers; then the therapist appeared and exposed the tricks of the "magician."

Among the Plains Indians, adolescent boys and men went on a vision quest that involved difficult ordeals with masochistic and exhibitionistic components. Finally, a supernatural being appeared in a vision and, as a guardian spirit, advised and inspired the supplicant. In his dreams, the patient identified the therapist with his guardian spirit. Because the guardian spirit was not believed to be omnipotent (any more than a father is), the therapist felt that in the transference relationship, he would not necessarily be expected to play the role of an omnipotent, infallible being.

Plains Indians had a certain number of highly stylized dreams that helped to build morale and reinforce various culturally standardized wishes. The manifest content of such dreams is usually so clear that they can easily be treated as real events. Devereux attempted to interpret the dreams of his acculturated patients in the traditional Plains Indian manner. This seemed to help the patients to do what members of their culture do naturally: feeling that the dreams are real events, they project their problems, wishes, and characteristic attitudes into their dreams. For example, one patient (the professional man) dreamed that a delivery wagon brought flowers to the house he was decorating. Then the wagon went on. When Devereux suggested that he himself might have been the wagon, the patient replied, "Of course: and where did you go from there?" Although this man had spent his adult years among intellectual white Americans, he still regarded the manifest content of dreams as genuine happenings. Therefore, Devereux felt that in working with patients from a Plains Indian background, it was never safe to ignore the manifest content of their dreams. He gave an example of how he had missed a crucial communication by not paying attention to the manifest content of a dream. Manifest content may be important for all patients, but for those from cultures in which dreams are the vehicles for stylized symbolism, they have a direct significance.

Devereux also employed other techniques to handle his patients' dreams. For example, he would point out the characterological aspects in a dream; the patient would indicate that he understood by saying that he knew he behaved in such a manner when awake. Plains Indian dreams may have didactic and autodidactic functions (advice giving). When unconscious aspects of this learning were pointed out to patients, they could easily accept them because their dreams and their interpretations are egosyntonic and have standard cultural emphases. The reality aspect of the interpretation helps them to build up their self-image enough to ward off taboo impulses. This supportive educative method has certainly been employed in other groups, including white Americans. But Devereux makes the suggestion that the supportive-interpretive method, as he calls it, is especially effective when the standard cultural patterns of relationships of authority figures, parents and peers, as well as the ways in which a culture makes use of or evaluates dreams are taken into account.

Transference in Other Cultural Groups

Maldonado-Sierra and Trent (1960) adapted another therapeutic technique to meet the needs of seriously and chronically ill (regressed schizophrenic) patients who had been hospitalized for at least five years in Puerto Rico. These patients had already had a variety of therapies—individual, group, physical, occupational, and social—but they were little improved.

In Puerto Rico, children and their mothers fear the father and husband, who has absolute authority (a situation that tends to change drastically when families migrate to the mainland). The mother suffers in silence, though she is able to manipulate the males in the household in passive-aggressive ways. The male children unconsciously resent male authority, but they need it to function, and they tend to relate to an older male sibling with whom they can discuss their difficulties (as they might wish to do with a father).

With this in mind, Maldonado-Sierra and Trent conceived of developing a special form of family-centered therapy for the male patients. Three groups of eight patients were selected. For three to four weeks they met with a resident physician, who became an elder sibling for the patients. The siblings were dressed alike, only first names were used and an attempt was made to form real relationships. (Transferences were minimized, but they must have been present.) Gradually the "older brother" (the therapist) introduced "Mama" and "Papa" (staff psychiatrists) to the group. The "Mama" fed the group, bringing candy and other good things to eat. The "older brother" became the spokesman for the group and told the parents about the younger brothers' feelings and their conscious attitudes. The investigators suggested that this kind of family therapy, which helped their schizophrenic patients more than any other that had been attempted, might be useful in work with other Latin American groups, but perhaps not with members of other cultures.

Group and family therapy may be much more effective in some cultures than in others. Mead (1951) discusses various ways in which the character structure, as it is developed in members of a specific culture (or version of a culture), may be relevant to the therapy and may markedly affect the responsiveness of patients to group therapy. She points out that styles of group participation vary and that spectatorship and exhibitionism may be attached to very different roles in different cultures. For example, in English culture exhibitionism is associated with dominance (the father) while children, the dependents and subordinates, take the spectator role. In this combination, exhibitionism takes the form of a continuous understatement of strength. In contrast, in American culture the dominant parents are the spectators who encourage their children's assertive exhibition of autonomy. In German culture the child's role is also exhibitionistic, but the child is expected to exhibit cheerful submission and control (Bateson 1972). Each of these combinations leads to a very different type of group organization and a very different conception of the roles of leader and follower, teacher and pupil, therapist and patient. The problems in handling transference and countertransference also are quite different.

Bustamente (1957), a Cuban psychiatrist, wrote about cultural variations in the behavior and dreams of patients in his country where (before the revolution) there was a caste-like division between well-to-do and educated people of European (Spanish) origin and the poor and uneducated people of African origin. However, as in all caste societies, areas overlap.[5] Bustamante describes the case of a highly intelligent patient from the upper class who was influenced by Afro-Cuban religious beliefs from the lower-class (or caste) version of the culture. This man was fickle and could form no close attachments to women. Moreover, he had become rebellious as a way of hiding his great dependence on his father, and he related in transference to the therapist in the same ambivalent way he related to his father. Since he resisted facing and giving up his dependency, he stalled in treatment. Then he had a dream. The patient was at a family gathering at his grandparents' home. His grandfather looked stern. The patient was pressured by an aunt to dance, but he wanted to retreat to his room. As he was leaving, another aunt (whom, in reality, he liked) gave him a small box like a snuffbox and told him to take some of the contents. The box contained bee's honey, which the patient could smell. The patient was unaware that "bee's honey" had any particular meaning, and it took Bustamante some time to catch on to its significance.

In fact, it stood for "Oshun's *aché*," a metaphor in the Afro-Cuban folk religion *Santería*, which incorporates, among other things, aspects both of Yoruba pantheonic beliefs and of Catholic beliefs. In the local version of Yoruba mythology, a goddess, Oshun, was granted by the chief god the power, *aché*, of complete love; she was believed to have unsurpassed sexual powers. Thus in the dream, the patient's aunt gave him *aché* (bee's honey)—that is, sexual liberation—freeing him from his father and from his neurosis—that is, from retreating to his room to avoid his oedipal conflicts.

The many covert communications that can be directed toward treatment and toward the therapist in dreams may reflect the cultural orientation of the patient, his cultural as well as his intrapsychic conflicts, and his ways of coping with these conflicts. The therapist may catch the latent meanings of such communications, but not knowing the patient's culture, he may misunderstand or misinterpret some aspects of the dream material.

A twenty-five-year-old Jewish woman came to her therapeutic session one day and related a dream she had had about candles burning in her mother's house. It was Friday, and the patient lit the candles. For once her married sisters, who were present in the dream, were not making disparaging remarks. The patient felt that the atmosphere was pleasant and that her friends, including the therapist, might have been present. Suddenly she felt something was wrong; she blew out the candles and woke up.

Over and above the symbolic meaning that the candles and blowing them out had for the patient, which was clear from her associations (male sex symbol and driving men away when they came close) there were relevant cultural factors, an understanding of which helped in the interpretation of aspects of the dream. First, why was the woman lighting candles in her mother's home? According to Jewish tradition, it is the role of the mother (who was present in the dream) to light the candles. Second, in her associations the patient said, "I guess I'd better explain about candles in a Jewish home," which, since her therapist was not Jewish, implied, "You don't appreciate my home." In reality, the patient had projected this attitude onto the therapist, for in fact, she left her home because she felt it was cold, crude, and unesthetic. When the therapist demonstrated that she understood her culture by asking, "What were you doing lighting the candles?" the patient disclosed much more information and expressed positive feelings for the therapist, who had "got the message."

Often messages in dreams are difficult to interpret, not only in terms of the various levels of intrapsychic conflict that are indicated, but also in terms of the significance of culturally relevant material. One of the psychologist authors (Abel) treated a well-educated Chinese patient from the rural gentry in south-central China (Abel 1962), who reported this dream in his twenty-fourth therapy session: "In same house—man, your husband. You in bed covered with bed cover. You are moving arms and legs all covered up. I urinated by the bed and woke up."

The patient's first association to the dream was that it was pleasant and that he had enjoyed himself. The therapist recalled at that point that the toilet training of Chinese children proceeded very gradually and that the young child was treated permissively. The child would not be scolded for urinating on the floor, as an American child would be. But this was only one aspect of the theme of urination. When the patient began to associate further to the dream, he said it was true that he had felt happy in the dream, playing and urinating, but that he also felt he had been discriminated against at home as a child and had not been allowed to do what he wanted. He said, "Never free play. Uncle six years older, had everything." Thus the dream reflects various aspects of Chinese culturally determined views (permissiveness toward urination, multiple household, favorite children, and so on) as well as intrapsychic conflicts (oedipal rivalry, jealousy, feeling cheated, hostility, sexual fantasies, and so on).

Obviously, this was an oedipal as well as a transference dream in which the therapist and her husband played the role of parents. The patient said he imagined that the therapist's husband was tall, since she was tall. His own mother and father were also tall. Then he became embarrassed and said, hesitantly, "This comes to my association, that you often turn your face aside as to avoid to look at me straight. I imagine you were shame at me a little." Here the patient's sexual feelings had been aroused, not only in the dream, but also as he was associating to it, and he projected his feelings onto the therapist. He used the face-turning image to convey this feeling. (The localization of shame in the face is a recurrent theme in Chinese culture.) Other transference aspects of the dream came up later in therapy when the patient recalled seeing his mother moving around in bed and having, as he thought, her arms twisted by his father. The patient also felt that in the dream he was somehow trying to please the therapist. In real life he believed he often tried to please people, but then he would say something against them behind their backs in order to please someone else. As a child, living as he did in a traditional Chinese household, he found it expedient to please a variety of authority figures—his grandfather's concubine, his father, his young uncle, his aunts—but behind their backs, he could speak disparagingly of them to his mother or to his paternal grandmother. The therapist seemed to be filling multiple transferential roles for the patient.

Nine

Dreams

Dreams are of considerable interest to psychotherapists because they reveal many aspects of the mental life of the individual under treatment. Dreams have been experienced, remembered in fragments or as wholes, and reported with more or less secondary elaboration by peoples at every level of cultural complexity from the earliest times.

Dreams are a form of communication that contains latent, overt, and transferential aspects. Such messages may be regarded as a kind of projective test, although the stimulus is not one standardized by investigators, like the Rorschach test, but is rather part of the mental life experience of an individual. Dreams may be touched off by the experiences of the day, external stimulation (such as temperature or noises), or by material presented by an experimenter to the subject before sleep. This material may be a suggestion about what to dream, or it may even be a projective test, such as a TAT card, which is shown to a subject before he goes to sleep (Fiss, Klein, and Bokert 1966). The presleep suggestion may also be given under hypnosis (Roffenstein 1951).

Dreaming has been found to take place under particular conditions while the individual is sleeping (Snyder 1963). In recent years, experiments have been conducted which indicate that some kind of mental activity goes on in all stages of sleep, but that dreaming in particular is associated with what is called REM (rapid eye movement) sleep.[1]

In Europe, prior to Freud, some scholars interested in mythology, rituals, and magic saw in dreams a reflection of animistic concepts, and some conceived of the idea that dreams might be one of the sources of religious beliefs that focused on ideas about the soul and the supernatural (see, for example, Frazer [1890] 1955). Freud's interpretation of dreams as disguised wishes and representations of motives, and his emphasis on dream symbolism, condensation, displacement, and other indirect clues pointing to the unconscious needs of and stresses on the individual, had a tremendous impact on certain aspects of cultural anthropology. As stated earlier, Róheim was the first psychoanalyst to go into the field, and he was one of the earliest investigators to collect dreams systematically from individuals in preliterate societies and to employ psychoanalytic principles to the interpretation of these dreams.[2]

Psychoanalytic Theory and Dreams

Psychoanalytic theory brought into focus a great many problems about dreams as universal or culturally determined phenomena. The question arose as to whether there are universal symbols in dreams, that is, symbols that stand for parts of the body, particularly the sex organs, the mouth and the eyes, or for birth, sexual intercourse, masturbation, and death. Then there are questions as to whether dreams can be used cross-culturally for purposes of comparison: are they a projection of the individual personality or a reflection of a particular culture. There has been a difference of opinion as to whether the latent content of a dream can be culturally determined, although it is agreed that a dream's manifest content—both its themes and its setting—obviously reflects cultural patterns. Róheim was the first to demonstrate that dreams can reveal cultural material that might otherwise escape the notice both of the dreamer and the investigator, that is, latent material. For example, the Aranda of Australia do not consciously recognize the man's contribution to reproduction, but in dreams, the process of impregnation seems to be understood.

Róheim demonstrated that oedipal conflicts, including hostility to the father and fears of castration, are expressed in the dreams of non-Western and preliterate peoples, as well as in the dreams of Western peoples. Kluckhohn and Morgan (1951), for example, present the dreams of a Navajo family in which these fears (castration, witnessing of primal scene, terror over punishment and so forth) are clearly expressed. Quite recently, Piotrowski (1983) interpreted dreams in an interesting way. In his interpretations of the Thematic Apperception Test, Piotrowski found that various aspects of his subject's personalities were reflected in the different characters in their stories. Likewise, Piotrowski found that each character described in the dream carries some aspect of the dreamer, either consciously or unconsciously. Piotrowski calls his method the Perceptanalysis Dream System. He devised a set of rules to help interpret dreams that cover such themes as dissent and assent, symbolism, and abstract words. Piotrowski's system offers promise as a method for the systematic exploration of cultural differences in manifest dream content.

Similarities and differences in dream symbolization and motivation have been reported from different parts of the world. Seligman (1924) collected dream symbols in various cultural groups in Africa, Southeast Asia, Japan, China, Western Europe, and elsewhere. Comparative analysis showed him that there is some universality in associated meaning, such as loss of a tooth representing illness or death and feces standing for money or wealth.[3] In general, however, it seems more appropriate for dreamers to make their own associations to their dreams, or for the investigators to look for additional confirmatory material from sources other than dreams (autobiographies, myths, interviews, rituals, projective materials, and therapy sessions) or at least from a series of dreams from different individuals before accepting the specific meaning of a dream symbol for the people of a given culture (Honigmann 1961; Lincoln 1935).

Kilborne (1981) has studied and reported extensively on the dreams of Moroccans. He points out that in general it is very difficult to determine whether the symbolism in dreams has some universal meaning, or whether it refers to individual or cultural concerns. He considers that some dreamers may know (consciously or unconsciously) what kind of dream is expected of them and what the interpretations might be. Kilborne also notes that in some cultures, interpreters may have set rules for interpreting dreams.

Kilborne carried out an interesting experiment working with Moroccan dream interpreters on some aspects of dream interpretation. In Moroccan culture, dreams are considered to be very important and there are professional dream interpreters. The interpretations are generally related to divination, illness, and healing. Moroccans also believe in the influence of saints, spiritual beings, and the *djinn* (a class of spirits with special powers).

Kilborne asked seven native interpreters—one of them a woman—to explain the meaning of a dream suggesting castration that Freud called a "type-dream." According to Kilborne, a universal type-dream should mean the same thing all over the world, but this premise had never been tested. The Freudian dream selected was the one about the pit and the tree: "The dreamer saw a deep pit in the vineyard which she knows had been caused by a tree being torn out" (Freud 1953). Interpretations of the dream of the pit and the tree revealed seven very different meanings. Some of the interpreters picked only two or three elements in the material; others used quite a few elements in their interpretations. The content of the dream interpretations varied greatly. For instance, to one interpreter the pit meant "the downfall of the director of a company"; to another, "There was too much drinking and the dreamer should avoid drunkenness."

Six of the seven dream interpretations suggested a threat; the dreamer should watch out for an obstacle, a prison, a trap, betrayal, or death. Only one dream was interpreted as something good happening in the present and in the next world. The six interpreters who felt a threat caught *mainly* the anxiety expressed in the dream and projected this onto the hostility of something or somebody external to the person who had related the dream. Most of these dream interpreters felt that the dream belonged to the individual reporting the dream to them (a Moroccan assistant of Kilborne).

Clearly, Freudian and Moroccan dream interpretations differ significantly. Freud drew on what he thought was a universal latent content: the uprooted tree and the hole it left behind were castration symbols. He felt there was a defense mechanism at work in the dream and in the secondary elaborations. The Moroccans explain dreams differently. The Moroccan dream interpreters rely on the dreamer's dependency needs, and on their own socially recognized position and particular narcissistic needs. In their interpretations, these professionals project what is bad in the dreams onto enemies of all kinds, including supernatural ones, or onto the danger of the dreamer's evil wishes.

Kilborne has not actually disproved the castration theme in the pit and tree dream. The castration threat may well have been present at some latent level in the Moroccans' interpretations. However, his experiment is interesting in that, with one exception, all the Moroccans saw the latent threat in the dream. None saw castration per se (only Freud did), but all did see serious harm. Not all current analytic thinkers would agree with Freud either. For example, Brenner (1982) cautions that the threat in this dream can represent, in addition to castration, loss of a loved one or loss of the love of a loved one, or a threat from one's own conscience.

Boyer (1979) takes the psychoanalytic position that the manifest content of a dream is a cryptic message that represents the latent content masked by the dreamer. Boyer studied intensively the Apache Indians on the Mescalero Reservation in New Mexico. His special interest was their folklore with its conscious and unconscious meanings; dreams, too, were included in his investigations. Sometimes it was not possible to tell whether a folktale or a dream was being reported, for the Apache patients with whom Boyer worked used both folktales and dreams in attempts to solve their intrapsychic conflicts.

Mescalero Apaches often have what they call power dreams that indicate ways of overcoming difficulties. They believe that dreams foretell good and bad luck. Preventive measures must be taken against bad dreams, the content of which may include a flood, a fire, a pig, falling teeth, the return of the dead, being chased by a wild animal or the colors red and black. However, some bad dreams may mean the opposite. For example, a person dreams that a snake will bite him; this means good luck. Or he dreams that he will die; this means that he will live a long life. There are also good dreams that mean good luck. Dreams about summer, about things growing, about everything green all have a positive meaning. Good luck symbols appear in dreams—for example, deer, horses, mules, and burros.

Mescalero Apaches have specific ways of warding off the effects of evil dreams. When they are uncertain what to do, they consult a shaman. Today, however, the shaman does not inquire about dreams; instead, he depends on visions, hypnosis, and hallucinations, with or without the aid of peyote. A patient's reverie may reveal to the shaman the presence of a witch or a conflict about which he feels guilty.

Mescalero Apache shamans reported that they study their own dreams intensively to be sure that their rivals are not using witchcraft against them. Of course, the dreams, and likewise the folktales, symbolize unconscious conflicts that only analytic work can unravel. Through work with patients and shamans on the reservation, Boyer was able to uncover the hidden meanings of certain symbols, such as the bat and the owl, which appear in the folklore. Once Boyer had mastered the Mescalero Apache myths and symbols, he found that he could introduce psychoanalytic methods, including dream interpretation, in his treatment of Apache patients.

Even where "universal" dreams have been reported, they may be given quite different emphases in different cultures. Griffith, Miyagi, and Tago (1958) reported that Japanese and American college students described parallel dreams, but expressed concern over different situations: Japanese students worried about responsibility and aggression, while American students worried about money, time, and physical freedom.

Clearly, fruitful research on the cultural interpretation of dreams, as well as other symbolic manifestations (for example, ritual, song, carving, curing, mythology, and so on), depends equally on the approach of the researcher and on the openness or secrecy with which symbolism is treated in the culture. In the early 1930s, Bateson's work (1958) with the only slightly acculturated Iatmul people of the Middle Sepik River in Papua New Guinea, proceeded very slowly because information crucial to the elucidation of symbolic material was the secret property of each of the several clans and was known only to initiated, adult men, among them some with highly specialized knowledge and training.

In contrast, Dorothy Eggan (1961) was able to carry out, over a period of several years, an intensive and very fruitful study of the dreams of Hopi Indians. She found that the Hopi did not find it difficult to report dreams because they encourage fantasy life and dreaming. Moreover, dream recitations have been one of the traditional ways in which individuals seek and obtain attention. Bad dreams must be confessed at once so that appropriate action can be taken. For these reasons, it was possible for her to work out both the individual patterns of dreaming and the cultural regularities within individual patterns.

In recent years, psychologists and psychoanalysts have dealt seriously with the manifest content as well as the latent meaning of dreams as ways of understanding the dynamics of personality (Brenneis and Roll 1975; Erikson 1970; Hall 1958). Interpretations of repeated dreams, dream series, and recurrent themes in successive dream series are essential to an understanding of the individual as well as to an understanding of a patient's changing relationships and ways of coping with conflicts in the course of therapy (French 1952, 1954, 1958).

Eggan, speaking from an anthropological standpoint, makes the point that in waking life individuals from extremely different cultures may have completely different attitudes toward a specific mode of behavior—for example, ritual killing viewed by an Aztec and by a Quaker. But she speculates that while the manifest content in the dreams would be very different for an Aztec and a Quaker, the latent dream content, a reflection of each one's conflict about aggression, might be less opposed. However, one must also take into account the fact that all known human societies have (and have had) basic cultural premises about killing members of the in- and out-group, and rules which define whether and when killing a human being is, or is not, murder.

O'Nell and O'Nell (1977) made a cross-cultural study comparing the manifest content of aggression in dreams. Their subjects were 132 Zapotec males and females from the ages of five to ninety-seven, from whom they obtained 660 dreams. The Zapotec are a rural Indian group living in the state of Oaxaca, Mexico. The comparison group consisted of 2,000 American males and females of a similar age range from whom Hall and Dumhoff (1963) had collected more than 3,000 dreams. For purposes of comparison, the total sample was divided into three age groups: ages 2–12, 13–30, and 31–95 (31–80 for the Americans). Unfortunately, other than the breakdown by age, the American sample was not described.

Analysis of the dreams indicated that for males in both groups there was no change in the relative frequency of aggression from one age group to another. There was an age-related decrease in the frequency of aggressive dreams among the females, but the decrease was decidedly less for the Zapotec females than for the American females. In addition, there was a greater difference in the frequency of dreams of aggression between American males and females than between Zapotec males and females: at all ages, American females ranked lowest in dreams of expressed aggression.

At all ages, the dreamer was more often the victim of aggression than the aggressor. This was particularly marked among children and adolescents in both cultures and, except among older adults, females were victims more often than males. In both cultures, male and female dreamers alike, whether as victims or as aggressors, had more frequent aggressive interaction with male than with female dream characters. A comparison was also made of the different kinds of dream aggression. Among the Zapotec, physical aggression was expressed in 75 per cent of the relevant dreams; among the Americans, physical aggression was expressed in approximately 50 per cent of the relevant dreams.

A comparative study of this kind raises a number of questions. First, one must ask to what extent these dreams of aggression at the manifest level relate to latent feelings of aggression, whether as victim or aggressor. Second, one must ask whether the individuals in the cultures compared—men, women, and children, persons of different ages—acted more or less aggressively or expected to be victimized more or less often or effectively in their dreams than in their waking lives. The Zapotec show so much physical aggression in their dreams—are their frustrations given more outlet in their dreams than in their waking lives? And how do they react, ordinarily, under provocation? These and other questions should be raised because they relate to the larger problem of the relationship of dreams to waking behavior.

A great deal has been written about the ways in which dreams are used in cultures around the world. Not uncommonly, dreams are believed to have predictive value and to be manifestations of various sorts of supernatural power. Supernatural beings may appear in dreams—and in visions—as mythological figures or ancestors (sometimes disguised as actual members of the group) in human, animal, or other well-recognized symbolic forms. They may threaten a catastrophe unless appropriate action is taken to offset the event; they may give help, for example by handing over power to the dreamer and suggesting how to perform rituals; they may make diagnoses (such as informing the dreamer about the cause and nature of an illness); they may be teachers (in some cultures, healers are believed to learn in dreams techniques and specific use of herbs and other materials as medicines); they may be the source of inventions (in some cultures, new techniques or styles are validated in dreams); and they may inspire creative endeavors (the dreamer may be given a song, an animal protector, or the design for a carving or painting).

Culturally Determined and Expected Dreams

In many societies the world over, individuals have been obliged—or permitted—to seek visions at some stage of life, to gain specific kinds of power, such as the powers of a shaman, or to gain strength, protection, or aid in some enterprise. Very often these visions are revealed in special dreams.

Throughout North America (except among the Pueblo Indians of the Southwest), supernatural power was sought in dreams and visions (Benedict 1923). Among the Indians of British Columbia, the vision quest was associated with puberty rites for both boys and girls. According to Benedict (1934:39–40), "The climax of the magic adolescent training for boys was the acquisition of a guardian spirit who by its gifts dictated the lifetime profession of the young man. . . . Girls also received guardian spirits representing their domestic duties." On the western plains, adult men sought visions through self-torture, fasting, and other extreme ordeals (Benedict 1934:81). However, although the idea of the vision quest and the search for a supernatural guardian was common to North American cultures, in its particulars it varied greatly from one culture to another.[4]

Dreams are not simply taken as indicators of supernatural and magical powers at work; the manner in which dreams are viewed and accounted for may reflect some understanding of their underlying psychodynamics. In North America, where the vision quest was associated with adolescence, the acquisition of a guardian spirit indicated that the individual (usually a boy) was emotionally and physically mature. In other words, through this kind of culturally determined dream, a boy could begin to solve his dependency conflicts.

In some societies, dreams may be a sign of social deviance. Among the

Sioux, a boy who dreamed of hermaphrodite buffalo or of taking hold of a woman's carrying strap hanging from the moon was destined to become a *berdache,* a man who might—or might not—wear woman's clothes and do woman's specialized, skilled work, but was not necessarily a homosexual. Such a man could not, or chose not to fulfill the male hunter-warrior role of his society. Erikson (1963) points out that in this respect, the Sioux take unconscious factors into account and legitimize certain deviant roles, such as the *berdache* and a kind of clown and a special type of prostitute. Although the group may look with horror or derision at the role, they are not attacking the individual but his fate, which is supernaturally determined. Since it is the unconscious that is attacked indirectly, and not the ego or the whole person, the deviant is not ostracized but given community support.

There are other ways in which dreams may be used therapeutically. The Navajo, for example, used dreams to reveal curing rituals which symbolically resolved unconscious conflicts (Lincoln 1935). Among Philippine Negritos, Stewart (1954) found that group support was given to an individual to symbolically master dangers represented in trances and dreams. The patient was encouraged by a group of shamans to go into trance and to meet and overcome the spirit that made him ill. In this way, the patient was able to overcome psychosomatic illness by having his conflicts externalized as spirits and by mobilizing strong group support behind his efforts.

Wallace (1958) describes how the Iroquois (as reported in the records of seventeenth-century missionaries) understood and took into account the latent meanings of dreams in order to avoid psychic and somatic illness. The Seneca, an Iroquois tribe, believed that sickness or disease could be brought about by natural causes or witchcraft, or by the mind itself out of a desire for something that made the person sick until he possessed it. Such desires were revealed in dreams, but often so indirectly that the group went through guessing rites in order to find out what the person longed for. In their view, it was essential to find out what he unconsciously wanted and give it to him. Although passive tendencies were so threatening to males that they could not allow themselves to dream directly about a need to be looked after, the signs and symbols of the dream, as well as what the person said about the dream (that is, his associations), permitted others to guess what he desired, which was then given to him.

Firth (1934) describes how among the Polynesian Tikopia of the Solomon Islands a dreamer may have a threatening dream—such as having intercourse with a taboo relative—but, knowing that the sex object of the dream is being impersonated by a spirit, he is not too upset. While sexual fantasies may be satisfied in an acceptable way in a dream, the individual also believes that sexual intercourse in dreams with an *atua* (spirit of nonhuman origin) can be debilitating; therefore, the same dream can be an explanation for an illness and a point of departure for healing. The Tikopia man is not consciously guilty about breaking a sexual taboo, but apparently he does feel unconscious guilt because such a dream can make him sick. The Melanesian Trobrianders react very differently to an incest dream. In their view, the dream represents reality and they become very emotionally disturbed (Malinowski 1962). They may see the dream as accidentally misapplied magic, but they cannot escape the emotional consequences.

Dreams of relatives, living or dead, or even of their animal namesake surrogates, are all considered significant by shamans among the Ute (Opler 1959). The shaman is expected to uncover the symbolic meaning of dreams. Dreams that are repeated are taken extremely seriously, and in interpreting these, the shaman attempts to isolate the dreamer's hidden wish or motive. As in the incest dreams of the Tikopia, blame is attached to "intruders" in the dream, not to the dreamer. But the patient then helps the shaman to exorcise the evil, with the result that the dreamer is rid of any guilt he may have about his wishes. However, the shaman also may translate some of the manifest content of a dream into its possible latent meaning, and relate it not to "intruders" but to the patient's own difficulties—the stresses within his family and his own motivations. This method is meant to eradicate drives or tendencies that are socially unacceptable. According to Opler, the Ute regard a dream as an indicator of mental and physical integration or a breakdown much as do psychoanalysts in Western societies.

Thus we see how in preliterate societies dreams may be incorporated in and organized by the culture to serve various purposes. They may be a way of maintaining health (physical and mental) through techniques that help the individual to cope with intrapsychic conflict or to overcome illness. Dreams may serve to validate change (as when a new idea originates in a dream), and they may provide ways of supporting cultural integration and continuity.

Investigations of dreams have generally been carried out within one society, sometimes with members of only one sex. Brenneis and Roll, in the interest of comparative research, planned a study based on work with Hispanic-Americans and American students, both men and women, at the University of New Mexico. The Americans were all born in the United States of nonimmigrant parents and came from homes in which no language other than English was spoken. The Hispanic-Americans were all born in the United States of nonimmigrant families but spoke Spanish at home. They identified themselves variously as Chicanos, Hispanic-Americans or Mexican-Americans; for purposes of the study all were grouped under the general term "Hispanic-Americans."

In a preliminary study, Brenneis and Roll (1975) investigated the manifest content in the dreams of the Hispanic-American students. For this study, the students (forty-two males and sixty-five females) were asked to describe in writing two to five dreams they had had during a two-week period. The manifest dream content was clearly differentiated by sex. The women's dreams, for example, made limited use of space, a response that is congruent with the traditional centering of the Hispanic-American woman in her home. The men's dreams concentrated more on activities outside the home. The men's dreams also contained more expressions of sexual and aggressive activities than did the women's dreams. The women's dreams incorporated fewer scenes of sex and aggression, but more frequent scenes of friendly interactions; these often took the place in the context of the home or with friends.

In the comparative study, Brenneis and Roll (1976), compared the reported dreams of the Hispanic-American students with those of other American students. The dreams were collected from both groups in an identical way. The American students (sixty-one males and seventy-four females) and the Hispanic students (forty-two males and sixty-five females) were asked to record their dreams over a two-week period.

Analysis of the manifest content of the dreams of the two groups showed that the Hispanic-American students of both sexes dreamed more often of familiar things than did the American students. They also had a relatively larger cast of characters in their dreams. In describing their dreams, the Hispanic-Americans discussed affect and sensory impressions more often than did the Americans; that is, the Americans much less often used terms that involved feelings (e.g., angry, sad, happy, confused) or sensations (e.g., hot, sweet, loud).

Roll, in collaboration with Rabold and McArdle (1976), carried out a further comparative investigation of the dreams of the same two groups of Hispanic-American and American students. In this research, the focus was on comparative passivity. Two previous psychometric studies of Mexicans in Mexico and Americans in the United States (Diaz-Guerrero 1975; Holtzman, Diaz-Guerrero, and Swartz 1975) found evidence of greater passivity among Mexicans than among Americans. This was sometimes manifested in the use of language. For example, the Mexican was more likely to say, "The plate was broken," whereas the American would say, "I broke the plate."

Roll and his collaborators focused their research on one special aspect of passivity, disclaimed activity. Claimed activity implies that a person sees himself as goal-directed and responsible for his actions. Disclaimed activity implies that responsibility for a person's actions is deflected onto something or someone else. For the purpose of this investigation, Roll and his collaborators defined disclaimed activity as responsibility deflected onto (1) another person; (2) the body (part of the body is held responsible for the action); (3) the psyche (part of the self or the mind is held responsible); (4) fate (an external force is held responsible); and (5), an object (an inanimate object is held responsible). It was predicted that a study of the manifest content of dreams would reveal instances of disclaimed activity, and that these could be compared for the two student groups. Some examples of disclaimed-activity dream reports are: "My mouth moved, and words came out by themselves"; "Fog was pulling me toward the pool"; "Suddenly, my pants came off by themselves." The claimed-activity versions of these dream reports would be: "I opened my mouth and spoke"; "I went toward the pool": "I took off my pants."

Significantly, there was a greater emphasis on disclaimed activity in the manifest content of the dreams of the Hispanic-Americans than in the manifest dream content of the other Americans. This was found to be equally true for both men and women. This finding appears to confirm the hypothesis that Hispanics respond with greater passivity than do Americans to coping with stress and problems as they are revealed in dreams. However, this must be accepted with a qualification. Americans define passivity negatively, but it may also have a positive connotation. In some circumstances, a passive response (disclaimed activity) may help an individual to cope with a difficult problem in ways that accepting personal responsibility (claimed activity) cannot.

By contrasting the dream reports of these two groups, Roll and his collaborators illustrated how cultural ties and identities significantly influence the internal lives of the members of the two groups. Psychodynamic psychotherapy—and, indeed, all therapy in which dreams and fantasies are important—has to take into account the influence of cultural identity on patients' reports.

Dream Communications to the Therapist

It has been stated in earlier chapters that in therapy all communications, latent, manifest, or transferential, may reflect cultural patterning to a greater or lesser degree. Dreams are included in such communications because both idiosyncratic wishes and culturally determined expectations and sanctions enter into them in some way. We would like now to go somewhat more fully into the way in which dreams are used in the course of psychotherapy, giving illustrations from two cases: the "Wolf" Indian patient treated by Devereux (1969) in a Veterans Administration hospital, and a Chinese professional man treated by Abel (1962), who was born and reared in pre-Communist China but who received his higher education in the United States and then settled here.

THE DREAM OF A PLAINS INDIAN PATIENT

"Wolf" is a fictitious tribal name adopted by Devereux to protect the identity of "Jimmy Picard" (also a fictitious name), his Plains Indian patient. Since Jimmy Picard's tribe is a small one, the use of fictitious personal names did not suffice. For the purposes of publication, Devereux combined features of Crow, Blackfoot, and Cheyenne (all Plains Indians cultures) that were appropriate to but not identical with Jimmy Picard's actual culture into a fictitious society he called the Wolf tribe. A few facts about the Wolf Indians need to be established in order to understand Devereux's patient's dreams. First, children growing up on the reservation were reared within the present-day version of their traditional culture, in which all that was recognized as manly and glorious lay in the lost past. Second, children living on a reservation were exposed to socially marginal white people who held the stereotypical view of Native Americans as shiftless, immoral, and alcoholic. Thus growing boys felt inferior: they could not identify with their warrior ancestors, and the external American world presented them with no acceptable image of what they might become.

The life of these Wolf Indians led to a curious oedipal situation. Since the father was often absent, the mother was the principal frustrating figure; therefore, boys repressed their oedipal hostility toward the father and projected it onto women in general. Although this seems like an inverted oedipal situation, there are other factors. Men were expected to seduce women, and women to resist men's advances. But without the sexual participation of the women, the men became impotent; they became more violent when they seduced the women and often punished them to assuage their guilt. However, there was also institutionalized rivalry between men and an institutionalized good relationship between a man and his female kin. This pattern gives the impression of a normal oedipal situation, but according to Devereux, this "normality" was a regression from the inverted oedipal conflict (great masculine hostility to women). Jimmy Picard was no exception. His dreams reflected many aspects of these variations in male-male and male-female relationships. Through associating to his dreams and understanding them, he was to some degree able to work out his underlying oedipal conflict. Some patients in American culture have inverted, or even more complicated, oedipal relationships, but this is not the normal oedipal relationship in American culture as it is in the present-day culture of these Plains Indians.

The Wolf child could leave his parental home if he felt frustrated and unhappy; he could take refuge in the home of kin. He was not shamed, and his kin were glad to take him in and raise him. This was the story of Jimmy Picard's experience. After the death of his father, he left home at the age of five. He had felt deeply frustrated by his mother and had also, apparently, witnessed a primal scene between his mother and her lover. He was accepted into the home of an elder sister and her husband. The sister, a puritanical Christian, was even more frustrating to the boy and thus became an object of hatred. Yet he tolerated the situation, for he remained in his sister's home for some time.

One of the patient's dreams and his associations to it illustrate male-female relationships among the Wolf. It also indicates the necessity of evaluating the implied homosexual relationship of two men, or a father and son, in terms of the culture—that is, without overestimating the homosexual tone. The dream was recounted in Session XIX (Devereux 1969:323):

> I had a short dream last night. I went to my country, where I live. I walked onto the open porch of a hotel, on top of a mountain, which overlooks the mountains. It was really pretty. I was surprised by the new landscape and wondered why I had never seen it before! Then I began to wonder whether others too may not have seen it, or know it. I decided that I would get someone else to come up here on a trip to look at the pretty scenery. That is all I dreamed.

Jimmy Picard made many associations to this dream, including another dream concerning religion. Then he began to think about marriage. He said that when a person gets married it is like a business proposition. In the dream he had not designated the person he would get to look at the scenery, whether it would be a man or a woman. He went on to say that the therapist was giving him new ways of figuring out things for himself, and he thought they might discuss figuring out marriage. He associated further:

> I think it is a good way to look at marriage, the way I see it. Of course,
> there is love in marriage. The same way, if you went downtown and saw a fel-

low and you decide he is pretty good for going into a business proposition
with him. It is like falling in love with a man, to go into business. It's the
same with a girl: you go into the marriage business, and build a home when
you are in love. Sometimes you meet a man and hardly care for his friendship
or for him. It is the same with a woman. You don't fall in love with each
woman you meet. Sometimes you meet a woman and love her when you
meet her, after a little time, or even the first time. There is something you like
in her. It is the same with a man. You figure he is a pretty good fellow to go
into business with (pp. 327–28).

He continued in this vein, saying that if the business partner or the wife
cheated you—or you cheated the partner or wife—you should go to court
and dissolve the business or get a divorce. It should not worry a person if he
cannot get along with a man or a woman. It was better to get out of the
situation; otherwise "it will wear on your mind, this thing."

In discussing these associations, Devereux points out that unique and
intense object cathexes are not typical of marriages in preliterate societies.
They are also not typical in complex societies where marriages are arranged
by parents or go-betweens. He suggests that Jimmy Picard was attempting to
give up theories about love and return to the realities of Wolf marriage. What
the patient was saying was not that business partnerships resemble love
relationships, but rather that love relationships resemble business partnerships. A misunderstanding of this point would lead one to overestimate the
homosexual aspect of his associations. There was certainly a homosexual
component, but given Wolf attitudes toward love and marriage, it would be a
mistake to give the same emphasis to the homosexual comparison that one
would certainly give to the case of an American man (or a man in any society
that heavily emphasized romantic love) who linked together love for a
woman and a male business partnership. The difference, as Devereux pointed
out, is a quantitative one.

Most therapists think that Plains Indian cultures—or, for that matter, any
culture based on traditions very different from their own—are remote and
difficult to approach. However, Devereux's handling of Jimmy Picard's case
illustrates how a therapist can help a patient from such an unfamiliar culture
by understanding his communications, particularly through his dreams and
his associations to them. Although Jimmy Picard did a great deal of the
work himself in attempting to reach a solution to his conflicts, he was aided
not only by the therapist's respect for him but also by the therapist's understanding of the salient features in his background—the typical patterns of

Wolf reservation culture and the traumatic and idiosyncratic patterns of the patient.

DREAMS OF A CHINESE PATIENT

Lee was a Chinese patient whom one of the coauthors (Abel 1962) treated once a week over a period of six years. Through an intensive study of his dreams, the therapist wanted to show how the dream work of a Chinese patient reflects both his motivational patterns and conflicts, past and present, and the values associated with the specific life style of a Chinese man from rural south-central China who was in the process of adapting to professional life in a large American city.

Lee was in his thirties and married (a marriage arranged in China), but he had never lived with his wife. He had grown up in the large household of an extended family that lived in the traditional style of the rural gentry. Before coming to the United States he had been converted to Roman Catholicism, and when he came to this country he attended a Catholic college. After completing college, he went on to obtain a master's degree in psychology and became a professional psychologist. He chose to remain in the United States and become an American citizen.

This discussion is an attempt to show the extent to which dreams reflected Lee's cultural background as well as his adaptations to American life. The therapist's knowledge of certain patterns characteristic of traditional Chinese culture helped her to understand the latent meanings in the dream symbolism and thus perhaps facilitated working through the transference. (At first, the patient had perceived the therapist as a stupid woman trying to be masculine, a "white devil" who asked too many questions, a woman who should be fooled.)

Lee centered many of his feelings in his head. For example, he reported that he often ground his teeth in the night; in fact, he had recently woken up doing so. His paternal grandmother had told him that he had had this habit as a child. He said that in China a pig's tail placed in the mouth was a way of preventing tooth grinding. At that time, he could not associate to the meaning of the pig's tail, but the therapist suggested that it might have represented a penis. It is her hypothesis that the Chinese have a strong tendency to sexualize the head by transferring the penis upward. This may account for the oral character so often ascribed to the Chinese (Muensterberger 1951). Lee had two dreams in which various feelings were relegated to the head.

Dream 15, Session 22: At camp dreamed of blood. Don't know if my blood or not, from the nose. Don't know if it is me or not. Associations: lately had some trouble with nose. That night lots of people sneeze, have hay fever. Then remembered my roommate had blood coming out of nose. Afraid my nose would bleed, too. I have fears my penis having blood coming out or break whenever pressing with hard surface.

Later in therapy, Lee remarked that he was afraid of intercourse: to him it meant coming up against a hard surface with too small an opening. He also feared he would not have the strength to penetrate the vagina. Later, he vaguely recalled fear of a sister's menstrual blood. When he was fifteen, he had slept for a time in the same bed with his sister (she was then thirteen). He denied at the time having any sexual feelings for his sister. The blood dream also suggested possible homosexual fears. In associating further, Lee remembered dreaming about the laboratory technician at his hospital, toward whom he had felt hostility, although he could not tell why. He said that one of this technician's jobs was to "take blood" from patients. (In China there was a traditional ritual of close friends—always male—exchanging blood, however Lee did not bring this up.)

Much later in therapy, Lee had a second dream centering in the head.

Dream 68, Session 58: Dreamed of an elephant's nose. I'm in the elephant's nose or might be. Elephant throws me out. I escape, turn around and fly. Associations: Not frightened, can get away from authority. The elephant was my father (father born under elephant sign), but I was able to escape and felt free.

This dream illustrates the upward displacement of the male sexual organ (the elephant's trunk). Lee also had a number of dreams about upward displacement of female sexual organs, such as the mouth substituting for the vagina and long black hair for pubic hair.

In traditional Chinese thought, continual sexual activity weakens the male.[5] Lee had a dream that seemed to incorporate this idea.

Dream 58, Session 55: I was in a Chinese rickshaw and the chaplain of the hospital was trying to pull it. Hard to pull. I thought the chaplain was tired and I asked him. He said, "A little." I said, "That's all right, you tired, you run around with too many women."

This dream could just as well be a quotation from the Chinese novel *Rickshaw Boy* by L. Shaw (1945). In the novel, the rickshaw boy talks about work and sex: "I'm going to tell you one sentence of the truth: people who follow our profession should never get married. It's the truth. . . . Once you get married, in the deep of the dark night and the brightest day, as well, you have to spend yourself; and the time comes when you're played out." Lee must have felt that the chaplain was weakened by his sexual excesses, but he might also have envied him his sexual prowess. This supposition was confirmed later by a dream Lee had about the chaplain surrounded by girls.

From the tenth century until their partial liberation in the twentieth century, Chinese women had bound feet—manifestly to keep the women at home and subservient, but latently, we may surmise, to prevent the full growth of penis-like objects. The tiny bound foot of the gentlewoman was a common image in Chinese poetry. In Dream 85, Session 65, Lee reported that a woman was lying in bed and that she had a large penis. He also had several dreams about being sexually aroused by women's feet. In his home, his paternal grandmother, whose favorite he was, was the only member of the household with bound feet. Perhaps this grandmother, who had lavished so much attention and affection on Lee, had aroused sexual feelings in him that included feelings about her feet. In Session 51, Lee reported that he had recently visited the home of a middle-aged woman and had been attracted by her dress and her feet. At other times, he mentioned the large feet of American women—the therapist's, for example.

Thus we see how the Chinese draw attention to the head (upward movement) and to the feet (downward movement) and away from the sexual areas, the source of anxieties. This diversion is very striking in Chinese sculpture of the feminine figure, which focuses on the head, the hands, and the feet. Of course, such shifts take place in patients from other cultures, but for the Chinese, it appears to be a cultural regularity (illustrated by such things as shame, concentrated in the face, and a face-saving and libidinized attitude toward the woman's bound foot).[6] Finally, Lee reported a dream in which he attempted to overcome his oedipal struggle.

Dream 53, Session 52: I push a Chinese wheelbarrow over a hill (not far from my home), and evidently lose my direction which way I should go. At a moment, I am confronted with a man who also pushes a wheelbarrow, but in the opposite direction. He told me I should not go forward and pointed to me that behind him there were so many soldiers (Chinese bandit soldiers or defeated soldiers) in line. They would capture me, of course. I thank him so kindly. I gave him money from my chest. He refused to accept it. I return to my original place and hide in my house. However, I feel he is in danger, as the other soldiers do not like him. I try to hide him in my place, but could not find a suitable corner until I finally find a small place. The soldiers seem close, but in a magic way then, there is one tall soldier in front of me, who finally is cut into pieces. These pieces made different piles of meat and all the people are ready to eat. Somehow or other, I don't want to eat, as I realize this is human meat.

Associations: During the day before read passage from words of Jesus, "Ye, you eat my flesh and blood."

Although this dream contains several aspects, including transferential ones to the therapist, only the oral fantasy and Lee's association to it are relevant here. The dream fantasy suggests a totem feast, for the person who was cut up into piles of meat was a tall soldier (Lee's father was tall). Kardiner (1939) states that oral fantasies of this kind may represent a desire to consummate and perpetuate a relationship with the object of dependency or to destroy the object. In the dream, Lee was struggling with his dependency conflict; he was trying to push a wheelbarrow over a hill from home (gain independence and manhood), but he became confused as to where to go. Since there was danger, he returned to his home and hid. At home there was danger also, but he resorted in his fantasy to a cannibalistic feast, thus attempting to destroy the threatening aspect of the father image. Although Lee did not say he ate the human meat in the dream—he reported that he found the idea repugnant—his association to the dream was the ritual of the Catholic sacrament, in which "flesh and blood"—both of Christ and God, the Father—are eaten symbolically.

Apparently Lee derived some strength from the dream, for the same night he had a second dream in which General MacArthur came up to him first on a beach where many people were waiting. The general was wearing old clothes and looked like a Chinese fisherman. Lee then sailed out to sea in a much larger boat than that of the general. Lee said that in the dream the boats were rolling, but "I felt no fear whatsoever. . . . When I woke up, I was quite calm."

Shortly after having these dreams, Lee had his first heterosexual experience. He soon had feelings of greater sexual freedom. At the same time, he became more successful at his job and was able to pay the therapist a larger fee. (This was indicated in Dream 53, reported above, in which Lee tried to pay the man who helped him.) Lee was on the road to becoming a man—a person in his own right, who could look after himself. He was coping not only with his intrapsychic childhood conflict, but also with his problems of acculturation.

Dream studies show how many of an individual's psychodynamics—his struggle against dependency needs and for autonomy, sexual freedom, and freedom from guilt and shame—are related to his cultural values and his personal idiosyncratic emphases and, as well, to values that are transcultural and universal.

Ten

Training in Cross-Cultural Therapy

The demand for culturally oriented therapeutic skills is steadily increasing. Worldwide communication, whether spelled out in the media or embodied in the artifacts of everyday life, deeply affect the lives even of those who live in relatively remote societies. In the United States, young Native Americans from many conservative tribes, young Hispanic-Americans and members of other ethnic groups that have hitherto lived somewhat apart now have moved into the mainstream; blacks and women demand the right and actively seek to enter virtually every field. Around the world, people are moving from one country to another as strangers in search of education and training, work, or simply another place to live. Above all there are the foreign workers, many of whom expect to return home soon or some day, and the refugees who have little choice in coming and little hope of returning. Their children, born in a society strange to their parents, may try to live simultaneously in two worlds. All these migrants and their children affect the lives of those among whom they now live, and they themselves may have almost unsurmountable difficulties adapting to a slightly familiar and yet an unknown way of life.

Therapists, too, are asked to go abroad as consultants, educators, and practitioners, particularly in the newer countries among peoples of whom they may know little or nothing. Yet most professionals must acquire the skills necessary to meet the demands of cross-cultural therapy on their own initiative. There are, of course, those therapists who choose not to take into account basic differences in cultural values, beliefs, and modes of thought

196

and behavior. Their choice is either to fit the patient or the client into their own partly recognized—or unrecognized—value system and overall cultural orientation or else to refuse to treat the person as someone "not suitable" for psychotherapy. Others, however, beginning with the generation of therapists who have practiced in the United States (and elsewhere) but who were reared and trained in Europe, have made a different and more difficult choice: they have come face-to-face with patients and clients reared in a culture—or version of a culture—different from their own. They have had to take what little was available in the clinical and research literature, call on their own cross-cultural experiences, and plunge in.

There is everywhere a shortage of training facilities for cross-cultural therapy, and the current training models are not yet fully adequate in depth or scope. There is, moreover, a shortage of professors trained and experienced in cross-cultural therapy on staff in standard teaching programs in psychiatry, psychology, and social work. Consequently, therapists in training must continue to make do with a combination of self-training, sporadic supervision, and consultation and discussion in workshops with colleagues who have given thought to and are working in cross-cultural areas.

The "psychotherapy" part of "cross-cultural psychotherapy" is not the problematic part. Training programs, while not perfect, are indeed geared to offer training and supervision in psychotherapy. Courses, seminars, supervision, a standard bibliography, and adequate training models are all available in good training programs. It is the "cross-cultural" part that is inadequate. There are some good programs available today, but these programs do not yet address the needs of the vast majority of practitioners and students. There are, however, some new aids.

First, there are newer texts, such as the *Handbook of Cross-Cultural Psychology,* edited by Triandis and Berry (1980). But even this extensive handbook does not—and cannot—address every relevant issue and certainly not every culture that may be important for the student of cross-cultural therapy. There is also a growing number of texts that offer some guidance to the cross-cultural practitioner: for example, Tseng and McDermott (1981), Jones and Korchin (1982), Marsella and Pedersen (1981), Sue and others (1981), Romanucci-Ross, Moerman and Tancredi (1982), and Walz and Benjamin (1978). Information is also becoming increasingly available in such journals as the *Journal of Cross-Cultural Psychology,* the *American Journal of Social Psychiatry,* the *International Social Science Journal,* and the *International Journal of Psychology.*

Anthropological journals contain accounts of current research and reviews of books that present much longer, more rounded, detailed discussions of contemporary cultures and special topics. In recent years, these journals have also included reviews of films that present visual data so necessary for those who are not acquainted with distant parts of the world or with the peoples with whom anthropologists work, both here and abroad. These journals include the *American Anthropologist,* the *American Ethnologist, Current Anthropology* (which contains articles by anthropologists of many nationalities), *Ethos* (the journal of the Society for Psychological Anthropology), *Anthropology and Humanism* (Journal of the Society for Humanistic Anthropology), and *Journal of Psychoanalytic Anthropology.* Occasionally, articles of special interest may also be found in *Human Organization* (the journal of the Society for Applied Anthropology).

It is more likely now that practitioners who are willing to do some research in the literature will find basic studies of the cultural group in which they are interested and perhaps clinical information as well. Nevertheless, it is still difficult to find information about the very specific cultural group and version of that culture to which a patient belongs. For example, general information about Latin Americans is not likely to be very relevant to the patient from Colombia. Not all information about Colombians will be relevant to the Colombian from the rural areas of the Pacific Coast, and not all information about Colombians from the Pacific Coast will be relevant to the Colombian who moved to the United States ten years ago, married a Jewish woman from the Bronx, and now lives in California.

Spiegel and Papajohn (1983) devised a system called "proximate differentiation" to coordinate cross-cultural information. According to this approach, the therapist finds research and other data (not excluding competent fiction by members of the culture) on the smallest relevant group on which there is available information, and then moves on to the next larger group, and so on. In our example, there is not likely to be information about Colombians from the Pacific Coast who marry women from the Bronx, but there is likely to be information about Colombians from different regions of Colombia and about Colombians in general; and, of course, there is a vast literature on Latin American society. At that point we must turn to community resources and to the patient himself to help us refine and correct the information available in the literature and research.

Most training in cross-cultural therapy will probably continue to take place outside the context of programs in the major disciplines. However, growing resources will modify the difficulties faced by the self-taught student and therapist. Increased sensitivity to culture as learned behavior, increased information about members of specific cultures, embedded subcultures, and ethnic groups, as well as an emphasis on actual value systems and clashes between and within value systems—all these can markedly increase the capacity of the therapist to work productively with patients and clients. Furthermore, an acquaintance with the research on culturally specific psychopathology and with the role of cultural factors in all psychopathology will increase the therapist's awareness of significant variations in the parameters of therapy. Acquiring skill in these and other aspects of cross-cultural psychotherapy are the therapist's self-training tasks.

Organized Training Programs

Even though practitioners will continue to self-train, systematic growth of the field, opportunities to evaluate specific components of training for cross-cultural therapy, encouragement and funding of research and the establishment of cross-cultural psychotherapy depends in large measure on organized programs. At this stage of development, programs should be diverse: they should vary considerably in intensity, diversity of cultural groups, treatment focus, and degree of closeness to the core training in traditional mental health fields like psychology and psychiatry.

One of the earliest training programs in cross-cultural psychotherapy was begun in the 1960s by one of the psychologist coauthors (Abel) and the anthropologist coauthor (Metraux) at the Postgraduate Center for Mental Health in New York City. They offered a two-hour-a-week course which was required of second-year candidates in psychoanalysis and psychoanalytic psychotherapy. Some candidates came from countries other than the United States; parents of others had immigrated from Europe or elsewhere; and there were Black Americans in the group.

Trainees were asked to write their personal culture histories: where they had grown up, where their parents had come from, and which different cultures or versions of American culture they had been exposed to. Keeping this information in mind, the anthropologist coauthor lectured on culture as defined in contemporary ethnology, emphasizing interpersonal relationships and American national character structure as a basis for discussion of case material from other cultures.

Trainees brought in cases from their practices in which they were having difficulties understanding a patient's beliefs, attitudes, and ideas. Among the questions raised was whether a patient resisted an interchange with the therapist for some reason related to the patient's own cultural expectations. One therapist wondered whether he, a conservative Jew, could help an older woman who was an ardent, practicing Catholic. Here the question was whether the therapist felt threatened by a woman the same age as his mother or whether he found her beliefs hard to accept.

Each year, several trainees were invited to volunteer for an intensive anthropological interview. These interviews served to give all the trainees more specific insights into both content and technique. Interest ran high when Jewish trainees from several different European backgrounds discovered that ritual language (which they shared) was, in each case, interpreted differently in behavior. Class discussion focused on the problem of how to work out the significance of a communication, verbal or nonverbal, by a patient from a culture unfamiliar to the therapist.

Koss and Canive (1982) give a course on family therapy with Hispanic-Americans in the psychiatry department of the University of New Mexico School of Medicine to mental health workers in the three basic disciplines, psychiatry, psychology, and social work. Koss and Canive select a few trainees with long experience in both Hispanic-American and American cultures; some of these are "just" Americans and some are Hispanic-Americans (that is, they were brought up in more traditional, Spanish-speaking homes).

Koss and Canive explain to the trainees certain important characteristics of Hispanic-American culture: the father is the authority both within and outside the home; the mother is the submissive one ("la sufrida"). Family interdependence stretches over three or more generations, and parental control and respect for elders are very important. Several topics, especially sex, cannot be discussed across generations or among strangers. Finally, it is explained that it takes time to gain the confidence of the family so that therapy can proceed.

The comparative method is used as the principal teaching technique. For example, a comparison is made of the different developmental tasks in the family life cycle among American-Hispanics and among members of the dominant American culture. Trainees are taught how to make both culturally syntonic and culturally asyntonic interpretations so as to understand more completely the cultural patterns sanctioned in these two sets of family relations. For the Hispanic-Americans, an important problem is the rift growing between the generations as young American-Hispanics emulate the behavior of American youth. Both trainees and trainers are encouraged to share descriptions of their immediate families and their families of origin. All find it easier to report on their families of origin than on their immediate families. This exercise helps each participant to understand the various aspects of culture that may help or impede a therapist attempting to understand family dynamics.

Several mental health professionals have attempted to coordinate the work of modern, professional practitioners with that of native healers (see especially Ruiz and Langrod 1976; Weidman 1978). Koss (1980) describes a training program in which a meaningful exchange of information took place between professional practitioners of psychotherapy and spiritist healers in Puerto Rico. In this program, three separate groups were seen for six hours a week over a ten-month period (thirty-six sessions). The core participants in the three groups (each from a different area of Puerto Rico) included, among the psychotherapists, twenty-two women and twelve men who were, by discipline, psychiatrists, psychologists, social workers, mental health workers, graduate nurses, and psycho-social technicians. Among the spiritists there were twenty-five women and eleven men; housewives predominated, but there were also clerks, retired school teachers, an auto-repair man, a taxi driver, and a lawyer, among others. Several onlookers—clergymen, physicians and others—were also included.

The weekly program consisted of one lecture each by a professional and a spiritist leader, followed by discussion. Lectures were interspersed with discussions throughout the training period. Many topics were covered, including anthropological perspectives on traditional and modern health systems; diagnosis and problem definitions in psychiatry, psychology, social work, and spiritism; physiological bases of emotional disorders and psychosomatic illnesses; and the use of pharmaceutical drugs and herbs. Initially there was skepticism among and suspicion between the therapists and healers. However, during the social hours, the participants became acquainted and gained confidence in one another.

Many cases were discussed, and the groups referred cases to each other. The therapists, including the psychiatrists, sent a few difficult cases to the spiritists. The spiritists, in turn, referred a few cases to the mental health center. A small number of participants in each group also came to individuals in the opposite group for therapy. For example, one spiritist woman felt she could be helped by a marriage counselor, and a severely psychotic woman was sent by a psychiatrist to a woman spiritist, who was able to get the patient to manage her life outside the hospital setting.

The resistance of therapists trained under the modern medical system was considerably modified by exposure to a system they had considered unscientific, erroneous, and old-fashioned. From an evaluation of the data on two of the three groups (data on the third group were not fully analyzed at the time of publication), it appeared that in quite a number of cases, the therapists recognized some value in cooperating with the spiritists. The spiritists, in turn, felt that they had learned much through their training and now better understood the concepts and services of mental health teams; to a degree, they believed that these services could help some of their clients and even themselves.

In the late 1970s, a very different program was developed at Brandeis University by Spiegel and Papajohn (1983), which was funded by a training grant from the National Institute of Mental Health. The program's aim was to train candidates from traditional programs in psychiatry, clinical psychology, and social work within an interdisciplinary format. The training model was based on an articulated set of principles.

One principle was that of proximate differentiation (see p. 198). This principle recognizes that we do not now have and never will have fully accurate, up-to-date information on the relevant aspects of all cultural groups and subgroups to which patients may belong. The technique calls first for an exploration of existing information on the most proximate group on which accurate information exists. Thereafter, it calls for extrapolation from this information, from the candidates' own fields of research and, together with the help of information provided by supervisors and cultural informants, from information given by the patients themselves.

Spiegel and Papajohn also incorporated into their training the principle of structural variation based on the work of Kluckhohn (Kluckhohn and Strodtbeck 1961). This technique attempts to view a cultural group—or to compare two cultural groups—within a neutral framework. For example, the American middle class (members of the version of American culture to which the trainees belong or to which they aspire) and another cultural group may be compared in terms of a set of value orientations. In regard to time, for instance, members of the American middle class emphasize the future, place less emphasis on the present, and place even less emphasis on the past. In contrast, Irish patients served by Spiegel and Papajohn were oriented primarily to the present, less to the past, and least to the future. Thematic comparisons of this kind in terms of activity, relationship to others, relationship to the natural world, and the basic structure of man provide a simplified technique for delineating certain contrasting aspects of different cultures. (See Table 1, Chapter 8, p. 157.)

Most training, however, will continue to take place in traditional post-graduate training centers, where there are many demands for service but as many limitations set by the accepted structure of standard programs. Accepting this restriction, Spiegel and Papajohn (1983) incorporated their program into the standard program by giving it a low profile; that is, a deliberate effort was made to keep the new program from interfering with other demands for service and training. Because cross-cultural training was meant to be an aid and not an additional responsibility, training was carried out, as far as possible, in the context of actual clinical work. Only after the clinical usefulness of cross-cultural training had been accepted were seminars and workshops added.

Like other training programs in cross-cultural psychotherapy, this one is essentially interdisciplinary in its organization. Spiegel and Papajohn take the position that the several professions can both benefit from and contribute to the training. Characteristically, those professionals who are interested in cross-cultural training are more eager than their colleagues disciplines to engage in open and innovative interdisciplinary work.

Still another training model has been developed by members of the Department of Psychology at the University of Hawaii in conjunction with the Institute of Behavioral Sciences and the East-West Cultural Learning Institute (Marsella and Pedersen 1981). In addition to the disciplines usually represented (psychiatry, psychology, and social work), this program includes personnel from public health, nursing, and the humanities. The program, entitled Developing Interculturally Skilled Counselors, involves a minimum of one year's training and includes formal course work in cultural psychology, culturally attuned psychopathology, diagnosis, and treatment.

The program is unique in several respects. It is closely tied to therapy techniques developed by one of the trainers (Pedersen 1977), rather than to psychoanalytic therapy (as at the Postgraduate Center for Mental Health) or to a version of behavioral therapy (as in the Spiegel and Papajohn program). The program has also trained many practitioners from Asia, Hawaii, and Samoa. The participants are strongly motivated to communicate their skills to others by organizing workshops on intercultural skills at other agencies in the Hawaiian islands and at various locations in the South Pacific.

We feel strongly that all training programs for cross-cultural therapy should take into account LeVine's approach discussed in Chapter 6, "Attitudes toward Therapy." He takes the position (assumed as a matter of course by contemporary anthropological fieldworkers) that within any culture or version of a culture there is a wide range in the acceptance (and in the denial) of any cultural belief, value, and mode of behavior among the members of the cultural group. One person may give only lip service to certain modes of behavior in the culture in which he was raised—for example, the idea that the father is the dominant member of the family or that it is a disgrace to discuss family problems with outsiders, except a priest. In contrast, another member of the same culture may adhere strictly to the norms prescribed by the culture. In all cultures, modifications of norms are known and accepted under circumstances that are also culturally defined. Moreover, it is essential to recognize that rejection of accepted values and modes of thought and behavior by a full member of a culture—or version of a culture—is nevertheless not random but closely related to the central core of values and their expressions in thought and behavior in that culture. In working in individual, marital, and group therapy, it is essential that the therapist be aware of and sensitive to both the range of cultural norms and the possibilities and circumstances of acceptable modifications of those norms. Therapists are fully aware that patients have their own intrapsychic and interpersonal conflicts, but the extent to which a particular individual adheres to or deviates from recognized cultural norms—and tolerates some measure of adherence and deviance in others—is often overlooked.

Long strides have been made in the last decade in the field of cross-cultural psychotherapy as evidenced in the emergence of some training programs and in the increased publication of research, handbooks, and new journals. However, acceptance of training in cross-cultural psychotherapy as an intrinsic part of a standard training program is still in the future. Those who support the new field of cross-cultural therapy have had to work against the sometimes open but often covert resistance to and rejection of cross-cultural perspectives by those who have an interest in retaining traditional training programs. The helping professions continue to be isolated from the field of contemporary anthropology. Individuals—and whole groups—are afflicted with covert, and sometimes overt, ethnocentricity. This resistance slows the development of the training programs that would, in time, alleviate the shortage of professionals in the relevant disciplines who are able and willing to conduct training in, and the practice of, cross-cultural psychotherapy.

We are living in a time of transition—a time of unprecedented social crisis of global proportions. Obviously, students of culture cannot pose as saviors; researchers and therapists alike must continually strive to combat their own rescue fantasies. At the same time, students of culture, and especially practitioners of cross-cultural psychotherapy, have a responsibility to champion the struggle against cultural stereotypes, sexism, racism, and ethnocentrism. Above all, they must combat the static, absolutist, and dangerously comfortable conservative conceptions of our own culture and the cultures of all the other inhabitants of this small spinning planet.

Notes

Chapter 2

1 A great deal has been, and continues to be, written on the question of the biological aspects of human diversity, matching the flood of new, important data. Unfortunately, the scientists chiefly concerned cannot yet settle on a mutually satisfactory descriptive term or set of terms which the layman in this field could safely use. Some wish to retain the term "race" in a new frame of reference; others wish to discard it altogether. Still others suggest that its use be confined to a sociocultural context, to stand for people's (former? contemporary? confused?) social designations. Where these differences arise, it is necessary to state one's own position. For discussion, see Alland (1971) Harris (1968) and Mead, Dobzhansky, Tobach, and Light (1968).

2 See Birdwhistell (1970) and the chapters on choreometrics in Lomax (1978); both contain extensive bibliographies. See also Lomax and Pauley (1976), a film on dance and body motion.

3 Lowenfeld (1954) includes illustrations from various cultures, but the book was published before the Mosaic test was widely used for field research. See especially Abel (1981) for a comparison of performance on the Mosaic Test and the Kaleidoblocs among high school Pueblo Indians in New Mexico, and Abel (1984) for a study of psychodynamics as reflected in the Mosaic Test among university students in five cultures.

4 See Mead (1953) for a discussion of work with a single format.

5 Based on fieldwork among the Eastern Iatmul, a middle Sepik River people, in 1967–68, 1971, 1972–73, and brief visits in 1979 and 1983, by Rhoda Metraux; for a study of Iatmul culture and personality a generation earlier, see Bateson (1958).

6 *Four Families,* produced and directed by Ian McNeill and narrated by Margaret Mead (1959), is a pioneer film in the visual presentation of multi-cultural data. There is a rapidly growing corpus of such films on many cultures, often filmed during fieldwork, and as simple movie and video cameras have become available, they are also being put into the hands of those who are the subject of study so they may record from their own visual and time perspective.

7 See, for example, the earlier work of the French philosopher, Levy-Bruhl ([1910] 1985); according to his theory, primitive, in contrast to civilized, thought was "prelogical," that is (in computer terminology), analogical, not digital. But in a volume of notes published post-humously (1949), he appeared finally to have rejected the theory of differences of kind in mentality. See also Chapter 3.

8 See Eglar (1960) for a discussion of caste identity and the interdependence of castes in a Muslim community in Pakistan; Carstairs (1967) has analyzed personality aspects of caste identity in an Indian community.

9 Yoors (1967) gives a nontechnical but insightful picture of gypsy life as seen through the eyes of a Belgian artist who spent most of his adolescence traveling with a gypsy band.

Among the best known of the dissenting religious groups in Europe from the early sixteenth century were the Anabaptists (Swiss Brethren), three of whose descendant religious groups (Hutterites, Amish and Mennonites) are represented in the United States; see Bennett (1967), Eaton and Weil (1955), Hostetler (1968), Hostetler and Huntington (1967), and Smith (1950).

On the East European Jewish cultural community, which bridged several national boundaries, see Zborowski and Herzog (1962).

10   See Leichter and Mitchell (1978) and Mitchell (1978) for an analysis of the Jewish family circle and cousin club, a contemporary kin-based social group which appears to have originated in New York after the turn of the century.

11   The prototype and, up to the present, the most detailed photographic study is one of Balinese adult–child interaction and adult–child parallels made by Gregory Bateson, analyzed by Bateson and Mead in *Balinese Character* (1942) and by Mead and Macgregor in *Growth and Culture* (1951). See also related films by Bateson and Mead, *A Balinese Family, Childhood Rivalry in Bali and New Guinea, Bathing Babies in Three Cultures,* and *Karba's First Years* (1952a–d).

12   For discussions of the child in the German family, see Metraux (1955a, 1955c and 1955d). On France, see Metraux and Mead (1954) and also Soddy (1955), which contains comparative material on infancy in France, Great Britain, and the United States. But a younger generation of parents in these countries has reacted strongly against traditional modes of rearing in handling their own children and new studies are needed to take into account and to compare these changes.

13   For a discussion of the way in which French models of the teacher–pupil relationship and of adult reciprocal relations enter into and provide a key to French attitudes toward Franco–American relations in the 1950s, see Dillon (1968).

14   On the question of redundance in culture and the relation of deviance to the model, see the section on "End Linkage: An Analytical Approach," in Mead and Metraux (1953), particularly the discussion by Bateson, pp. 367–78.

15   The principal evaluation of Ruth Benedict's work is found in Mead (1959a). Two early field work approaches to problems of culture and personality are Mead (1935), in which cultural definitions of masculinity and femininity are explored, and Bateson and Mead (1942), in which the process of enculturation and redundancy in the statement of cultural themes are explored photographically. See also Mead (1972) for a further discussion of Benedict's conception of temperamental fit and the exploration of this in Mead's field work.

16   See Metraux and Abel (1957) for a discussion of deviance in one culture, that of peasant Montserrat in the West Indies, as seen from the viewpoint of members of the culture, the anthropologist and the clinical psychologist.

17   George Devereux (1961:260–85) presents illuminating material on this type of deviance among the Mohave in his discussion of deviant children whose particular "pattern of misconduct" marks them as either budding shamans or transvestites, and whose delinquent behavior "cannot therefore be controlled, either by an act of will on the part of the child, or by familial and/or social pressures. 'It is his nature, he cannot help it.'" Devereux suggests that "the conflicts of the future shaman are rooted in the unconscious segment of his 'ethnic personality' and differ from those of other individuals only in their intensity" and that, as a shaman, such an individual does not have to develop other idiosyncratic symptoms. See particularly Devereux's supporting case material.

18   The autobiographical account by Evelyn West Ayrault (1963) of her rearing as a child afflicted with cerebral palsy illustrates the point. The unremittingly rigid physical training by

her Marine officer father on the model of a Marine recruit and, in later years, the difficulty the parents had in acknowledging the autonomy they had worked so hard to foster, as well as the young woman's own difficulties in making a life of her own, demonstrate the interrelated responses of parent and child in such circumstances.

19   Based on research by the anthropologist co-author on the rearing and education of the blind and the deaf child in Great Britain, France, and the United States. For an unusual book addressed to the parents of handicapped American children, see Mitchell (1982).

20   In anthropological field work it is not unusual to find individuals whose talents are given little, if any, formal recognition in their culture and who may discover a congenial role in particular types of informant relations with fieldworkers. Thus, in a culture in which there is little interest in abstraction, an individual with a very high capacity for abstraction may very rapidly learn to become a sophisticated linguistic informant (see Mead 1968b).

21   Based on field studies in Haiti (see Rhoda Metraux 1951 and, on Voodoo, Alfred Metraux 1959).

22   This is based on unpublished field observations of the anthropologist co-author. A full analysis of a culture must, of course, include what is overtly rejected as well as the forms through which the rejection is given expression. On the question of the negation of manifest patterns and central values, see Devereux (1967, especially pp. 212ff.).

Chapter 3

1   In the considerable literature on the subject of drug use by members of the armed forces during the war in Vietnam no special point has been made of the fact that, in addition to the knowledge about and easy availability of almost innumerable over-the-counter drugs intended to relieve pain, modify tension, cure a host of minor ailments, induce or overcome sleepiness, and so on, it was also common knowledge that chemotherapy had become the treatment of choice for the alleviation of various forms of mental disturbance.

2   See especially Spencer and Gillen (1899). It is worth noting that Spencer, while at Oxford, studied under E. B. Tylor, but in fact was trained—and first went on an expedition to Central Australia in 1894—as a zoologist. Gillen, who already had twenty years' experience in Australia when he met Spencer there, was a station master of the transcontinental telegraph and a "subprotector" of the local aborigines, with whose language and way of life he had gained some familiarity (Stocking 1983). This greatly facilitated the field research carried out by Spencer and Gillen; their work, in turn, made possible the detailed analysis of kinship and marriage carried out by Malinowski ([1913] 1963) before he himself had done fieldwork. It was the initially slow accumulation of precise data and modern kinds of analysis that transformed older conceptions about so-called primitive peoples.

3   A large body of ethnographic data exists on the Indians of the area. On the problem of windigo, see Cooper (1933, 1934), Hallowell (1934, 1936, 1938, and 1976b) and Landes (1938 and 1961) of which the former is a summary article that outlines the immediate cultural context of windigo beliefs, but not within the wider area context. Teicher (1960) and Fogelson (1965) have published summary data, but fail to state that their interpretations are based on secondhand accounts, a fact corroborated by Hallowell (personal communication). Brown (1971) refutes a hypothesis that links nutrition to the causes and occasional cures of the windigo psychosis; Hay (1971) attempts to place the windigo victim's desire to eat human flesh within a wider context of ritual cannibalism, drawing on selected literature.

4　This discussion is based on unpublished field data recorded by the anthropologist co-author.

5　Four years later, at a period when there had been an unusual number of deaths in the community, it was whispered about that there was, after all, a sorcerer in the village, but no direct accusation was made.

6　See also, for example, the summary article on Bali by Ketter (1983), which is valuable both for its concise statements about Balinese personality and Balinese cultural categorizations of mental disturbance and for a brief description of the contemporary medical organization, including traditional as well as Western-trained personnel. Ketter provides an extensive bibliography.

Chapter 4

1　For a recent thorough study of Freud and the early influences on the development of his ideas as well as criticisms of these ideas, see Wallace (1983).

2　Here we shall deal chiefly with the Oedipus complex as it affects the boy, since this has been the focus of most discussions and conflicts about the universality of the phenomenon. In fact, of course, cultural differences in the ways in which a girl strives for self and sex identity (e.g., penis envy) are equally important.

3　As is well known today, parents may communicate one set of values to their children verbally, such as "sex is fun," while nonverbally they may express the opposite, owing to such factors as their own upbringing or the values they believe to exist in their society, as exemplified by what neighbors will say, social custom, the dictates of religious groups, oral tradition, folklore, and so on.

4　Malinowski's fieldwork and his evolving theoretical position have been widely discussed. For discussions of his work and a representative bibliography of his own publications, see Firth (1960), Metraux (1968), Stocking (1983) and Weiner (1976).

5　See Malinowski (1953, 1954, 1962) for statements of his own position as taken as early as 1916 and as late as 1927 and 1929. For recent comments, see Spiro (1982), who reinterprets Trobriand data to challenge Malinowski's argument with regard to the Oedipus complex; see also Weiner's (1985) critique of Spiro in the light of her more specialized knowledge of Trobriand culture.

6　Van Gennep's *The Rites of Passage* (1960, first published in French in 1909) is the classic study of ritual. Whiting, Kluckhohn, and Anthony (1958) discuss psychodynamic factors in male initiation rites in various cultures. See Allen (1967) for a critique of older analyses of initiation and other ceremonies; and for articles on, discussion of, and references to a wide range of male rituals of initiation in Papua New Guinea and elsewhere, see the articles in Herdt (1982b) as well as the editor's preface and the introduction by Keesing in the same volume. See also Tuzin (1980) whose analysis of the secret men's cult of the Ilahita Arapesh, a Papua New Guinea people, places initiation rites in a global context.

7　From a presentation by George Devereux, 1962, The Post-Graduate Center for Mental Health, New York.

8　Melanie Klein (Klein, Heinemann, and Money-Kyrle 1957) considered that the Oedipal struggle and superego development begin in the first months of infancy; this is a different concept from that under discussion here.

Chapter 5

1   The full research records of this program, Columbia University Research in Contemporary Cultures, and successor projects, are now located in the Margaret Mead archive, Manuscript Division, Library of Congress. See Mead and Metraux, eds. (1953); also Metraux (1980).

2   One set of records of this research, based on 100 China-born Chinese life histories carried out 1954–1957, are located in the Margaret Mead archive, Manuscript Division, Library of Congress.

3   Many French Canadians have migrated to the United States, settling primarily in New England. This group is not included here. See Langlier (1982) French Canadian Families.

4   This was found to be true also among the Greek-Americans in the United States. They often returned to Greece, where they had to teach people living in Athens how to do the traditional dances. See Abel and Major (1981).

5   The Institute of Anthropos in Athens, headed by George and Vassou Vassiliou, finds that Athenians are not reluctant to come for therapy for their children, for themselves, and for the whole family.

6   Thomas and Znaniecki wrote about Polish peasants. Mondykowski does not mention this, nor does he state from which socioeconomic level the Polish-American families he discusses came.

Chapter 6

1   Personal communication in Beirut, 1967, to one of the psychologist coauthors (Abel).

2   Some of these students came from villages where a woman never appeared in public with her head uncovered. Unmarried girls were strictly chaperoned and were never seen with a male companion or suitor. In 1965, a student spotted his sister as she walked, bareheaded, on the boardwalk in Beirut in the company of a young man. Later he beheaded her and returned to his native village carrying her head. The villagers considered his course was the correct one.

3   One of the authors (Abel) received a communication from the brother of a psychiatric nurse, Leila Farhood, in Beirut. He had talked to his sister on the telephone from the United States in January, 1984, and reported that she, despite the continuing warfare, was still running an outpatient mental health clinic at the American Hospital. Nasr, Racy, and Flaherty (1983) described the effects of the 1975–76 civil war in Lebanon. Admissions to psychiatric hospitals decreased considerably, as did office consultations, during the war. But there was an increase in admissions of patients with psychiatric complaints to general hospitals, where the care was generally minimal. This shift was perhaps due to the stigma attached to entering a psychiatric hospital while the civil war continued. After the war, the number of patients entering psychiatric hospitals increased. There were many psychiatric complaints, including insomnia, depression, and gastrointestinal disturbances due to post-traumatic effect. Office consultation increased considerably, apparently because there had recently been much more open discussion of psychiatric issues in the media.

4   For a thorough discussion of attitudes toward treatment in various socioeconomic groups, see S. L. Sharma, *The Therapeutic Dialogue* (1986).

Chapter 7

1 The words *psychotherapy* and *psychotherapist* are used frequently here to include psycho-analysis and the psychoanalyst. When a specific form of treatment is referred to, the appropriate terms will be used.

2 For a review of different kinds of psychiatric treatment in less economically developed countries, see Kiev (1964) and Romanucci-Ross, Moerman, and Tancredi (1982).

3 In recent years, several publications have appeared that discuss the Morita method and its modifications; see, for example, Caudill (1959), Caudill and Doi (1966), Jacobson and Berenberg (1952), Kondo (1953), and Mivra and Usa (1970).

4 See the films Bateson and Mead, *Bathing Babies in Three Cultures* (1952b) and McNeill, *Four Families* (1959).

5 But the timing may vary. For example, the French, who do not encourage the infant to explore, emphasize fine tactile learning at an age when Americans teach children large muscle control (in nursery school and kindergarten).

6 Comprehensive and sophisticated research has been carried out in the larger field of kinesics, the study of body-motion communication (Birdwhistell 1970). Through the use of films and tapes it is possible to make microanalyses of combined body movement and speech. Such studies include a worldwide comparative study of styles of body-motion patterning using the choreometric methods developed by Alan Lomax and his associates (Lomax 1978, Chapters 10–12 and Lomax and Pauley 1976) as well as various studies, in progress, using sound film and, more recently, video tape, concerned with communication in the therapeutic process (Scheflen 1965). Research of this kind is being brought together under the general title of kinesics, a discipline concerned with the total communication process (Sebeok, Hayes, and M. C. Bateson 1964; see also the bibliography in Birdwhistell 1970).

7 The reader may be interested in the discussion by Jungreis and Speik (1965), of the case of an Orthodox Jewish family (parents and a schizophrenic son in his twenties) who were treated, in family therapy, in their own home. The son attempted to control his parents by means of religious rituals. He was reinforced in his practices by an outside physician who also used Jewish Orthodoxy in a compulsive way. The fact that one of the cotherapists was interested in, and believed in, Orthodox Judaism made it possible for him to identify the points at which the son's pathology (as well as that of the parents) distorted particular religious practices.

8 Diaz-Guerrero (1955) has discussed this subject (a virile male has *muchos huevos* in his testicles) and other topics, including how fathers feel about having a baby daughter, what is said about girls' intellectual ambitions and so on.

9 In this connection, see also Wolfenstein (1955), in which she compares French and American children on the basis of observations of French children at play and of adult controls over children's play.

Chapter 8

1 Kluckhohn and Strodtbeck (1961) carry the analysis of value orientation further and present an analysis of the value constellations of the people in five contiguous but culturally distinct communities in the southwestern United States. Kluckhohn refers to a sixth problem, orientation in space, which was not studied but which she suggests is also a universal problem.

2   But efforts by social scientists to create a context for better understanding go back to the 1930s, in such studies as those carried out by Dollard (1937) and by Davis, Gardner, and Gardner (1941).

3   Minuchin and his collaborators (1967) were able to get several lower-class Puerto Rican and black families in New York into therapy. They also spelled out recommendations for conducting family therapy.

4   See also Devereux (1961), a study of the Mohave, and Devereux (1969) for the full account of the therapy of a Plains Indian patient, in which the author deals at greater length with these and other topics.

5   It is characteristic of caste societies that each caste incorporates (as a negative) the enjoined behavior of other castes. For a discussion of this aspect of caste relationships see Carstairs (1967).

Chapter 9

1   In the REM stage there can also be physiological manifestations of dreaming (changes in pulse and respiration rates, blood pressure, muscle tone and, in males, erection). For a discussion of REM sleep, see especially Aserinsky and Kleitman (1953) and Dement and Kleitman (1957a, 1957b).

2   Róheim has written extensively on this topic; see especially *Gates of the Dream* (1952b). See also the discussion in Fisher, "Psychoanalytic Implications of Recent Research on Sleep and Dreaming" (1965).

3   Among the Polynesian Tikopia, dreaming of feces was understood to predict a good catch of fish, that is, wealth. See Firth (1934).

4   This idea is discussed in many ethnographic monographs, but the classic analysis was made by Ruth Benedict in "The Concept of the Guardian Spirit in North America" (1923).

5   Actually, anxiety did not center on sexual activity per se, but on the loss of semen—a very ancient Chinese idea. See Needham's discussion (1956) of conceptions of sex and sexual practices in early Taoism (pp. 146ff.) and in Chinese Tantrism (pp. 428–29).

6   Personal communication from a Polish physician who worked in rural areas of central China before World War II who described his experiences in examining the older women. These women were willing to expose the whole of their bodies, except their feet, to the physician. Their feet remained bound in rags.

References

Abel, T. M. 1958. "The Szondi Profile of the Negro Peasants of Montserrat, B.W.I.," *Szondi Newsletter*, 6:3–9.

———— 1960. "Differential Responses to Projective Testing in a Negro Peasant Community: Montserrat, B.W.I.," *International Journal of Social Psychology*, 6:218–24.

———— 1962. "The Dreams of a Chinese Patient," *Psychoanalytic Study of Society*, 2:280–309.

———— 1978. "Introducing Family Therapy in Iran," *Transnational Mental Health Research Newsletter*, 20:1–8.

———— 1981. "A Comparison of Two-Dimensional and Tri-Dimensional Designs of High School Pueblo American Indians in New Mexico," *Transnational Mental Health Research Newsletter*, 22:9–15.

———— 1982. "Teaching Increased Skills in Crosscultural Psychotherapy," paper read at the Annual Meeting of the Society for the Study of Psychiatry and Culture, San Miguel Regla, Mexico.

———— 1984. "Psychodynamics as Reflected in the Lowenfeld Mosaic Test Among University Students in Five Cultures," *Hiroshima Forum for Psychology*, 9:3–16.

Abel, T. M., and F. L. K. Hsu 1949. "Some Aspects of Personality of Chinese as Revealed by the Rorschach Test," *Rorschach Research Exchange and Journal of Projective Techniques*, 13:285–301.

Abel, T. M., J. Belo and M. Wolfenstein 1954. "An Analysis of French Projective Tests," in *Themes in French Culture*, R. Metraux and M. Mead, eds. (Stanford, Calif.: Stanford University Press), pp. 109–18.

Abel, T. M., and R. Metraux 1959. "Sex Differences in a Negro Peasant Community, Montserrat, B.W.I.," *Journal of Projective Techniques*, 23:127–33.

Abel, T. M., and J. Major 1981. "Greeks in Albuquerque, New Mexico 1980–1981: A Pilot Study," *Transnational Mental Health Research Newsletter*, 23:6–9.

Adams, W. A. 1950. "The Negro Patient in Psychiatric Treatment," *American Journal of Orthopsychiatry*, 20:305–10.

Alland, A. 1971. *Human Diversity* (New York: Columbia University Press).

Allen, M. R. 1967. *Male Cults and Secret Initiations in Melanesia* (London and New York: Cambridge University Press).

American Journal of Social Psychiatry, Journal of American Association of Social Psychiatry.

American Anthropologist, Journal of the American Anthropological Association.

American Ethnologist, Journal of the American Ethnological Association.

Aries, P. 1962. *Centuries of Childhood: A Social History of Family Life*, R. Boldick, trans. (New York: Knopf).

Aserinsky, E., and N. Kleitman 1953. "Regularly Occurring Periods of Eye Motility and Concomitant Phenomena during Sleep," *Science*, 118:273–74.

Ayrault, E. W. 1963. *Take One Step* (Garden City, N.Y.: Doubleday).

Barbarin, O. A. 1984. "Racial Themes in Psychotherapy with Blacks: Effects of Training on the Attitudes of Black and White Psychiatrists," *The American Journal of Social Psychiatry,* 4:13–20.

Bateson, G. 1953. "Formulation of End Linkage," in *The Study of Culture at a Distance,* M. Mead and M. Metraux, eds. (Chicago: University of Chicago Press), pp. 367–78.

——— 1958. *Naven,* 2nd ed. (Stanford, Calif.: Stanford University Press). First edition 1936.

——— 1972. "Morale and National Character," in *Steps to an Ecology of Mind* (San Francisco: Chandler), pp. 88–106. First published in 1942.

Bateson, G., and M. Mead 1942. *Balinese Character: A Photographic Analysis* (New York: Special Publications of the New York Academy of Sciences), vol. 2.

——— 1952a. *A Balinese Family,* in *Character Formation in Different Cultures,* narrated by M. Mead, 16 mm, black and white, sound, 17 min. (New York: New York University Film Library).

——— 1952b. *Bathing Babies in Three Cultures,* in *Character Formation in Different Cultures,* narrated by M. Mead, 16 mm, black and white, sound, 9 min. (New York: New York University Film Library).

——— 1952c. *Childhood Rivalry in Bali and New Guinea,* in *Character Formation in Different Cultures,* narrated by M. Mead, 16 mm, black and white, sound, 20 min. (New York: New York University Film Library).

——— 1952d. *Karba's First Years,* in *Character Formation in Different Cultures,* narrated by M. Mead, 16 mm, black and white, sound, 20 min. (New York: New York University Film Library).

Benedict, R. 1923. "The Concept of the Guardian Spirit in North America," *Memoirs of the American Anthropological Association,* no. 29, pp. 1–97.

——— 1934. *Patterns of Culture.* (Boston: Houghton Mifflin).

——— 1959. "Anthropology and the Abnormal," in *An Anthropologist at Work: Writings of Ruth Benedict,* by M. Mead (Boston: Houghton Mifflin) pp. 262–83. First published 1934.

——— 1969. *Zuni Mythology* (New York: AMS Press). First published 1935.

Bennett, J. W. 1967. *Hutterian Brethren: The Agricultural Economy and Social Organization of a Communal People* (Stanford, Calif.: Stanford University Press).

Bernard, V. W. 1953. "Psychoanalysis and Members of Minority Groups," *Journal of the American Psychoanalytic Association,* 1:256–67.

Bettelheim, B. 1959a. "Feral Children and Autistic Children," *American Journal of Sociology,* 64:455–67.

——— 1959b. "Rejoinder," *American Journal of Sociology,* 68:76.

——— 1962. *Symbolic Wounds: Puberty Rites and the Envious Male,* rev. ed. (New York: Collier Books). First published 1954.

Birdwhistell, R. L. 1970. *Kinesics and Context: Essays on Body Motion Communication* (Philadelphia, Pa.: University of Pennsylvania Press).

Bishop, M. McF., and G. Winokur 1956. "Cross-Cultural Psychotherapy," *Journal of Nervous and Mental Diseases,* 123:369–75.

Bleuler, M., and R. Bleuler 1935. "Rorschach's Ink Blot Test and Racial Psychology: Mental Peculiarities of Moroccans," *Character and Personality,* 4:97–114.

Boas, F. 1964. *The Central Eskimo* (Lincoln, Nebr.: University of Nebraska Press). First published 1888 in English.

—— 1974a. "The Principles of Ethnological Classification," in *The Shaping of American Anthropology, 1883–1911: A Boas Reader,* G. W. Stocking, ed. (New York: Basic Books), pp. 61–67. First published 1887.

—— 1974b. "The History of Anthropology," in *The Shaping of American Anthropology, 1883–1911: A Boas Reader,* G. W. Stocking, ed. (New York: Basic Books), 23–36. First published 1904.

Bosch-Kohrer, E. 1984. "On Difficulties Assessing Transference and Countertransference When Analyst and Analysand Have Different Socio-Cultural Backgrounds," *International Review of Psychoanalysis,* 11:61–67.

Boszormeny-Nagy, I., and G. M. Spark 1973. *Invisible Loyalties: Reciprocity in Inter-Generational Family Therapy* (New York: Harper and Row).

Boyer, R. M. 1964. "The Matrilocal Family Among the Mescalero: Additional Data," *American Anthropologist,* 66:593–602.

Boyer, L. B. 1978. "On Aspects of the Mutual Influences of Anthropology and Psychoanalysis," *Journal of Psychological Anthropology,* 1:265–96.

—— 1979. *Childhood and Folklore: A Psychoanalytic Study of Apache Personality* (New York: Library of Psychological Anthropology).

Brenneis, C. B., and S. Roll 1975. "Ego Modalities in the Manifest Dreams of Male and Female Chicanos," *Psychiatry,* 38:172–85.

—— 1976. "Dream Patterns in Chicano and Anglo Young Adults," *Psychiatry,* 39:280–90.

Brenner, C. 1982. *The Mind in Conflict* (New York: International Universities Press).

Brown, J. 1971. "The Cure and Feeding of Windigos: A Critique," *American Anthropologist,* 73:20–22.

Burgum, M. 1957. "Values and Some Technical Problems in Psychotherapy," *American Journal of Orthopsychiatry,* 27:338–48.

Bustamente, J. A. 1957. "Importance of Cultural Patterns in Psychotherapy," *American Journal of Psychotherapy,* 11:803–12.

Carstairs, G. M. 1961. "Cross-Cultural Psychiatric Interviewing," in *Studying Personality Cross-Culturally,* B. Kaplan, ed. (Evanston, Ill.: Row, Peterson), pp. 533–46.

—— 1967. *The Twice-Born.* (Bloomington, Ind.: Indiana University Press). First published 1957.

Caudill, W. 1959. "Observations on the Cultural Context of Japanese Psychiatry," in *Culture and Mental Health,* Marvin K. Opler, ed. (New York: Macmillan), pp. 213–42.

Caudill, W., and L. T. Doi 1966. "Psychiatry and Culture in Japan," in *International Trends in Mental Health,* Henry F. David, ed. (New York: McGraw-Hill), pp. 129–46.

Caudill, W., and H. Weinstein 1969. "Maternal Care and Infant Behavior in Japan and America," *Psychiatry,* 32:12–43.

Chess, S., K. B. Clark, and A. Thomas 1953. "The Importance of Cultural Evaluation in Psychiatric Diagnosis and Treatment," *Psychiatric Quarterly,* 27:102–14.

Cohen, Y. A. 1964. *The Transition from Childhood to Adolescence* (Chicago: Aldine Publishing Co.).

—— 1966. "On Alternative Views of the Individual in Culture-and-Personality Studies," *American Anthropologist,* 68:355–61.

Cooper, J. M. 1933. "The Cree Witiko Psychosis," *Primitive Man,* 6:20–24.

—— 1934. *The Northern Algonquian Supreme Being* (Washington, D.C.: Catholic University Press).

Crapanzano, V. 1973. *The Hamadsha: An Essay in Moroccan Ethnopsychiatry.* (Berkeley, Calif.: University of California Press).

———— 1980. *Tuhami: Portrait of a Moroccan* (Chicago: University of Chicago Press).

———— 1982. "Rites of Return: Circumcision in Morocco," in *The Psychoanalytic Study of Society,* W. Muensterberger and L. B. Boyer, eds., S. A. Grolnick, assoc. ed. (New York: Psychohistory Press Publishers), 19:15–36.

Current Anthropology, sponsored by the Wenner-Gren Foundation for Anthropological Research (Chicago: University of Chicago Press).

Daniloff, R. 1984. "Softening the Strains of Soviet Life," *Psychology Today,* 18:46–50.

Davis, A., B. Gardner, and M. Gardner 1941. *Deep South* (Chicago: University of Chicago Press).

Davis, K. 1949. *Human Society* (New York: Macmillan).

Dement, W., and N. Kleitman 1957a. "Cyclic Variations in EEG during Sleep and Their Relation to Eye Movements, Body Motility, and Dreaming," in *Electroencephalography and Clinical Neurophysiology,* 9:673–90.

———— 1957b. "The Relation of Eye Movements During Sleep to Dream Activity," *Journal of Experimental Psychology,* 53:339–46.

Deutsch, F., and W. F. Murphy 1955. *The Clinical Interview,* 2 vols. (New York: International Universities Press).

Devereux, G. 1951a. "The Primal Scene and Juvenile Heterosexuality in Mohave Society," in *Psychoanalysis and Culture,* G. B. Wilbur and W. Muensterberger, eds. (New York: International Universities Press), pp. 90–107.

———— 1951b. "Three Technical Problems of the Pyschotherapy of Plains Indian Patients," *American Journal of Psychotherapy,* 5:411–23.

———— 1961. *Mohave Ethnopsychiatry and Suicide: The Psychiatric Knowledge and Psychic Disturbances of an Indian Tribe,* Smithsonian Institution, Bureau of American Ethnology, Bulletin 175 (Washington, D.C.).

———— 1962. "The Cultural Implementation of Defense Mechanisms," unpublished paper read at the Post-Graduate Center for Mental Health, New York.

———— 1967. *From Anxiety to Method in the Behavioral Sciences* (Paris and the Hague: Mouton).

———— 1969. *Reality and Dreams,* 2nd ed. (Garden City, N.Y.: Doubleday). First published 1951.

———— 1978. *Ethnopsychoanalysis—Psychoanalysis and Anthropology as Complementary Frames of Reference* (Berkeley, Calif.: University of California Press).

———— 1980. *Basic Problems of Ethnopsychiatry,* M. Gulati and G. Devereux, trans. (Chicago: University of Chicago Press).

———— 1982. "Socio-Cultural and Reality Factors in Displaced Pubertal Oedipality," *The Journal of Psychoanalytic Anthropology,* 5:379–82.

DeVos, G., and L. Romanucci-Ross, eds. 1982. *Ethnic Identity: Cultural Continuities and Change* (2nd ed. Chicago: University of Chicago Press). First published 1975.

Diaz-Guerrero, R. 1955. "Neurosis and the Mexican Family Structure," *American Journal of Psychiatry,* 112:411–17.

———— 1975. *Psychology of the Mexican: Culture and Personality* (Austin, Texas: University of Texas Press).

Dillon, W. S. 1968. *Gifts and Nations* (The Hague and Paris: Mouton).

Doi, L. T. 1963. "Some Thoughts on Helplessness and the Desire to Be Loved," *Psychiatry,* 26:266–72.

Dollard, J. 1937. *Caste and Class in a Southern Town* (New Haven, Conn.: Yale University Press).

Dolto, F. 1955. "French and American Children as Seen by a French Child Analyst," in *Childhood in Contemporary Cultures,* M. Mead and M. Wolfenstein, eds. (Chicago: University of Chicago Press), pp. 408–23.

Eaton, J. W., and R. J. Weil 1955. *Culture and Mental Disorders* (Glencoe, Ill.: Free Press).

Edwards, J. W. 1983. "Semen Anxiety in South Asian Cultures: Cultural and Transcultural Significance," *Medical Anthropology,* 7:51–67.

Eggan, D. 1961. "Dream Analysis," in *Studying Personality Cross-Culturally,* Bert Kaplan, ed. (Evanston, Ill.: Row, Peterson), pp. 551–77.

Eglar, Z. 1960. *A Punjabi Village in Pakistan* (New York: Columbia University Press).

Elwin, V. 1939. *The Baiga* (London: Murray).

Erikson, E. H. 1963. *Childhood and Society,* 2nd ed. (New York: Norton). First published 1950.

——— 1970. "The Dream Specimen in Psychoanalysis," in *Psychoanalytic Psychiatry and Psychology,* R. P. Knight and C. R. Friedman, eds. (New York: International Universities Press), pp. 131–70. First published 1954.

Ethos, Journal of the Society for Psychological Anthropology.

Falicov, C. J. 1982. "Mexican Families," in *Ethnicity and Family Therapy,* M. McGoldrick, J. K. Pearce and J. Giordano, eds. (New York: The Guilford Press), pp. 134–63.

Fenichel, O. 1954. *The Concept of Trauma in Contemporary Psychoanalytic Theory,* in *The Collected Papers of Otto Fenichel,* second series, collected and edited by H. Fenichel and David Rapaport (New York: Norton).

Field, M. J. 1955. "Witchcraft as a Primitive Interpretation of Mental Disorder," *Journal of Mental Science,* 101:826–33.

——— 1958. "Mental Disorder in Rural Ghana," *Journal of Mental Science,* 104:1043–51.

——— 1960. *Search for Security: An Ethnopsychiatric Study on Rural Ghana* (Evanston, Ill.: Northwestern University Press).

Firth, R. 1934. "The Meaning of Dreams in Tikopia," in *Essays Presented to C. G. Seligman,* E. E. Evans-Pritchard et al., eds. (London: Kegan Paul, Trench and Trubner), pp. 63–74.

Firth, R., ed. 1960. *Man and Culture: An Evaluation of the Work of Bronislaw Malinowski* (London: Routledge and Kegan Paul).

Fisher, C. 1965. "Psychoanalytic Implications of Recent Research on Sleep and Dreaming," *Journal of the American Psychoanalytic Association,* 13:197–303.

Fiss, H., G. S. Klein, and E. Bokert 1966. "Waking Fantasies Following Interruption of Two Types of Sleep," *Archives of General Psychiatry,* 14:543–51.

Fogelson, R. D. 1965. "Psychological Theories of 'Windigo' Psychosis and a Preliminary Application of a Models Approach," in *Context and Meaning in Cultural Anthropology,* M. E. Spiro, ed. (New York: Free Press), pp. 74–79.

Fortes, M. 1960. "Malinowski and the Study of Kinship," in *Man and Culture: An Evaluation of the Work of Malinowski,* R. Firth, ed. (London: Routledge and Kegan Paul), pp. 157–88. First published 1957.

Frank, J. D. 1961. *Persuasion and Healing: A Comparative Study of Psychotherapy* (Baltimore, Md.: Johns Hopkins Press).

Frank, L. K. 1956. "Tactile Communication," *Genetic Psychology Monographs,* 56:209–55.

Frazer, J. G. 1955. *The Golden Bough: A Study in Magic and Religion,* 3rd ed., rev. and enl., 13 vols. (New York: St. Martin's Press). First published in 1890.

Freeman, D. M. A., E. F. Foulks, and P. A. Freeman 1978. "Child Development and Arctic Hysteria in the North Alaskan Eskimo Male," *Journal of Psychological Anthropology*, 1:203–10.

French, T. 1952. *Basic Postulates*, vol 1 of *The Integration of Behavior*, 5 vols (Chicago: University of Chicago Press).

——— 1954. *The Integrative Process in Dreams*, vol. 2 of *The Integration of Behavior*, 5 vols (Chicago: University of Chicago Press).

——— 1958. *The Reintegrative Process in a Psychoanalytic Treatment*, vol 3 of *The Integration of Behavior*, 5 vols (Chicago: University of Chicago Press).

Freud, A. 1965. *Normality and Pathology in Childhood* (New York: International Universities Press).

Freud, S. 1950a. "On Psychotherapy," in *Collected Papers*, 4 vols. (London: Hogarth Press), vol. 1, pp. 249–263. First published 1904.

——— 1950b. "Turnings in the Ways of Psycho-Analytic Therapy," in *Collected Papers*, 4 vols. (London: Hogarth Press), vol. 2, pp. 392–402. First published 1919.

——— 1953. The Interpretation of Dreams, vols. 4–5 of *The Standard Edition of the Complete Psychological Works of Sigmund Freud* (London: Hogarth Press). First published 1900.

——— 1959. Totem and Taboo, in vol. 13 of *The Standard Edition* (London: Hogarth Press), pp. ix–162. First published 1913.

——— 1961. The Ego and the Id, in vol. 19 of *The Standard Edition* (London: Hogarth Press), pp. 12–63. First published 1923.

——— 1963. Introductory Lectures on Psychoanalysis *........ of *The Standard Edition* (London: Hogarth Press). First published 1915–1916.

Fromm, E. 1949. "Psychoanalytic Characterology and Its Application to the Understanding of Culture," in *Culture and Personality*, S. S. Sargent and M. W. Smith, eds. (New York: Viking Fund), pp. 1–12.

——— 1953. "Individual and Social Origins of Neurosis," in *Personality in Nature, Society, and Cultures*, 2nd ed., C. Kluckhohn and H. A. Murray, eds. (New York: Knopf), pp. 515–21.

Fromm-Reichman, F. 1950. *Principles of Intensive Psychotherapy* (Chicago: University of Chicago Press).

Gomez-Palacio, M., E. Padilla, and S. Roll 1982. *WISC-R Mexicano* (Mexico City: Dirección General de la Educación Especial).

Gorer, G. 1964. *The American People*, rev. ed. (New York: Norton). First published 1948.

Griffith, R. M., O. Miyagi, and A. Tago 1958. "The Universality of Typical Dreams: Japanese vs. Americans," *American Anthropologist*, 60:1173–79.

Griffith, R. M., and E. Jones 1979. "Race and Psychotherapy: Changing Perspectives," in *Current Psychiatric Therapies*, J. Masserman, ed. (New York: Grune & Stratton).

Hall, C. S. 1958. *The Meaning of Dreams* (New York: Harper and Row).

Hall, C. S., and B. Domhoff 1963. "Aggression in Dreams," *International Journal of Social Psychiatry*, 9:259–67.

Hall, E. T. 1963. "A System of Notation of Proxemic Behavior," *American Anthropologist*, 65:1003–26.

Hall, E. T., and W. F. Whyte 1966. "Intercultural Communication: A Guide to Men of Action," in *Communication and Culture*, A. G. Smith, ed. (New York: Holt, Rinehart & Winston), pp. 567–75.

Hallowell, A. I. 1934. "Culture and Mental Disorder," *Journal of Abnormal and Social Psychology,* 29:1–9.

——— 1936. "Psychic Stresses and Culture Patterns," *American Journal of Psychiatry,* 92:1291–1310.

——— 1938. "Fear and Anxiety as Cultural and Individual Variables in a Primitive Society," *Journal of Social Psychology,* 9:25–47.

——— 1956. "The Rorschach Technique in Personality and Culture Studies," in *Developments in Rorschach Techniques,* 2 vols, B. Klopfer et al., eds. (Yonkers-on-Hudson, N.Y.: World Book), 2:458–544.

——— 1976a. "On Being an Anthropologist," in *Contributions to Anthropology: Selected Papers of A. Irving Hallowell* (Chicago: University of Chicago Press), pp. 3–14. First published 1972.

——— 1976b. "Ojibwa World View and Disease," in *Contributions to Anthropology: Selected Papers of A. Irving Hallowell,* with introductions by R. D. Fogelson et al. (Chicago: University of Chicago Press), pp. 391–448. First published 1963.

Harris, M. 1968. "Race," in *International Encyclopedia of the Social Sciences,* 13 D. L. Sills, ed. (New York: Macmillan & Free Press), pp. 263–69.

Hartmann, H. 1958. *Ego Psychology and the Problem of Adaptation,* D. Rapaport, trans. (New York: International Universities Press).

Hartmann, H., E. Kris, and R. Loewenstein 1951. "Some Psychoanalytic Comments on Culture and Personality," in *Psychoanalysis and Culture,* G. B. Wilbur and W. Muensterberger, eds. (New York: International Universities Press), pp. 3–31.

Hay, T. H. 1971. "The Windigo Psychosis: Psychodynamic, Cultural and Social Factors in Aberrant Behavior," *American Anthropologist,* 73:1–19.

——— 1963. *Culture against Man* (New York: Random House).

Herdt, G. H. 1981. *Guardians of the Flute: Idioms of Masculinity* (New York: McGraw-Hill).

——— 1982a. "Sambia Nosebleeding Rites and Male Proximity to Women," *Ethos,* 10:189–231.

———, ed. 1982b. *Rituals of Manhood: Male Initiation in Papua New Guinea* (Berkeley: University of California Press).

——— 1982c. "Fetish and Fantasy in Sambia," in *Rituals of Manhood: Male Initiation in Papua New Guinea,* G. H. Herdt, ed. (Berkeley: University of California Press), pp. 44–98.

Herskovits, M. J. 1938. *Dahomey: An Ancient African Kingdom,* 2 vols. (New York: Augustin).

Herskovits, M. J., and R. Herskovits 1957. "Sibling Rivalry, the Oedipus Complex and Myth," *Journal of American Folklore,* 71:1–15.

Hes, J. P. 1966–1967. "From Native Healer to Modern Psychiatrist. Afro-Asian Immigrants to Israel and Their Attitudes Towards Psychiatric Facilities," *International Journal of Social Psychiatry,* 13:21–27.

Hinkle, Jr., L. E., et al. 1957. "Studies in Human Ecology: Factors Governing the Adaptation of Chinese Unable to Return to China," in *Experimental Pathology* (New York: Grune & Stratton), pp. 170–86.

Hofstadter, R. and M. Wallace, eds. 1970. *American Violence: A Documentary History* (New York: Knopf).

Holden, D. 1972. *Greece Without Columns: The Making of Modern Greece* (New York: Lippincott).

Holtzman, W. H., R. Diaz-Guerrero, and J. D. Swartz. 1975. *Personality Development in Two Cultures: A Cross-Cultural Longitudinal Study of School Children in Mexico and the United States* (Austin, Tex.: University of Texas Press).

Honigmann, J. J. 1961. "The Interpretation of Dreams in Anthropological Field Work," in *Studying Personality Cross-Culturally,* B. Kaplan, ed. (New York: Harper & Row), pp. 579–85.

Hostetler, J. A. 1968. *Amish Society,* rev. ed. (Baltimore, Md.: Johns Hopkins Press). First published 1963.

Hostetler, J. A., and G. E. Huntington 1967. *The Hutterites in North America* (New York: Holt, Rinehart & Winston).

Human Organization, Journal of the Society for Applied Anthropology.

International Journal of Psychology, Journal of International Union of Psychological Science.

International Social Science Journal, Journal of United Nations Educational, Scientific and Cultural Organization (UNESCO).

Itard, J. M. G. 1932. *The Wild Boy of Aveyron* (New York and London: Century).

Jackson, A. 1973. "Psychotherapy: Factors Associated with the Race of the Therapist," *Psychotherapy: Theory, Research and Practice,* 10:273–77.

Jacobson, A., and A. N. Berenberg 1952. "Japanese Psychiatry and Psychotherapy," *American Journal of Psychiatry,* 109:321–29.

Jalali, B. 1982. "Iranian Families," in *Ethnicity and Family Therapy,* M. McGoldrick, J. K. Pearce and J. Giordano, eds. (New York: The Guilford Press), pp. 289–309.

Jilek, W. G. 1984. Abstracts of D. Dutta, H. R. Phookan and P. D. Das: "The Koro Epidemic in Lower Assam," *Indian Journal of Psychiatry,* vol 24; and Ajita Chakroborty: "An Epidemic of Koro in West Bengal," manuscript (1983), with comments by abstracter, *Transcultural Psychiatric Research Review,* 2:59–61.

Johanson, D., and M. Edey 1981. "The Early Fossil Finds," in *Lucy: The Beginnings of Mankind* (New York: Simon & Schuster). See also for bibliography.

Jones, E. 1964. "Mother-Right and the Sexual Ignorance of Savages," 2 vols (New York: International Universities Press), vol. 2, pp. 145–173. First published 1925.

Jones, E. E., and S. Korchin 1982. *Minority Mental Health* (New York: Praeger).

Jones, N. F., and M. W. Kahn 1964. "Patient Attitudes as Related to Social Class and Other Variables Concerned with Hospitalization," *Journal of Consulting Psychology,* 28:403–08.

Journal of Cross-Cultural Psychology, Journal of the Center for Cross-Cultural Research and International Association for Cross-Cultural Psychology.

Journal of Psychoanalytic Anthropology, Journal of the Institute of Psychohistory.

Jungreis, J. E., and R. V. Speik 1965. "The Ritual Family," in *Psychotherapy for the Whole Family,* A. Medman et al., eds. (New York: Springer-Verlag), pp. 80–105.

Kahn, M. W., et al. 1963. "A Factorial Study of Patient Attitudes Toward Mental Illness and Psychiatric Hospitalization," *Journal of Clinical Psychology,* 19:235–41.

Kahn, M. W., et al. 1966–1967. "A Comparison of Korean and American Mental Patients' Attitudes toward Mental Illness and Hospitalization," *International Journal of Social Psychiatry,* 13:14–20.

Kardiner, A. 1939. *The Individual and His Society* (New York: Columbia University Press).

Kardiner, A., et al. 1945. *Psychological Frontiers of Society* (New York: Columbia University Press).

Kardiner, A., and L. Ovesey, 1951. *The Mark of Oppression: A Psychological Study of the American Negro* (New York: Norton).

Karon, B. P. 1958. *The Negro Personality: A Rigorous Investigation of the Effects of Culture* (New York: Springer-Verlag).

Keesing, R. N. 1982. "Introduction," in *Rituals of Manhood: Male Initiation in Papua New Guinea,* G. H. Herdt, ed. (Berkeley: University of California Press), pp. 1–43.

Keniston, K. 1967. *The Uncommitted: Alienated Youth in American Society* (New York: Dell).

Ketter, T. 1983. "Cultural Stylization and Mental Illness in Bali," *Transcultural Psychiatric Research Review,* 20:87–106. Overview article; see especially for bibliography.

Kiev, A., ed. 1964. *Magic, Faith and Healing* (New York: Free Press of Glencoe).

Kilborne, B. 1981. "The Handling of Dream Symbolism: Aspects of Dream Interpretation in Morocco," in *The Psychoanalytic Study of Society,* W. Muensterberger and L. B. Boyer, eds., S. A. Grolnick, assoc. ed. (New York: Psychohistory Press Publishers), 9:1–14.

Klein, M., P. Heinemann, and R. E. Money-Kyrle, eds. 1957. *New Directions in Psychoanalysis* (New York: Basic Books).

Kluckhohn, C., and W. Morgan. 1951. "Some Notes on Navaho Dreams," in *Psychoanalysis and Culture,* G. B. Wilbur, and W. Muensterberger, eds. (New York: International Universities Press), pp. 120–331.

Kluckhohn, F. R. 1958. "Family Diagnosis: Variations in the Basic Values of Family Systems," *Social Casework,* 39:63–72.

Kluckhohn, F. R., and F. L. Strodtbeck 1961. *Variations in Value Orientations* (Westport, Conn.: Greenwood Press).

Kohut, H. 1975. *The Reconstruction of the Self* (New York: International Universities Press).

Kondo, A. 1953. "Morita Therapy: A Japanese Therapy for Neurosis," *American Journal of Psychoanalysis,* 13:31–37.

Koss, J. D. 1980. "The Therapist-Spiritist Training Project in Puerto Rico: An Experiment to Relate the Traditional Healing System to the Public Health System," *Social Science and Medicine,* 148:255–66.

Koss, J. D., and J. Canive 1982. "A Program for Teaching Family Therapy for Hispanic Americans," paper presented at the Annual Meeting of the Society for the Study of Psychiatry and Culture, San Miguel Regla, Mexico.

Kroeber, T. 1970. *Alfred Kroeber: A Personal Configuration* (Berkeley: University of California Press).

Lacan, J. 1966. *Ecrits I* (Paris: Editions du Seuil).

—— 1971. *Ecrits II* (Paris: Editions du Seuil).

Landes, R. 1938. "The Abnormal among the Ojibwa Indians," *Journal of Abnormal and Social Psychology,* 33:14–33.

—— 1961. "The Ojibwa of Canada," in *Cooperation and Competition,* 2nd ed., M. Mead, ed. (Boston: Beacon Press), pp. 87–126. First published 1938.

Langham, I. 1981. *The Building of British Social Anthropology* (Dordrecht, Holland: D. Reidel Publishing Co.).

Langlier, R. 1982. "French Canadian Families," in *Ethnicity and Family Therapy,* M. Goldrick, J. K. Pearce and J. Giordano, eds. (New York: Guilford Press), pp. 229–46.

Lasswell, H. D. 1948. *Power and Personality* (New York: Norton).

Leichter, H. J., and W. E. Mitchell 1978. *Kinship and Casework: Family Network and Social Intervention,* enl. ed. (New York: Teachers College Press).

Lerner, D. 1961. "An American Researcher in Paris: Interviewing Frenchmen," in *Studying Personality Cross-Culturally,* B. Kaplan, ed. (New York: Harper & Row), pp. 427–42.

Lerner, H. E. 1983. "Female Dependency in Context: Some Theoretical and Technical Considerations," *American Journal of Orthopsychiatry,* 53:697–705.

Lessa, W. A., and E. Z. Vogt, eds. 1965. *Reader in Comparative Religion: An Anthropological Approach,* 2nd ed. (New York: Harper & Row). First published 1958.

LeVine, R. A. 1982. *Culture, Behavior, and Personality,* 2nd ed. (New York: Aldine Publishing Co.).

Levy-Bruhl, L. 1949. *Les carnets de Levy-Bruhl* (Paris: Presses Univerisitaires de France).

—— 1985. *How Natives Think.* Lilian Clare, trans. (Princeton: Princeton University Press). First published 1910.

Lewis, O. 1966. *La Vida* (New York: Random House).

Lidz, T., and R. W. Lidz 1984. "Oedipus in the Stone Age," *Journal of the American Psychoanalytic Association,* 32:507–27.

Lincoln, J. S. 1935. *The Dream in Primitive Cultures* (London: Cresset Press).

Lomax, A. 1978. *Folk Song Style and Culture* (New Brunswick, N.J.: Transaction Press [Rutgers University]). First published in 1968.

Lomax, A., and F. Pauley 1976. *Dance and Human History,* in the *Movement Style and Culture Series,* 16 mm, color, sound, 40 min. (Berkeley, Calif.: University of California Media Center).

Lowenfeld, M. 1954. *The Lowenfeld Mosaic Test* (London: Newman Neame).

Lowie, R. H. 1935. *The Crow Indians* (New York: Farrar & Rinehart, Inc.).

McGoldrick, M., J. K. Pearce, and J. Giordano, eds. 1982. *Ethnicity and Family Therapy* (New York: The Guilford Press).

McNeill, I. 1959. *Four Families,* two parts. M. Mead, narrator and consultant. 16 mm, black and white, sound, 60 min. (Toronto: National Film Board of Canada; New York: McGraw-Hill Films).

Maldonado-Sierra, E. D., and R. D. Trent 1960. "The Sibling Relationships in Group Psychotherapy with Puerto Rican Schizophrenics," *American Journal of Psychiatry,* 117:239–44.

Malinowski, B. 1935. *Coral Gardens and Their Magic,* 2 vols (New York: American Book Company).

—— 1953. *Sex and Repression in Savage Society* (New York: Harcourt Brace). First published 1927.

—— 1954. "Baloma: The Spirits of the Dead in the Trobriand Islands," in *Magic, Science and Religion and Other Essays* (Garden City, N.Y.: Doubleday), pp. 149–274. First published 1916.

—— 1961. *Argonauts of the Western Pacific* (New York: Dutton). First published 1922.

—— 1962. *The Sexual Life of Savages in Northwestern Melanesia.* (New York: Harcourt Brace). First published 1929.

—— 1963. *The Family among the Australian Aborigines* (New York: Schocken Books). First published 1913.

Mandelbaum, D. G. 1943. "Wolf-Child Histories from India," *Journal of Social Psychology,* 17:25–44.

Marsella, A. J., and P. B. Pedersen, eds. 1981. *Cross-Cultural Counseling and Psychotherapy* (New York: Pergamon Press).

Mead, M. 1951. "Group Psychotherapy in the Light of Anthropology," *International Journal of Group Psychotherapy,* 1:193–99.

—— 1953. "The Single Informant," in *The Study of a Culture at a Distance,* Margaret Mead and Rhoda Metraux, eds. (Chicago: University of Chicago Press), pp. 41–49.

——— 1959a. *An Anthropologist at Work: Writings of Ruth Benedict* (Boston: Houghton Mifflin).

——— 1959b. "Feral Children and Autistic Children," *American Journal of Sociology,* 65:75.

——— 1964. *Continuities in Cultural Evolution* (New Haven, Conn.: Yale University Press).

——— 1965. *And Keep Your Powder Dry,* rev. ed. (New York: Morrow). First published 1942. See especially bibliography.

——— 1968a. *Sex and Temperament in Three Primitive Societies* (New York: Dell). First published 1935.

——— 1968b. *The Mountain Arapesh, I: The Record of Unabelin with Rorschach Analyses* (Garden City, N.Y.: Natural History Press). First published 1949.

——— 1972. *Blackberry Winter* (New York: Morrow).

——— 1978. *Culture and Commitment,* rev. ed. (New York: Columbia University Press). First published 1970.

Mead, M., T. Dobzhansky, E. Tobach, and R. E. Light, eds. 1968. *Science and the Concept of Race* (New York: Columbia University Press).

Mead, M., and F. C. Macgregor 1951. *Growth and Culture* (New York: Putnam).

Mead, M., and R. Metraux, eds. 1953. *The Study of Culture at a Distance* (Chicago: University of Chicago Press).

Mead, M., and M. Wolfenstein, eds. 1955. *Childhood in Comtemporary Culture* (Chicago: University of Chicago Press).

Melgoza, B., S. Roll, and R. Baker 1983. "Conformity and Cooperation in Chicanos: The Case of the Lost or Missing Susceptibility to Influence," *Journal of Community Psychology,* 11:323–33.

Meltzoff, J., and M. Kornreich 1970. *Research in Psychotherapy* (New York: Alberton Press).

Metraux, A. 1959. *Voodoo in Haiti,* H. Charteris, trans. (New York: Oxford University Press).

Metraux, R. 1951. "Kith and Kin: A Study of Creole Social Structure in Marbial, Haiti," unpublished doctoral dissertation, Columbia University.

——— 1955a. "The Consequences of Wrongdoing: An Analysis of Story Completions by German Children," in *Childhood in Contemporary Cultures,* M. Mead and M. Wolfenstein, eds. (Chicago: University of Chicago Press), pp. 306–23.

——— 1955b. "Life Stress and Health in a Changing Culture," in *Family Mental Health and the State, Proceedings of the 8th Annual Meeting of the World Federation for Mental Health* (London: World Federation for Mental Health), pp. 113–26.

——— 1955c. "Parents and Children: An Analysis of Contemporary German Child-Care and Youth-Guidance Literature," in *Childhood in Contemporary Cultures,* M. Mead and M. Wolfenstein, eds. (Chicago: University of Chicago Press), pp. 204–28.

——— 1955d. "A Portrait of the Family in German Juvenile Fiction," in *Childhood in Contemporary Cultures,* M. Mead and M. Wolfenstein, eds. (Chicago: University of Chicago Press), pp. 253–76.

——— 1968. "Bronislaw Malinowski," in *International Encyclopedia of the Social Sciences,* vol 9, D. L. Sills, ed. (New York: Macmillan and The Free Press), pp. 541–49.

——— 1980. "The Study of Culture at a Distance," *American Anthropologist,* 82:362–72.

Metraux, R., and T. M. Abel 1957. "Normal and Deviant Behavior in a Peasant Community: Montserrat, B.W.I.," *American Journal of Orthopsychiatry,* 27:167–84.

Metraux, R., and M. Mead 1954. *Themes in French Culture* (Stanford, Calif.: Stanford University Press).

Minuchin, S., et al. 1967. *Families of the Slums: An Exploration of Their Structure and Treatment* (New York: Basic Books).

Mitchell, J. S. 1982. *Taking on the World: Empowering Strategies for Parents of Children with Disabilities* (New York: Harcourt Brace Jovanovich).

Mitchell, W. E. 1978. *Mishpokhe: A Study of New York City Jewish Family Clubs* (The Hague: Mouton).

Mivra, M., and S. Usa 1970. "A Psychotherapy of Neurosis, Morita Therapy," *Yonaga Acta Medica,* 14:1–17.

Moloney, J. C. 1953. "Understanding the Paradox of Japanese Psychoanalysis," *International Journal of Psycho-Analysis,* 34:291–303.

Mondykowski, S. M. 1982. "Polish Families," in *Ethnicity and Family Therapy,* M. McGoldrick, J. K. Pearce, and J. Giordano, eds. (New York: Guilford Press), pp. 293–411.

Morita, S. 1917. "The True Nature of Shinkeishitsu and Its Treatment," in *Anthology of Theses Commemorating the Twenty-Fifth Anniversary of Professor Kure's Appointment to His Position* (Tokyo: Jikei University).

Moitoza, E. 1982. "Portuguese Families," in *Ethnicity and Family Therapy,* M. McGoldrick, J. K. Pearce and J. Giordano, eds. (New York: Guilford Press), pp. 412–35.

Muensterberger, W. 1951. "Orality and Dependence: Characteristics of Southern Chinese," in *Psychoanalysis and the Social Sciences,* 5 vols, G. Róheim, ed. (New York: International Universities Press), 3:37–69.

Myers, J. K., L. L. Bean, and M. P. Pepper 1968. *A Decade Later: A Follow-Up of Social Class and Mental Illness* (New York: Wiley).

Nasr, S., J. Racy, and J. A. Flaherty 1983. "Psychiatric Effects of the Civil War in Lebanon," *Psychiatric Journal of the University of Ottawa,* 8:208–12.

Needham, J. 1956. *History of Scientific Thought,* vol 2 of *Science and Civilization in China* (Cambridge: University Press).

Newman, Philip L. 1964. "'Wild Man' Behavior in a New Guinea Highlands Community," *Amerian Anthropologist,* 66:1–19.

Oberholzer, E. 1944. "Rorschach's Experiment and the Alorese," in *The People of Alor,* by C. DuBois (Minneapolis, Minn.: University of Minnesota Press), pp. 449–54.

Ogburn, W. F. 1959. "The Wolf Boy of Agra," *American Journal of Sociology,* 64:588–640.

O'Nell, C. W., and N. D. O'Nell 1977. "A Cross-Cultural Comparison of Aggression in Dreams: Zapotecs and Americans," *International Journal of Social Psychiatry,* 23:35–41.

Opler, M. K. 1959b. "Dream Analysis in Ute Therapy," in *Culture and Mental Health,* M. K. Opler, ed. (New York: Macmillan), pp. 97–117.

—— 1967. "Social and Cultural Influences on the Psychotherapy of Family Groups," in *Family Therapy and Disturbed Families,* G. H. Zuk and I. Boszormenyi-Nagy, eds. (Palo Alto, Calif.: Science and Behavior Books), pp. 133–58.

Padilla, A. M., and R. A. Ruiz 1973. *Latino Mental Health: A Review of the Literature* (Washington, D.C.: U.S. Government Printing Office).

—— 1975. "Personality Assessment and Test Interpretation of Mexican-Americans: A Critique," *Journal of Personality Assessment,* 39:103–09.

Papiasvili, A. 1984. "Psychodrama in Eastern Europe and the USSR," a paper read at the symposium on Transcultural Crossroads in Group Psychotherapy at the VIIth International Congress in Group Psychotherapy, Mexico City, D.F.

Parker, S. 1962. "Eskimo Psychopathology in the Context of Eskimo Personality and Culture," *American Anthropologist*, 64:76–96. See also for the extensive bibliography.

——— 1969b. "Is the Oedipus Complex Universal? The Jones-Malinowski Debate Revisited," in *Belief, Magic, and Anomie* (New York: Free Press), pp. 3–36.

——— 1969c. "Paternal and Maternal Authority of the Neapolitan Family," in *Belief, Magic, and Anomie* (New York: Free Press), pp. 67–97.

Pedersen, P. 1977. "The Triad Model," *The Personnel and Guidance Journal*, 56:94–100.

Pelto, P. J. and G. H. Pelto 1975. "Intra-Cultural Diversity: Some Theoretical Issues. *Ethnology* 2:1–18.

Piotrowski, Z. A., in collaboration with A. M. Biele 1983. "The Perceptanalytic Dream System (P.D.S.) as a Tool in Personality Assessment," *Advances in Personality Assessment*, 2:1–12.

Pollack, O., et al. 1952. *Social Science and Psychotherapy for Children* (New York: Russell Sage Foundation).

Powdermaker, H. 1953. "The Channeling of Negro Aggression by the Cultural Process," in *Personality in Nature, Society, and Culture*, 2nd ed., C. Kluckhohn and H. A. Murray, eds. (New York: Knopf), pp. 597–608.

Radin, P. 1958. "Introduction," in *The Origins of Culture*, pt. 1 of *Primitive Culture* by E. B. Tylor (New York: Harper & Row), pp. ix-xv.

Redlich, F. C., 1958. "Social Aspects of Psychotherapy," *American Journal of Psychiatry*, 114:800–04.

Redlich, F. C., A. B. Hollingshead, and E. Bellis 1955. "Social Class Differences in Attitudes Toward Psychiatry," *American Journal of Orthopsychiatry*, 25:60–70.

Riesman, D. 1973. *The Lonely Crowd* (New Haven, Conn.: Yale University Press). First published 1950.

Roffenstein, G. 1951. "Experiments on Symbolization in Dreams," in *Organization and Pathology of Thought*, D. Rapaport, ed. (New York: Columbia University Press), pp. 249–56.

Róheim, G. 1934. *The Riddle of the Sphinx*, R. Money-Kyrle, trans. (London: Hogarth Press).

——— 1939. "Racial Differences in Neuroses and Psychoses," *Psychiatry*, 23:375–90.

——— 1941. "Psycho-Analytic Interpretation of Culture," *International Journal of Psycho-Analysis*, 22:147–69.

——— 1943. *The Origin and Function of Culture*, Journal of Nervous and Mental Disease, no. 69.

——— 1946. "The Oedipus Complex and Infantile Sexuality," *Psychoanalytic Quarterly*, 15:503–08.

——— 1952a. "The Anthropological Evidence and the Oedipus Complex," *Psychoanalytic Quarterly*, 21:537–42.

——— 1952b. *Gates of the Dream* (New York: International Universities Press).

Roll, S. 1970. "Conservation of Number: A Comparison Between Cultures and Subcultures," *Interamerican Journal of Psychology*, 4:13–18.

Roll, S., R. Hinton, and M. Glazer 1974. "Dreams of Death: Mexican-American vs. Anglo-Americans," *Interamerican Journal of Psychology*, 8:111–15.

Roll, S., and C. B. Brenneis 1975. "Chicano and Anglo Dreams of Death: A Replication," *Journal of Cross-Cultural Psychology*, 6:377–83.

Roll, S., and M. H. Irwin 1976. "Manipulation of Subject Involvement and Conservation of Number and Liquid," *Revista latinoamericana de psicología*, 6:157–60.

Roll, S., K. Rabold, and L. McArdle, 1976. "Disclaimed Activity in the Dreams of Chicanos and Anglos," *Journal of Cross-Cultural Psychology*, 7:335–45.

Roll, S., L. Millen, and R. Martinez 1980. "Errors in Psychotherapy with Chicanos: Extrapolations from Research and Clinical Experiences," *Psychotherapy: Theory, Practice and Research*, 17:158–68.

Romanucci-Ross, L., D. E. Moerman, and L. E. Tancredi 1982. *The Anthropology of Medicine* (South Hadley, Mass.: Bergin and Garvey).

Ruesch, J. 1955. "Nonverbal Language and Therapy," *Psychiatry*, 18:323–330.

Ruiz, P., and J. Langrod 1976. "The Role of Folk Healers in Community Health Services," *Community Mental Health Journal*, 12:392.

Samuda, R. 1975. *Psychological Testing of American Minorities* (New York: Dodd & Mead).

Sanua, V. D. 1966. "Sociocultural Aspects of Psychotherapy and Treatment: A Review of the Literature," *Progress in Clinical Psychology*, 7:151–90.

Sapir, E. "Why Cultural Anthropology Needs Psychiatrists." In *Selected Writings of Edward Sapir*. Language, Culture and Personality. D. G. Mendelboun, ed. (Berkeley: University of California Press).

Satow, R. 1983. "A Severe Case of Penis Envy: The Convergence of Cultural and Individual Intrapsychic Factors," *Journal of the American Academy of Psychoanalysis*, 2:547–56.

Schachter, J. S., and H. F. Butts 1968. "Transference in Interracial Analyses," *Journal of the American Psychoanalytic Association*, 16:792–808.

Scheflen, A. E. 1965. *Stream and Structure of Communicational Behavior: Context Analysis of a Psychotherapy Session* (Commonwealth of Pennsylvania: EPPI, Behavioral Studies), monograph no. 1.

Schwartz, T. 1962. "The Paliau Movement in the Admiralty Islands, 1946–1954," *Anthropological Papers of the American Museum of Natural History*, 49, Pt. 2, pp. 207–421.

——— 1982. "Cultural Totemism: Ethnic Identity, Primitive and Modern," in *Ethnic Identity: Cultural Continuities and Change*, 2nd ed., G. DeVos and L. Romanucci-Ross, eds. (Chicago: University of Chicago Press), pp. 106–31.

Sebeok, T. A., A. S. Hayes, and M. C. Bateson, eds. 1964. *Approaches to Semiotics* (London, The Hague and Paris: Mouton).

Seligman, C. G. 1924. "Anthropology and Psychology," *Journal of the Royal Anthropological Institute*, 54:13–46.

Seward, G. 1956. *Psychotherapy and Culture Conflict* (New York: Ronald Press).

Sharma, S. L. 1986. *The Therapeutic Dialogue* (Albuquerque, N. Mex.: The University of New Mexico Press).

Shaw, L. (Shu Ch'ing-ch'un) 1945. *Rickshaw Boy*, E. King, trans. (New York: Reynal and Hitchcock).

Singal, D. J. 1982. *The War Within: From Victorian to Modernist Thought in the South* (Chapel Hill: University of North Carolina Press).

Smith, C. H. 1950. *The Coming of the Russian Mennonites* (Newton, Kans.: Mennonite Publishers).

Snyder, F. 1963. "The New Biology of Dreaming," *Archives of General Psychiatry*, 8:381.

Soddy, K., ed. 1955. *Mental Health and Infant Development*, 2 vols (New York: Basic Books).

Spencer, W. B., and F. Gillen 1899. *The Native Tribes of Central Australia* (London: Macmillan).

Spiegel, J. P. 1959. "Some Cultural Aspects of Transference and Countertransference," in *Indi-*

vidual and Familial Dynamics, J. H. Masserman, ed. (New York: Grune & Stratton), 2:160–82.

Spiegel, J., and J. Papajohn 1983. *Training Program in Ethnicity and Mental Health* (manuscript, the Florence Heller School, Brandeis University).

Spiro, M. E. 1965. "Religious Systems as Culturally Constituted Defense Mechanisms," in *Context and Meaning in Cultural Anthropology,* M. E. Spiro, ed. (New York: Free Press), pp. 100–13.

———— 1982. *Oedipus and the Trobriands* (Chicago: University of Chicago Press).

Srole, L., et al. 1962. *Mental Health in the Metropolis* (New York: McGraw-Hill).

Stewart, K. 1954. *Pygmies and Dream Giants* (New York: Norton).

Stocking, G. W., Jr. 1983. "The Ethnographer's Magic: Fieldwork in British Anthropology from Tylor to Malinowski," in *Observers Observed, History of Anthropology,* vol 1, G. W. Stocking, Jr., ed. (Madison, Wis.: University of Wisconsin Press), pp. 70–120.

Sue, D. W., et al. 1981. *Counseling the Culturally Different* (New York: Wiley-Interscience).

Swartz, M. J. 1982. "Cultural Sharing and Cultural Theory: Some Findings of a Five-Society Study." *American Anthropologist,* 84:314–38.

Tatara, M. 1974. "Problems of Separation and Dependency: Psychotherapy in Japan and Some Technical Considerations," *Journal of the American Academy of Psychoanalysis,* 2:231–42.

Teicher, M. I. 1960. "Windigo Psychosis," in *Proceedings of the 1960 Annual Spring Meeting of the American Ethnological Society,* V. F. Ray, ed. (Seattle, Wash.: University of Washington Press), pp. 1–129. See for comprehensive bibliography on Windigo phenomenon.

Thomas, W. I., and F. Znaniecki 1927. *The Polish Peasant in Europe and America,* 2nd ed., 2 vols (New York: Knopf). First published 1918–1920.

Thompson, L. 1948. "Attitudes and Acculturation," *American Anthropologist,* 50:200–15.

Ticho, G. E. 1971. "Cultural Aspects of Transference and Countertransference," *Bulletin of the Menninger Clinic,* 35:313–34.

Tseng, W. S., and J. McDermott, Jr. 1981. *Culture, Mind, and Therapy: An Introduction to Cultural Psychiatry* (New York: Bruner/Mazel).

Turner, V. W. 1969. *The Ritual Process* (Chicago: Aldine Publishing Co.).

Tuzim, D. F. 1980. *The Voice of the Tambaran* (Berkeley, Calif.: University of California Press).

Tylim, I. 1982. "Group Psychotherapy with Hispanic Patients: The Psychodynamics of Idealization," *The International Journal of Group Psychotherapy,* 32:339–66.

Tylor, E. B. 1958. *The Origins of Culture,* pt. 1 of *Primitive Culture,* 2 vols (New York: Harper & Row). First published 1871.

Van Gennep, A. 1960. *The Rites of Passage,* B. Vizedom and G. L. Caffee, trans. (Chicago: University of Chicago Press). First published 1909.

Wallace, A. F. C. 1958. "Dreams and Wishes of the Soul: A Type of Psychoanalytic Theory Among the Seventeenth-Century Iroquois," *American Anthropologist,* 60:234–48.

Wallace, E. R. 1983. *Freud and Anthropology: A History and Reappraisal.* Psychological Issues Monograph, No. 55. (New York: International Universities Press).

Wallerstein, R. S. 1969. "Psychoanalysis and Psychotherapy," *International Journal of Psychoanalysis,* 50:117–26.

Walz, G. R., and L. Benjamin 1978. *Transcultural Counseling: Needs, Programs and Techniques* (New York: Human Sciences Press).

Warner, W. L., et al. 1941–1959. *Yankee City Series,* 5 vols (New Haven, Conn.: Yale University Press).

Weidman, H. 1978. *The Miami Health Ecology Project Report* (Miami, Fl.: University of Miami).

Weiner, A. B. 1976. *Women of Value, Men of Renown: New Perspectives in Trobriand Exchange* (Austin, Tex.: University of Austin Press).

———— 1985. "Oedipus and Ancestors," *American Ethnologist,* 12:758–62.

Welts, E. P. 1982. "Greek Families," in *Ethnicity and Family Therapy,* M. McGoldrick, J. K. Pearce and J. Giordano, eds. (New York: Guilford Press), pp. 269–88.

West, J. 1945. *Plainville, U.S.A.* (New York: Columbia University Press).

Whiting, J. W. M., R. Kluckhohn, and A. Anthony 1958. "The Function of Male Initiation Ceremonies at Puberty," in *Readings in Social Psychology,* 3rd ed., E. E. Maccoby, T. M. Newcomb and E. J. Hartley, eds. (New York: Holt, Rinehart & Winston), pp. 359–70.

Winn, R. B. 1962. *Psychotherapy in the Soviet Union* (New York: Grove Press).

Wolberg, L. R. 1967. *The Techniques of Psychotherapy,* 2 vols, 2nd ed. (New York: Grune & Stratton). First published 1954.

Wolfenstein, M. 1955. "French Parents Take Their Children to the Park," in *Childhood in Contemporary Cultures,* M. Mead and M. Wolfenstein, eds. (Chicago: University of Chicago Press), pp. 99–117.

World Health Organization 1979. *Schizophrenia: An International Follow-Up Study* (New York: Wiley).

Yoors, J. 1967. *The Gypsies* (New York: Simon & Schuster).

Zborowski, M., and E. Herzog 1952. *Life Is with People: The Jewish Little Town in Eastern Europe* (New York: International Universities Press).

Index

Abel, Theodora M., 5–6, 89, 113, 152, 174, 191
Abel, T. M., and F. L. K. Hsu, 5, 65
Abel, T. M., and J. Major, 153
Abel, T. M., and R. Metraux, 6
Abel, T. M., J. Belo, and M. Wolfenstein, 5, 65
acculturation, 136, 140, 169–70, 181, 195
aché, 173
Adams, W. A., 164–66
Admiralty Islands, 47, 68
African culture, 9, 44, 164, 167, 172–73, 178
Akan tribes, 58–59
Algonkian Ojibwa culture, 53, 53–54, 54
Alland, A., 9, 16
Allen, M. R., 86
Alor Island, 65
Alorese culture, 75
amae, 134–35
American Anthropologist, 198
American culture, 3–15 passim, 20–23, 30, 32–33, 34, 36, 41, 46–47, 49, 65, 71, 73, 81, 89, 91–92, 98–99, 104, 107, 113, 115, 121, 124–25, 127, 131–32, 137, 140–47, 156–59, 164, 172, 180–82, 185–94, 199, 200, 202, 207 note 19, 210 note 5. *See also* United States
American Ethnologist,, 198
American Indians, 39, 46, 51, 60, 147–48. *See also* Plains Indian culture; Pueblo Indian culture
American Journal of Social Psychiatry, 197
American University at Beirut, Lebanon, 125, 209 note 3
analysts, 10–11. *See also* therapists
Anglos, 150–51, 152
anthropology, 12, 13, 70–71, 79–81, 83–93

passim, 95, 177, 197–98, 207 note 20; anthropologists, 49–51, 69, 75
"Anthropology and the Abnormal," (Benedict), 39
Apache culture, 75. *See also* Mescalero Apache culture
Arabic culture, 125, 140
Aranda culture, 177
Arapesh, 66. *See also* Ilahita Arapesh culture
Argentina, 118
Aries, Phillipe, 35
Arizona, 72
Armenian culture, 125
Ashanti culture, 58–59
Asia, 203
Assam, 67
Atimelang culture, 65
atua, 185
Australia, 72, 73, 177
Australian aborigine culture, 50, 61
Austria, 159
autonomy, 14. *See also* individuality
Ayrault, Evelyn West, 206 note 18
Ayurvedic medicine, 66–67
Aztec culture, 181

Baiga culture, 84
Baker, R. *See* Melgoza, Roll, and Baker
Balinese culture, 69, 206 note 11, 208 note 6
"Baloma: Spirits of the Dead in the Trobriands," (Malinowski), 84
Barbarin, O. A., 163
Bateson, G., 62, 92, 172, 181
Bateson, G., and M. Mead, 62, 69
Bean, L. L. *See* Myers, Bean, and Pepper
Bechterev Institute of Leningrad, 120

bee's honey, 173
behavior, 7, 11, 13, 20–22, 25, 99, 110–16,
    127–28, 157, 172, 202–3; aberrant, 38–45,
    52–64, 206 note 14; aggressive, 55, 72, 163,
    164, 181–82; amok, 56, 60; autistic, 29;
    claimed/disclaimed, 187; dissimulating, 61;
    distantiation, 107; group, 11; histrionic,
    58; infant/adult or mother/infant, 30, 77–
    83, 99, 106–7, 137–38, 206 note 11; patri-
    cide, 72; phylogenetic, 11; sexual, 132–33;
    temperamental misfits, 43–44; women
    and, 91, 131–32, 148. *See also* deviance; so-
    ciety; traumas
Bellis, E. *See* Redlich, Hollingshead, and
    Bellis
Belo, J. *See* Able, Belo, and Wolfenstein
Benedict, Ruth, 5, 20, 38–40, 68, 74, 86,
    100, 183
Benjamin, L. *See* Walz and Benjamin
berdache, 61–62, 184
Bernard, Viola W., 160
Bettelheim, B., 29, 73
biology, 16–17, 205 note 1
Birdwhistell, R. L., 9
birth, 31
Bishop, M. McF., and G. Winokur, 146
black Americans, 13–14, 46, 96, 148, 160–67
Bleuler, M., and R. Bleuler, 65
Boas, Franz, 51, 71, 74
Bokert, E. *See* Fiss, Klein, and Bokert
Bosch-Kohrer, 166–167
Boston, (Massachusetts), 156
Boszormeny-Nagy, I., and G. M. Spark, 127
Boyer, L. Bryce, 68, 141–42, 179–80
Boyer, Ruth, 68
Brandeis University, 202
Brazil, 159
Brenneis, C. B., and S. Roll, 181, 185–86
Brenner, C., 81, 179
Britain. *See* British culture *and* English cul-
    ture
British Columbia Indian culture, 183
British culture, 43, 59, 65. *See also* English
    culture
Browning, Elizabeth Barrett, 42

Buber, the philosopher, 120
Buddhist monastery, 62–63
Burgum, Mildred, 155
Burma, 62–63
Bustamente, J. A., 172
Butts, H. F. *See* Schachter and Butts

Calcutta, 67
Cambridge Expedition, 71
Cambridge, Massachusetts, 152
Canada, 53–54
Canadian culture (English), 22
Canive, J. *See* Koss and Canive
cannibalism, 53–54, 72
cantometrics, 28. *See also* communication,
    nonverbal
Caribbean culture, 164
Carstairs, G. M., 112–13
Caudill, W., and H. Weinstein, 30, 32
Central Eskimo, The, (Boas), 71
Centuries of Childhood, (Aries), 35
Chaouia plains, Morocco, 65
Chess, S., K. B. Clark, and A. Thomas, 160
children, 11–15, 29–35; child rearing, 77–79,
    80–83. *See also* behavior: infant/adult or
    mother/infant
Chinese culture, 5–6, 9, 23, 26, 30, 35, 36,
    66–67, 89, 92, 100, 102–5, 111, 112, 119, 125,
    137, 155–56, 162, 174–75, 178, 191–94
choreometrics, 28, 205 note 2, 210 note 6.
    See also communication, nonverbal
Christian Syrians, 108–10
circumcision, 88–89
Civil Rights, 47
Clark, K. B. *See* Chess, Clark, and Thomas
client, the, 8. *See also* patients
cognition and intelligence studies, 6
Cohen, Yehudi A., 90, 93
Colombia, 6, 149
Columbia University, (Research in Contem-
    porary Cultures), 5, 100, 209 note 1
communication, 8–9, 15, 17–19, 24, 27, 37–
    38, 49, 94, 99, 104, 132–33, 137–38, 143, 173
communication, nonverbal, 8–9, 18, 22, 27,
    30–32, 94, 136–38, 167, 205 note 2

Concept of Trauma, The, (Fenichel), 82
Coral Gardens and Their Magic, (Malinowski), 84
Crapanzano, Vincent, 69, 88–89
creativity, 28
Cree Indians, 53
Crow Indians, 51
Cuba, 149
Cuban culture, 172–73
culture: abstractions, 19–22; artifacts, 13, 15, 18; attributes, 8, 16, 18, 71; changes, 5, 19, 44, 45–46; character structure (social), 5, 76–77, 202; coordinating information on, 198, 202; counterculture, 47; discontinuity in, 3–4, 44; discrimination, 165, 166; formal culture, 51, 68, 84, 105; hidden, 131–32; identity, 14; as neurosis, 12, 73; relativism, 38–40; styles, 22, 30, 39; universals, 24, 26, 156, 177, 178, 180
Culture, Behavior and Personality, (LeVine), 127
curandero, 149
Current Anthropology, 198
Czechoslovakia, 119
Czechoslovakian culture, 100

Dahomey, 90
Damascus, 109
dance, 28
Daniloff, R., 119
Darwin, Charles, 12, 70
Davis, Kingsley, 95
da Vinci, Leonardo, 12
deaf-mutism, 24
death, 27
Deutsch, F., and W. F. Murphy, 94
Developing Interculturally Skilled Counselors, 203
Devereux, George, 12, 13, 40, 42, 51–52, 62, 64, 75, 76, 79, 82–83, 90, 144, 147, 162, 169–71, 188–90
deviance, 7, 38, 38–40, 40–45, 183–84, 206 note 14. *See also* behavior: aberrant
DeVos, G., and L. Romanucci-Ross, 47, 132
Diaz-Guerrero, R., 186

divorce, 85, 92–93
djinn, 178
Dobuan culture, 39
Doi, L. T., 134–35
Dollard, J., 14
Dolto, Françoise, 99, 145
Domhoff, B. *See* Hall and Domhoff
dreams, 6, 10, 169–71; latent content, 177, 179, 181; manifest content, 170–75, 177–81, 186–87; vision seeking, 183–84
drug use, 49
Dubois, Cora, 65
dynamic psychotherapy, 118–20. *See also* therapy

Easter Island, 44
Eastern European culture, 42, 99, 100, 100–102, 206 note 9
East Germany, 119
East Indies, 65. *See also* Alorese culture
East-West Cultural Learning Institute, 203
economics, 112. *See also* socioeconomics
Edwards, J. W., 52, 66–67, 133
Eggan, Dorothy, 181
ego, 81–83
Ego and the Id, The, (Freud), 81
Egypt, 125
Egyptian culture, 109, 162
Electra, 12
Elwin, V., 84
emotions, 82, 112–13, 136, 149
enculturation, 7, 15, 29
endocrinology, 120
English culture, (England), 42, 104, 112, 133, 172. *See also* British culture
environment, 28–33, 54, 55, 61, 147, 157. *See also* natural world
Erikson, Erik H., 12, 13, 29, 52, 77–79, 80, 181, 184
Eskimo culture, 35, 53, 54–56
ethnicity, 14, 16–17, 46–47, 148, 148–49, 152–53
ethnic psychoses, 40
ethnocentricity, 204
Ethos, 198

Europe, 35, 49, 65, 118, 120, 134, 176, 197
European culture generally, 11, 141, 172, 178, 200
European gypsies, 24, 205 note 9
evolution, 12, 70. *See also* society: evolutionary
existentialism, 120

Falicov, C. J., 115
family, the, 26, 82–93 passim, 114–16, 128, 148–52, 156–59, 171–72, 200, 211 note 3
Fenichel, O., 82, 136
Field, M. J., 58–59, 64
film in research, 69, 198, 205 note 6, 206 note 11, 210 notes 4 and 6
Firth, R., 184–85
Fiss, H., G. S. Klein, and E. Bokert, 176
folktales, 179–80
formal culture, 51, 68, 84, 105
Fortes, M., 84
Foulks, E. A. *See* Freeman, Foulks, and Freeman
Four Families, (McNeill), 22, 205 note 6
France, 133. *See also* French culture
Frank, Jerome D., 132
Frank, L. K., 137–38
Frazer, James G., 12, 70, 71, 177
Freeman, D. M. A., E. A. Foulks, and P. A. Freeman, 55
Freeman, P. A. *See* Freeman, Foulks, and Freeman
French, T., 181
French Canadian culture, 209 note 3
French culture, 5, 20, 22, 29, 33–34, 35, 36, 43, 99, 100, 104, 105–8, 120, 145, 164, 206 notes 12 and 13, 210 note 5
Freud, Anna, 81–83
Freud, Sigmund, 11–12, 70–72, 83, 84, 90, 91, 117–18, 119, 130, 134, 154, 162, 176–77, 178–79; criticisms of, 73, 74, 83
Fromm, Erich, 12, 76–77, 132
Fromm-Reichman, Frieda, 148

generation gap, 4, 38, 114, 131, 200
Germany, 119
German culture, 33, 172, 206 note 12

Ghana, 58–59, 64
Ghanaian culture, 164
Giordano, J. *See* McGoldrick, Pearce, and Giordano
Glazer, M. *See* Roll, Hinton, and Glazer
Gold Coast culture, 59
Golden Age, 26
Gomez-Palacio, M., E. Padilla, and S. Roll, 6
Gorer, G., 14, 92
Great Britain, 71. *See also* British culture; English culture
Great Russian culture, 80, 81, 100
Greek culture, 119
Greek-Americans, 105, 114, 153, 209 note 4
Griffith, R. M., and E. Jones, 163
Griffith, R. M., O. Miyagi, and A. Tago, 180
guidance, 7
Gururumba culture, 56–58
gypsy culture, 205 note 9

Haitian culture, 35, 36, 42, 43–44, 60, 64
Hall, C. S., 181
Hall, C. S., and B. Domhoff, 182
Hall, E. T., 139–40
Hall, E. T., and W. F. Whyte, 139
Hallowell, A. Irving, 52, 53–54, 75, 146
Hamadsha brotherhood, 69
Handbook of Cross-Cultural Psychology, (Triandis and Brislin), 197
handicapped children, 29, 32–33. *See also* physical incapacity
Hartmann, H., 81
Hartmann, H., E. Kris, and R. Loewenstein, 83
Hawaii, 203
health service, 67
Heidegger, the philosopher, 120
Henry, Jules, 142, 143
Herdt, G. H., 86–88
Herskovits, Melville, 90
Hes, J. P., 123–24
Hindu culture, 113
Hinkle, L. E., Jr., 6
Hinton, R. *See* Roll, Hinton, and Glazer

Hispanic culture, 25, 149–50
Hispanic-Americans, 149, 151, 152, 185–87, 200. *See also* Mexican-Americans
Hofstadter, R., and M. Wallace, 21
Holden, D., 153
Hollingshead, A. B. *See* Redlich, Hollingshead, and Bellis
Holtzman, W. H., R. Diaz-Guerrero, and J. D. Swartz, 186
Homo ferus, 29
Honigmann, J. J., 1/8
Hopi Indians, 75, 181
hospitalization, 121–25
Hsu, F. L. K. *See* Abel and Hsu
humanization, 16
human nature, 157
Human Organization, 198
Husserl, the philosopher, 120

Iatmul culture, 19, 30–31, 57, 62, 77, 181, 205 note 5
id, 81–83
ideals, 23, 44, 165
identity, 14, 23; insecurity/neurosis, 112–13; national, 134, 153; sexual, 74, 81–93. *See also* individuality; personality
idiosyncrasies, 8, 12, 30, 38, 75
Ilahita Arapesh culture, 208 note 6. *See also* Arapesh
illness, (physical condition), 59, 124, 149, 184–85
immigrants, 45–46, 46, 148, 164, 166
Indian culture, (Asian), 22, 66–67, 84, 112, 133, 205 note 8
individuality, 4–5, 7–9, 11–13, 18, 20, 23, 26–28, 36, 41–42, 75–76, 82, 118, 126–28, 131, 134, 135, 141, 143, 146, 153, 157–58, 203–4, 205 note 4. *See also* personality
infants, 29–32, 73–74, 206 note 12. *See also* behavior: infant/adult or mother/infant
initiation rites, 85–88, 183
Institute of Behavioral Sciences, 203
International Congress of Group Psychotherapy, 119
International Journal of Psychology, 197
International Social Science Journal, 197

Interpretation of Dreams, The, (Freud), 81
interviewing, 9–10, 94–95, 115–56, 200; group, 102, 103; review of management of, 110–16
intrapsychic conflict, 10, 97–98. *See also* traumas
Iranian culture, 152–53
Irish culture, 9, 140
Irish-Americans, 156–59
Iroquois culture, 184
Irwin, M. H. *See* Roll and Irwin
Isleta Pueblo, 150
Israel, 123
Italian culture, 90–91, 98–99, 102, 127, 140–41, 143
Italian-Americans, 127–28, 156–58
Itard, J. M. G., 29, 106

Jackson, A., 163
Jalali, B., 152–53
Japan, 119, 133, 134–36
Japanese culture, 22, 30, 32, 35, 78, 134–36, 136, 137, 146–47, 178, 180
Jaspers, the philosopher, 120
Jemez Pueblo, 150
Jerusalem, 141
Jesup North Pacific Expedition, 71
Jewish culture, 10, 12, 24, 25, 98, 99, 100, 100–102, 111, 119, 121, 141, 155, 173–74, 200, 206 notes 9 and 10
Jikeikai School of Medicine, 135
Jilek, W. G., 67
Johanson, D., and M. Edey, 12
Jones, E. E., and S. Korchin, 197
Jones, Ernest, 48, 85. *See also* Griffith and Jones
Jones, N. F., and M. W. Kahn, 122–23, 124
Jordan, 125
Journal of Cross-Cultural Psychology, 197
Jungle Book, The, (Kipling), 29

Kahn, M. W., et al., 122, 124–25
Kaleidoblocs, 18
Kardiner, Abram, 12, 74–76, 194
Kardiner, A., and L. Ovesey, 162
Karon, B. P., 163

Keesing, R. N., 86
Keniston, K., 131
Kilborne, B., 178–79
killing, 53–54, 61, 63, 181
kinesics, 210 note 6. *See also* communication, nonverbal
kinship, 26, 144, 157–58
Kipling, (Rudyard), 29
Klein, G. S. *See* Fiss, Klein, and Bokert
Klein, Melanie, 208 note 8
Kluckhohn, C., and W. Morgan, 177
Kluckhohn, Florence R., 156–57, 202
Kluckhohn, F. R., and F. L. Strodtbeck, 156, 202
knowledge, 5
Kohut, H., 81
Kokutai no Honji, 134
Korean culture, 124–25
Kornreich, M. *See* Meltzoff and Kornreich
koro, 52, 67
Koss, J. D., 201
Koss, J. D., and J. Canive, 151, 200
Kroeber, Alfred L., 52, 80
Kroeber, T., 51
Kwakiutl Indian culture, 39, 74
Kyoto, Japan, 135

Lacan, J., 118, 120
Lamarck, the biologist, 70
Lang, Andrew, 12, 70
Langham, I., 71
Langrod, J. *See* Ruiz and Langrod
language, 14, 20–21, 24, 104, 109, 112, 142, 149–50, 155–56, 186, 200
Lasswell, H. D., 120
Latin America, 118
Latin American culture, 139, 149, 164, 172
Latin culture, 90–91
learning, 13, 16, 27, 28–35, 83, 167; swaddling experience, 31, 80
Lebanon, 125, 209 note 3
Lebanese culture, 108
lebenstüchtig, 33
Lee, the Chinese patient, 191–94
Lerner, D., 107–8
Lerner, H. E., 131

Lessa, W. A., and E. Z. Vogt, 61
LeVine, R. A., 127–28, 203
Levy-Bruhl, L., 205 note 7
Lewis, O., 167
Lidz, T., and R. W. Lidz, 88
Lincoln, J. S., 178, 184
Linnaeus, the biologist, 29
literature (fiction) in research, 198
Loewenstein, R. *See* Hartmann, Kris, and Loewenstein
Lomax, Alan, 28
Lomax, A., and F. Pauley, 28
Lowenfeld, Margaret, 18, 65, 66
Lowenfeld Mosaic test, 18, 65
Lowie, Robert H., 51

McArdle, L. *See* Roll, Rabold, and McArdle
McDermott, J., Jr. *See* Tseng and McDermott
McGoldrick, M., J. K. Pearce, and J. Giordano, 153
McNeill, Ian, 22
machismo, 130
Major, J. *See* Abel and Major
Malayan-Indonesian culture, 67
Maldonado-Sierra, E. D., and R. D. Trent, 171
Malinowski, Bronislaw, 48, 69, 84–85, 185
Mandelbaum, D. G., 29
Manhattan (New York City), 121. *See also* New York City
Manus, 66
Marmor, Judd, 168
Marsella, A. J., and P. B. Pedersen, 197, 203
Martinez, R. *See* Roll, Millen, and Martinez
Martinique, 164
Mead, Margaret, 14, 15, 27, 29, 39, 44, 45, 62, 64, 66, 100, 131, 172, 206 note 15. *See also* Bateson and Mead
Mead, M., and R. Metraux, 5, 108. *See also* Metraux and Mead
Mead, M., and M. Wolfenstein, 32
medicine, 66–67, 120, 122, 133, 201–2
Mekeel, H. Scudder, 52, 80
Meknes, Morocco, 88
Melanesian culture, 39, 48, 85–86, 185

Melgoza, B., S. Roll, and R. Baker, 6
Melikian, Levon, 125
Meltzoff, J., and M. Kornreich, 122
mental health professionals, 7–8, 11, 15. See also therapists
mental illness, 7–8, 49–52, 62, 64–69, 73. See also illness (physical condition); symptoms; traumas
Mescalero Apache culture, 68, 141–42, 179–80
Metraux, A., 60
Metraux, Rhoda, 5–6
Metraux, R., and T. M. Abel, 6
Metraux, R., and M. Mead, 5, 20. See also Mead and Metraux
Mexico, 118, 167, 181
Mexico City, 119
Mexican culture, 145, 186
Mexican-Americans, 14, 115. See also Hispanic culture; Hispanic-Americans
Millen, L. See Roll, Millen, and Martinez
minorities, 46–47. See also immigrants
misinterpretation, 20–21, 41–42, 64–66
Miyagi, O. See Griffith, Miyagi, and Tago
Mohave Indian culture, 82–83, 206 note 17, 211 note 4
Moloney, J. C., 134
Mondykowski, S. M., 115
Montagnais-maskapi Indian culture, 53
Montserrat culture, 6, 35, 36, 44, 206 note 16
Moreman. See Romanucci-Ross, Moreman, and Tancredi
Morgan, W. See Kluckhohn and Morgan
Morita, S., 135
Morita Therapy, 134–36
Moitoza, E., 114, 152
Morocco, 65, 69
Moroccan culture, 88–89, 123–24, 141, 178–79
Moses, 12
Mowgli, 29
Muensterberger, W., 191
Mundugumor culture, 62
Murphy, W. F. See Deutsch and Murphy
Muslim Indian culture, 133

Muslim Pakistan, 205 note 8
Muslim Syrian culture, 108–10
Myers, J. K., L. L. Bean, and M. P. Pepper, 122
myths, 12

Naples, Italy, 90
National Institute of Mental Health, 202
Native Americans, 108. See also American Indians
Native American culture, 162. See also American Indians
natural world, 25. See also environment
Naturphilosophie, 70
Navajo culture, 177, 184
neonate. See infants
Neurological Institute, (Shiraz, Iran), 152
New Guinea, 62, 72, 77. See also Papuan New Guinea
New Haven, Connecticut, 121–22
Newman, Philip L., 56–57, 63
New Mexico, 141, 149, 151, 152, 179
New World, 54
New York, 97, 102, 109, 167
New York City, 9, 121, 149, 199
New York Hospital-Cornell Medical Center, 6, 125
Nietzsche, the philosopher, 70
North American culture, 139, 160, 183–84. See also American culture; Canadian culture; Plains Indian culture; Pueblo Indian culture
Northwest Coast Indian culture, 51

Oaxaca, Mexico, 181
Oberholzer, E., 65, 75
Oediupus, 12
Oedipus complex (oedipal conflicts), 48, 72, 74, 79, 83, 83–93, 141, 144, 165, 173, 174, 177, 188–89, 193–94
Ogburn, W. F., 29
Ojibwa Indian culture, 53–55
O'Nell, C. W., and N. D. O'Nell, 181
opinion polls, 96
Opler, Marvin K., 79–81, 185
Origin of Species, (Darwin), 70

orphans, 37
Ovesey, L. *See* Kardiner and Ovesey

PAT, (Tomkins-Horn Picture Arrangement Test), 163–64
Padilla, A. M., and R. A. Ruiz, 9
Padilla, E. *See* Gomez-Palacio, Padilla, and Roll
Pakistan, 205 note 8
Pakistani culture, 127
Papajohn, J. *See* Spiegel and Papajohn
Papiasvili, A., 119–20
Papua New Guinea, 19, 49, 56–58, 85–86, 86–88, 181, 208 note 6
Parker, S., 53, 55
Parsons, Ann, 48, 90
patients, 117, 118, 122–23, 128–29, 158
Patterns of Culture, (Benedict), 38–40
Pauley, F. *See* Lomax and Pauley
Pavlovian model, 119
Peace Corps, 21
Pearce, J. K. *See* McGoldrick, Pearce, and Giordano
Pedersen, P., 203. *See also* Marsella and Pedersen
Pelto, P. J. and G. H. Pelto, 128
Pepper, M. P. *See* Myers, Bean, and Pepper
Perceptanalysis Dream System, 178
personality, 7, 8, 12, 22, 23, 48, 51–52, 74–79, 81–83, 146, 177–78, 181
Philippine Negrito culture, 184
photography in research, 30, 206 note 11
physical incapacity, 24, 38, 40–41, 42–43, 59. *See also* illness (physical condition)
physicians, 8
Picard, Jimmy, 188–91
Piotrowski, Z. A., 177–78
Plains Indian cultures, 39, 51, 61–62, 79, 144, 147, 169–71, 188–91. *See also by tribes*
pluralist society, 4–5, 22–23, 46–47, 164
Poland, 119, 120
Polish culture, 35, 100, 115, 123–24
Polish-Americans, 115
politics, 109
Pollak, O., 141, 155
Polynesian culture, 44, 184–85, 211 note 3

Portuguese-Americans, 114, 152
Postgraduate Center for Mental Health, 6, 199, 203
Powdermaker, H., 164
Primitive Culture, (Tylor), 71
projective techniques, 18, 64–66, 75, 163–64, 176, 205 note 3; testing generally, 9, 125
proxemics, 139
proximate differentiation, 198, 202
psychiatric nursing, 7
psychiatry, 7
Psychoanalytic Anthropology, 198
psychoanalytic theory, 11–15
psychodrama, 119–20
psychology, 7
psychopathology, 7–8, 52–60
psychoses, 49, 52. *See also* traumas
Psychotherapy and Culture Conflict, (Seward), 168
psychotics, 138
Pueblo Indian culture, 39, 150–51, 205 note 3
Puerto Rico, 167, 201
Puerto Rican culture, 130, 149, 171–72

Quaker culture, 181
questionnaires, 100, 100–101, 121, 122, 124, 125

REM sleep, 176
Rabold, K. *See* Roll, Rabold, and McArdle
race, 16–17, 205 note 1
Radin, P., 71
reciprocity, 104
Redlich, F. C., 120
Redlich, F. C., A. B. Hollingshead, and E. Bellis, 121
religion, 43–44, 49, 58–59, 60, 61, 62–63, 66, 69, 108–10, 121, 127, 133, 149, 172–73, 177, 206 note 9, 210 note 7
research, 17–18, 30, 153, 197–204, 205 note 4
Rickshaw Boy, (Shaw), 192
Riesman, D., 14
rites of passage, 85–88, 183
Rites of Passage, The, (Van Gennep), 208 note 6
Roffenstein, G., 176

Róheim, Géza, 12, 61, 72–74, 84, 177
Roll, Samuel, 6. *See also* Brenneis and Roll
Roll, S., and C. B. Brenneis, 6
Roll, S., and M. H. Irwin, 6
Roll, S., R. Hinton, and M. Glazer, 6
Roll, S., L. Millen, and R. Martinez, 6, 118, 130
Roll, S., K. Rabold, and L. McArdle, 6, 186–87
Romanucci-Ross, L. D. *See* DeVoss and Romanucci-Ross
Romanucci-Ross, L. D., E. Moerman, and L. E. Tancredi, 197
Rorschach test, 9, 62–63, 65, 66, 75, 103, 104, 107, 176
Ruesch, J., 138
Ruiz, P., and J. Langrod, 201
Ruiz, R. A. *See* Padilla and Ruiz
Russian (Great) culture, 80, 81, 100

Sambia culture, 86–88
Samoa, 203
Samuda, R., 9
Sansei Hospital, 135
Santa Ana Pueblo, 150
Santería, 173
Santo Domingo Pueblo, 150
Sanua, V. D., 117, 167
Sapir, E., 128
Satow, R., 130
Schachter, J. S., and H. F. Butts, 162
Schwartz, T., 47, 68
secularization of life, 36–37
self-psychology, 81
Seligman, C. G., 178
Seneca Indians, 184
Seoul, Korea, 124
Seward, Georgene, 168
shamans, 60–61, 180, 184, 185, 206 note 17
Shaw, L., 192
shtetl, 42
Siberian culture, 60–61. *See also* Eskimo culture
Sicilian culture, 140–41
Singal, D. J., 14
Singapore, 67

Sioux Indian culture, 52, 79, 80, 184
Skinner, the psychologist, 119
Snyder, F., 176
society, 17; aberrance in, 41; caste, 23, 163–67, 172–73, 205 note 8; cohesion in, 23; double alienation, 46; enclaves, 24; ethnic distortions of, 105; evolutionary, 22, 70–72, 205 note 7; institutions, 42, 74–77, 93; life-stages, 27, 29–36; national culture, 23, 46–47, 148–49; nuclear complex, 90, 92; panic, 67; poverty, 167–69; race and, 16–17, 205 note 1; roles for mentally ill, 60–63; socialization, 32–35; social work, 7, 140–41; stability in, 44; taboos, 90. *See also* behavior; family, the
Society for Applied Anthropology, 198
Society for Psychological Anthropology, 198
socioeconomics, 118, 121, 121–23, 129, 167–69, 209 note 4. *See also* economics
Soddy, K., 106
Solomon Islands, 184
Somaliland, 72
song, 28
South American culture, 160. *See also* Latin American culture
Southeast Asian culture, 178
South Pacific, 75, 203
Soviet Union, 119–20. *See also* Russian (Great) culture
space, 34, 139–40
Spain, 42, 43
Spanish-Americans, 118. *See also* Hispanic culture *and* Hispanic-Americans
Spark, G. M. *See* Boszormeny-Nagy and Spark
Spiegel, J. P., 156–59
Spiegel, J., and J. Papajohn, 153, 156, 157, 198, 202–3
Spiro, M. E., 62
Srole, L., 117, 121
Steel, James, 63
Stewart, K., 184
stigmata, 49
Strodtbeck, F. L. *See* Kluckhohn and Strodtbeck
students, 125–26, 148, 180, 185–87, 205 note 3

Sue, D. W., et al., 197
suicide, 45
superego, 81–83, 91–92, 130, 134, 158
Swartz, M. J., 128
Switzerland, 65
Symbolic Wounds, Puberty Rites and the Envious Male, (Bettelheim), 73
symbolism, 73–74, 171, 177, 178, 180–81
symptoms, 118, 135–36, 141
Syria, 125
Syrian culture, 100, 108–10

TAT, 176; Thematic Apperception Test, 75, 177
Tago, A. *See* Griffith, Miyagi, and Tago
Tambunam Village, 19, 62
Tancredi, L. E. *See* Romanucci-Ross, Moreman, and Tancredi
Tatara, M., 135
teaching, 6
Teicher, M. I., 53
testing, 9, 125; projective techniques, 18, 64–66, 75, 163–64, 176, 205 note 3
Thailand, 67
Thematic Apperception Tests, 75, 177; TAT, 176
therapists, 8–9, 113, 128–29, 158; community, 56–58, 63; priests, 58–59, 62–63, 149; self-awareness of, 10–11, 126–28, 150, 160–67; shamans, 60–63
therapy: acting-out, 139; countertransference, 150, 163; goals, 132–33, 134, 145–48, 158; groups, 148–52, 172, 184; methods, 113 (note-taking), 133, 134–36 (Japanese-Morita), 138 (action and analogic), 145 (children's play), 171 (supportive-interpretive); new directions for, 69; regression, 149; resistance, 136, 144–45, 156, 165, 199, 201–2; transference, 107, 134–35, 149–50. *See also* treatments
Thomas, A. *See* Chess, Clark, and Thomas
Thomas, W. I., and F. Znaniecki, 115
Thompson, Laura, 169
Ticho, G. E., 159–60
Tikopian culture, 184–85, 211 note 3
time, 25–26, 139–40, 157, 159

Tokyo, Japan, 135
Tomkins-Horn Picture Arrangement Test (PAT), 163–64
Torres Strait, 71
Totem and Taboo, (Freud), 12, 72, 73
totemism, 72
traumas, 12, 50, 53–59, 63, 65, 66–67, 73–74, 83, 90, 112–13, 134–35, 142, 171–72
treatments, 63–64, 120–22; attitudes toward, 10, 122; community, 56–58; hypnosis, 176; ritual, 86–88; trance, 43–44, 58–59. *See also* therapy
Trent, R. D. *See* Maldonado-Sierra and Trent
Triandis, H. C. and J. W. Berry, 197
Trinidad, 164
Trobriand Island culture, 48, 84–85, 90, 185
Truffaut, François, 29, 106
Tseng, W. S., J. McDermott, Jr., 197
Tuhami, 69
Turkish culture, 109
Tylim, I., 149–50
Tylor, E. B., 70, 71

unforeseeable, the, 26
United States, 13, 23, 78, 92–93, 100, 105, 108, 117, 118, 120–22, 129, 133, 134, 136, 139, 148, 149, 156, 159, 164, 191, 196, 197, 206 note 9. *See also* American culture
University of Hawaii, 203
University of New Mexico, 185
Ute Indian culture, 80, 185

values, 140–44, 146, 147, 155, 156–59, 167, 203–4; profile chart, 157, 202
Vancouver Island, 39
Van Gennep, A., 88
Vassiliou, George, and Vassou Vassiliou, 209 note 5
Veterans Administration, 188
Vienna, Austria, 12
Vietnam, 49
Vogt, E. Z. *See* Lessa and Vogt
Voodoo, 43–44, 60

Wallace, A. F. C., 184

Wallace, M. *See* Hofstadter and Wallace
Wallerstein, R. S., 154
Walz, G. R., and L. Benjamin, 197
Warner, W. L., et al., 14
Weidman, H., 201
Weiner, Annette B., 48, 85
Weinstein, H. *See* Caudill and Weinstein
Welts, E. P., 114, 153
West, J., 14
West African cultures, 26, 58
West Bengal, 67
Western culture generally, 12, 22, 41, 48–49, 52, 83, 112, 118, 134, 138, 146, 177, 185
Western Europe, 29, 49, 50
Western medicine, 49, 52, 133
West Indian cultures, 35. *See also* Montserrat culture
Whyte, W. F. *See* Hall and Whyte
Wild Boy of Aveyron, The, (Itard), 106
Wild Child, The, (Truffaut), 29

Winn, R. B., 119
Wolberg, L. R., 94, 160
Wolfenstein, M. *See* Abel, Belo, and Wolfenstein; Mead and Wolfenstein
Wolf Indian culture, 188–91
world view, 5, 12, 14–15
World War I, 49
World War II, 3, 49, 68

Yale University, 152
Yemenite culture, 123–24, 141
Yoruba culture, 173
Yuma Indian culture, 72
Yurok culture, 52, 80

Zapotec culture, 181–82
Zen, 136
Znaniecki, F. *See* Thomas and Znaniecki
zonal-modal chart, 77–79
Zuñi culture, 39, 68, 80, 81